GOLIATH

GOLIATH

The Life of
Robert Schuller
by James Penner

New Hope Publishing Company, Inc

Published in The United States of America by
New Hope Publishing Company, Anaheim, Ca   92642

Library Of Congress Cataloging in Publication Data

Penner, James.

GOLIATH

The Life of Robert Schuller.

ISBN 1-879989-06-9

92-073271

1992

PRINTED IN THE UNITED STATES OF AMERICA

To Gretchen and Julia, the joys of my life.

This book would not have been possible without the help of some very special people. For their hard work and dedication to this project, I would like to take this opportunity to thank the following:

Richard Baltzell
Tim Kirchner
Linda Adams

This is a love story. It is the true story of a man and a woman who overcame great obstacles and personal tragedy to realize their hopes and dreams. Their love made a difference to millions of people all over the world.

This is the story of a family who never gave up on each other. No matter how hard it got, no matter how unfairly they were treated, they kept their family together through it all.

This is the story of Robert Schuller, a man who faced GOLIATH.

GOLIATH

Prologue

He rose from his bed into the light. His frail body struggled to break the confines of the hospital bed. His eyes searched for the window in the corner, trying desperately to catch a brief glimpse of home.

It was there, just outside his window, a mile down the road. The place that he called home. A place where dreams came true. Where his dream came true.

He smiled gently as he watched it shimmer in the setting sun. Robert Schuller was home, almost. As he leaned back in his bed, he closed his eyes, shutting out the world around him, reflecting, wondering if anything would ever be the same again.

I rode up the elevator to the intensive care section of the hospital. The silence was eerie. The waiting was awful. I knew that I would be one of the first to get there, the first to see him. The hollow click-click of my own footsteps echoed down the long, empty corridor to his room. It felt so cold, so lonely.

As I entered his room, it surprised me how warm and soft it was. The late afternoon sun came through the window and washed the walls with a gentle, mellow glow. There was really nothing remarkable about the room. It was just a hospital room, like any other. Simply furnished with only a bed, a nightstand, a television, all those flowers, and that mirror. There was always that mirror. It made everything look bigger than it really was.

He hardly noticed me as I came into the room. He sat upright in bed, dressed only in a blue and white striped gown. It was a light, flimsy material that strained to cover his tall massive body. Even sitting down, it always caught me off-guard how big a man he actually was. Broad shoulders centered over a massive chest. He wasn't like anyone else I had ever known.

A person had to look right into his eyes to really see how soft and brown they were. His thick glasses hooded and guarded the brightness that was so natural to him. His eyes were fascinating. Always searching, always looking around, always planning. Examining every detail, every item, checking them off one by one and filing them away for some future plan or project. When he looked at you, a quiet power captivated you. It happened so fast that you were caught off guard, as if a warrior had grabbed you and held you with all his might.

There was a wonderful mystery about him. Like so

many others, I always wanted to know what made him tick. I knew where he came from. I had read all of his books. I had met his friends. I was a member of his family. Yet, I never quite understood the power of his dreams. Where did he get those wonderful dreams that helped so many millions of people? How could he dream so big?

Even now, when he was lying in a hospital bed, you could feel the quiet power. His silvery-white hair had been shorn away for the surgery. Now only a cap of snow-white bristles showed in the fading afternoon sunlight. The ugly scar from the surgery was covered with a simple white bandage.

Arvella stood quietly in the corner studying her husband's every move. I could feel the worry and pain deep within her. It hurt. It hurt me to watch her struggle, forcing a smile to her face as I entered. I reached for something to say, something comforting, something hopeful. Yet I was helpless, frustrated that the right words would not come.

Somehow, in my silence she sensed my anxiety. Her arm gently wrapped around my waist as she said, "He's very tired after the twelve-hour plane ride."

I looked into her eyes, searching for reassurance.

"Is he going to be okay? He looks so frail."

She paused briefly and turned back to her husband.

"He's alive."

As she spoke, I heard the rustle of footsteps as the family began to file into the room. Sheila, his first born, entered carrying a white birthday cake full of candles. His only son Robert Anthony followed close behind, with his wife Donna. The middle daughter Jeanne, and her husband Paul Dunn walked in, arm in arm. Carol, and her husband Tim arrived next. And the youngest daughter, my wife Gretchen, came to stand beside me.

The sweetest melody I have ever heard filled the air

as they slowly filed in. A soft smile creeped onto his lips as he quietly listened to his family. "Happy Birthday to you, Happy Birthday to you, Happy Birthday, dear Dad, Happy Birthday to you!"

Sheila set the cake down in his lap and said, "Make a wish, Dad!"

The three youngest daughters rang out in a chorus saying, "Yeah, come on Dad, make a wish and blow out the candles!"

Although grown and married, they were as happy as school girls to see their father home again in Southern California.

He picked up the cake crowned with burning red candles and held it away from his tapered jaw. Every movement was steady and sure. I saw him start to smile as he read the simple inscription 'Happy 65th Birthday Dad!' As he blew out the candles, Arvella said, "Carol has a special present for you Bob." His eyes became bright, as he quietly said, "Did you get your new prosthesis? Let's see you walk!"

What happened next was the greatest birthday present I had ever seen. Excitedly, Carol hopped up and began to demonstrate the miracle of modern technology. With the grace of a runway model, Carol strode across the hospital room floor as her siblings cheered her on from behind. For the first time in almost fifteen years, he nearly forgot the artificial limb she wore as her left leg. As she walked, the wound that had ripped through a leg, and the heart of a father, was once again a bright and shining star. His face filled with emotion as he said, "Congratulations, sweetheart, I'm proud of you."

That infectious smile inherited from her father appeared on Carol's face as she knelt next to his bed. Her eyes glistened as she fought back the tears. "Daddy, you spent a lot of hours by my bedside–I think it's time for me to return the favor!" She held him tightly as he closed his eyes, embracing her warmth. He didn't say a word; he didn't have to.

As the family hugged and kissed him goodbye, I stood in the doorway and watched his every move. He was looking away, not out the window this time, but into the mirror. I hardly recognized him because it was a look I had never seen in him before. Or had I? I stood there, waiting. Expecting him to say something, expecting him to do something. That's the way it was, that's the way it always was. Everybody always waited for him.

I watched him carefully as he looked into the mirror across the room. I got the feeling of walking through a deep, dark forest at night, waiting to feel the gaping steel jaws of a bear trap *snap!* against the bone of my leg. Once again I felt Arvella's arm hold me close to her side. I watched her look deep within her husbands soul. Quietly she whispered to me,

"He's afraid."

Her voice was strong and gentle, full of spirit and backbone. Arvella was always there, always supportive, always ready, always dependable. She was his constant companion, she was his friend, she was his partner for life. She was glad he was finally home.

"He's afraid no one wants him anymore."

Her words sent a shiver down my spine.

"Who wants a tired old man?"

I couldn't believe it. I couldn't believe he could feel that way.

"He can't really believe that, can he?" I asked.

"Trust me, Jim." Her eyes closed in prayer.

As she spoke, his eyes, always twinkling with love and laughter, took on a dull, lifeless look. It was as if a battle raged on within him, a battle that he believed was his alone, a great fight that could only belong to Robert Schuller.

He looked deep into the mirror, deep into its crevices, the lines on his face drew taut. There was something cold and terrifying in the air between him and the darkness in the mirror. I followed his gaze deep into the reflection. I reached into the blackness that he had immersed himself in. And for one brief, fleeting moment, I caught a glimpse of it. I saw what he was so afraid of. I saw what lurked in the darkness.

I saw the Giant.
I saw GOLIATH.

Book I

Bigger Dreams

- 1 -

Arvella's Love Letters

Amsterdam survives as a romantic fairy tale from the 16th Century. Canals line tidy red brick houses trimmed with white shutters. Flowers of every conceivable color, decorate the windows of each house. Inside, golden sunlight quietly pours over the simple Dutch furniture. Outside, the sound of hymns float across the water, rendered in beautiful harmony by young school boys.

When night falls, the city quiets down so lovers can stroll along the summer waterways. Who would have thought Goliath would pick such a beautiful place to try to kill Robert Schuller?

The phone *rang!* in my nightmare. I hung suspended in that purgatory place between the light and darkness, where you're not sure whether you're dead or alive. And you can't do anything about it, anyway, no matter where you are, no matter who you are.

The phone *rang!* again and jerked me back into the real world of 4:30 a.m. in warm, safe California.

"Jim, it's Arvella."

Her voice strained for control. I remember it vividly as I pinched the sleep from my eyes. She tried to keep her voice soft and soothing, but even half-awake, I knew something was terribly wrong.

"What's happened?" I asked, propping myself up in bed. Gretchen's face awoke against the clean, white pillow when she heard my voice deepen.

"There's been an accident in Amsterdam. Bob's in the hospital. They're going to operate." Arvella's voice strained for control again. "Jim, it's brain surgery. I need to leave for the airport."

"We'll be right there."

Suddenly her voice became quiet as she said, "Jim I need to tell Gretchen."

I handed my wife the phone. She sat next to me staring into my eyes with that puzzled look.

"What's the matter?" was her first question.

I looked down into her young frightened face as her mother gave her the news. I knew that look was the same one that gripped Arvella. Her expression suddenly changed as the tears began to roll off her cheeks. Her hands began to shake as she dropped the phone and fell into my arms.

Gretchen had grown up with her father gone. He was always off somewhere. She always wished she had spent more time with him.

Gretchen is so close to her Mom that it even scares me sometimes. She knows what Arvella is thinking almost before Arvella does. They have something between them that I guess I'll never understand. If it were the forties again, she could slip into one of her Mom's dresses and no one would know the difference.

Gretchen sprang from our four-poster bed and flung her housecoat on. I grabbed my robe and thrust an arm into it.

"Don't forget your slippers," I said.

"Forget my slippers," she shot back. "Let's go!"

Our house sits exactly eighty-six feet from the Schuller's property line. I know this because I had to tape off the distance just last spring for the final building permit on our house. They wouldn't let us build it before I measured the distance. I spent almost half-an-hour checking and rechecking that distance.

In the blackness of the night, Gretchen and I must have covered that run in less than thirty seconds. We ran past the wrought-iron gates that surrounded the pool, past the sleeping Koi ponds, past the wooden decking. Amber and Tasha, our two family dogs, snapped to attention as we ran by. They didn't know why, but they knew we were both on an important mission. Gretchen held one-year old Julia in her arms, being careful not to wake her. Julia slept pretty soundly, but we didn't need any more problems right now.

The light over the breakfast table was already on when we got to the house. Arvella stood there in the kitchen, silhouetted against the oak cabinets.

I pushed open the kitchen door.

"Don't be worried," she coaxed with a warm smile. "We've been through worse than this. We'll make it."

Gretchen put Julia in my arms and threw her arms around her mother. They held each other for what had to last an eternity. It was a long way to Amsterdam.

"I'll help you pack, Mom," she whispered.

*   *   *

A Waiting Room in a hospital in Amsterdam is no different from the ones in America. They show every detail in a cold, unforgiving manner.

Michael Nason stood next to Paul David Dunn. Michael slowly wadded his gray Pierre Cardin tie into a sweaty, crumpled mess. His usually impeccable suit, already looked like he had slept in it for three straight nights. He was on his fourth cup of coffee for the afternoon and had already looked through every magazine in the waiting room twice. For a man who was about to celebrate his fiftieth birthday, Michael Nason looked the picture of a thirty-five-year-old, torn from the pages of GQ magazine. Steel-blue eyes, trim, muscular figure. Steady, patient hands that contrasted with his ever-searching eyes.

The Dutch wall clock held it's arms at ten after twelve. Mike checked his gold wrist-watch. It showed exactly the same time. Ten after twelve. The afternoon sunlight streamed in over the simmering coffee pots and bounced off the pay phone.

Paul David Dunn paced the floor like a tiger. A big, barrel-chested man, he filled a doorway with his imposing six-foot figure. He was only thirty-three, but he carried the manner and maturity of a man many years older. He stroked and pulled at the heavy, brown beard that gripped his face, pulling deeper and longer with every stroke. But it didn't matter. It didn't make anything any easier. It didn't make the sharp pointed arms on the clock move any faster. All he could do was wait while his father-in-law struggled for his life.

Mike looked up at the clock for the fiftieth time. Twelve after twelve. An hour had passed since Paul had made the call to Arvella. In the twenty-one years Nason had served as Robert Schuller's closest aide and confidant, this waiting was the worst job he'd ever had.

The three of them had arrived in Amsterdam ten hours earlier. This first leg of the trip was supposed to be pretty much routine. Stop off in Amsterdam to review the new European office before heading on to Rome. The meeting with the Pope had been set for Thursday to allow plenty of time to rest before going on to Moscow for the meeting with Valentin Lazoutkin, the head of Soviet Television. The meeting in Moscow was the reason for the whole trip. Amsterdam was just trying to kill another bird with the same stone.

"How much longer do you think now?" Paul asked Mike.

"How should I know?" Mike snapped back. "We're just along for the ride."

Paul backed off. He knew that edge in Mike's voice. It was just as painful for him. Paul stuffed his tie into his coat pocket. He loosened his collar and rolled up his shirt sleeves, more to the way he liked it.

Paul David Dunn was one of the most influential men in the ministry. As the writer and producer of the world famous stage productions of *The Glory of Christmas* and *The Glory of Easter* presented every year at the Crystal Cathedral, Paul was a true entrepreneur, a man who liked to be in control of every situation. But right now, even Paul David Dunn had no control over what went on in the emergency operating room down the hall.

*   *   *

"What about this sweater, Mom? Do you want to take this sweater?"

Gretchen held the white sweater out and away from the rack of clothes in the closet. She waited for Arvella's answer.

"No, I don't think so. I'd rather take the light blue one. Could you pack the light blue one for me?"

Gretchen fitted the white sweater back onto the clothes rack and lifted out the lighter-weight blue one. She slowly removed it from the hanger, folded the long slender arms behind the body of the sweater and neatly placed it in the suitcase, open on the bed. Julia slept soundly nestled in her blue-pink blanket against the pillows. She opened her tiny mouth and grabbed another breath of life.

Arvella stood over the open top drawer of Schuller's dresser. She had selected a few things he would need - socks, two fresh white shirts and a gold tie the grandchildren had given him last June that he still hadn't worn. These things were easy. The tough choice was the hat.

Which hat would he want? Which one would he have taken? There were so many to choose from. His collection of baseball caps had grown enormously over the last five years. Ever since he had started his morning jogging. What had started as an idea about dropping off a few pounds had turned into a daily constitutional overnight. Two miles every morning at Seven a.m. Even in her deepest dreams, Arvella felt the bed lighten as he left every morning, "Just going to get some fresh air, Dear."

She decided on the dark blue, Los Angeles Rams hat he had gotten as a gift from the teams' owner. That had been years ago, but it was still one of his favorites. The fall season had just started and it would cheer him up to know how his team was doing. The special NFL badge on the right side was a nice touch. *Yes, the L.A. Rams hat.* She put it next to the other selections on the dresser.

"I wish I was going with you," Gretchen offered. She had stopped packing.

"You have your own family to think of now. Your place is here with Jim and Julia."

"I know." Gretchen agreed. "But I want to be with Dad so much."

Arvella put the Rams hat atop the red-striped jogging suit she knew was Bob's favorite and carefully found a place for them both in the suitcase. She looked up at Gretchen.

"Do you remember when you asked me what I thought about you marrying Jim?"

Gretchen smiled. "You told me I'd be stupid if I didn't."

Arvella smiled back at her. "I also told you he wasn't perfect. Remember?" She held Gretchen tightly with a look from her deep brown eyes. "As much as we all want them to be, they're not perfect, Gretchen. Your father was with you as much as he could be, honey. But he's not perfect."

Arvella's gaze drifted out into the gardens that protected the bedroom. Amber, a large red doberman, stood just beyond the walk-way, looking lonely next to the small statue of the Chinese elephant.

She folded her arms against herself and gently rubbed away the sudden chill. Tears began to well up behind her eyes. "As much as everyone wants him to be, as much as everyone always expects of him, your father's not perfect." She gripped herself tighter. "As much as I pray that he can be, he's not perfect."

Gretchen moved close to her mother. She grasped her hand warmly and said with all the strength she could muster, "He'll be okay, Mom." The feeling of dread was gone from Gretchen's voice. She put her arms around her Mother and said through the tears, "I love Daddy, Mom. He's all the perfect I ever wanted."

Arvella pulled Gretchen in close and wrapped her arms around her. She stroked her daughter's soft, brown hair. "Me, too, sweetie. Me, too."

*   *   *

"Did you call Jeanne yet?" Mike Nason said across the hospital room to Paul Dunn.

Paul looked over to Nason. He thought about his wife, alone with their two kids halfway around the world. He looked at his watch and made a quick calculation. It was two in the morning in Hawaii, but he was sure his wife Jeanne would be waiting near the phone.

"What am I going to tell her, Mike? We're still here in the waiting room at the hospital? We don't have any word from the Doctor to report. Right now, we can't tell anything for sure."

"I guess you're right, Paul." Nason said. "They say the most important thing is to stop the bleeding into the brain."

Nason thought about the Doctors latest report. They had diagnosed a subdural hematoma. That meant blood clots in the thin membrane between the skull and brain tissue. All the Doctors knew for sure was that he was still in a coma.

"I can't believe that he came within thirty minutes of dying." Nason said under his breath. Paul Dunn heard every word as he paced back over to the corner of the waiting room. They resumed their silent vigil. There was nothing else they could do.

*   *   *

While Gretchen helped Arvella pack, I wandered into the library. I loved being in Schuller's library. I loved the high ceilings and the rich woodwork. I loved the homey, family room feel of the place. If not for that haunting picture of John Wayne that hung in the hallway, it would have been perfect for me.

John Wayne had called Schuller to his hospital room the night before Wayne's cancer surgery. Schuller and the Duke had been close friends and Wayne thought he was losing his battle with cancer, "The Big C", as he called it.

Schuller went right away. Afterwards, a close friend of John Wayne's sent Schuller a special photograph of the Duke. It's a profile of John Wayne staring into the darkness. All you can see is Wayne's face. You can't make out what he sees in the darkness.

I would sit and stare at that picture. I always wondered what Wayne was looking at in the darkness. That question haunted me.

The library was a long room lined from floor to

ceiling with books. One entire twenty foot wall was filled with row after row of beautiful books. Schuller liked to tell everybody he could that he had read them all, but no one ever believed him. It was that smile he had on his face when he made the claim. I didn't believe him either.

The front and the back of the library had large windows that spilled out into the lush gardens. The ceiling was coffered with heavy oak beams. Schuller had always dreamed of having a library like this.

You stepped down into the library from the main hallway of the house, so once inside, you felt protected from the world beyond. To me, the library was a world within a world.

Schuller and Arvella had added the library onto the main house, almost fifteen years ago. His books were selling well, and he needed a place to write. The room became a favorite spot for the whole family as soon as it was done.

Schuller's big wooden desk stood at one end of the library. This was the business end of the room. Early on, the major decisions of the Ministry were made right here at that desk.

On the other side of the library sat a long, comfortable couch and two easy chairs. You could get lost forever in the pages of a good book in their deep, overstuffed cushions. Above the chairs are two stained glass windows, each a graceful peacock. They throw a soft and inviting light onto the chairs. Many a night I had watched Schuller and Arvella cuddle up like two love-struck teenagers on their first date.

A pile of open letters lay on the little table under the lamp between the chairs. I recognized them right away. They were Arvella's Love Letters. They were the letters that Schuller had written to Arvella when he was away at school after the War. We all knew about the love letters and how special they were to her.

Some were complete letters, some were short poems, others were just yearnings of a lonely young man plowing through the duties of an education for the future, the future that would be the foundation for both of them and all of us. In the family, Arvella's Love Letters were nothing secret. We all knew what was in them.

Arvella had told me she had burned a whole suitcase full of his letters for fear of her brothers and sisters discovering them. The few that were left, were precious.

The letters were over forty years old. The pages were completely stained and yellowed. The edges had started to wither away. They were hard and brittle like leaves that had fallen and lain on the cold winter ground. You could feel how tightly the gentle structures tried to hold themselves together. But the slightest touch of your hand could crush them into tiny, broken pieces, never to be restored again.

Every time Arvella took the letters out of their special storage place, they became a little more worn, a little more damaged. I was very careful as I picked up the first stack. Yet as I did, something about the top one captured me. It was one written in Dutch in Schuller's own hand.

He wrote the early letters to her in Dutch so that her brothers and sisters couldn't read them.

Mijn Lieve Arvella, the letter began, *De dagen fiejken langer nu dat we verderen verder weg hjn. Jk hie de regen buiten vanwit het klas raam en denk of you. Jk zit avonds alleen in het donker en denk aan jou.*

The words had been written with a fountain pen and were difficult for me to decipher.

Jk ril wanneer ik denk aan de warne en hart verwarmende tijden we samen hadden. De by elkaar jehaaled herinningen, lijken op bellen, vul my hart met melodies. Het is de toon van genoe gen, dieper dan een sympony. Net een bijbelvers het kalms alle zorgen, aloe malle bezorgd heden . . .

"He wrote that to me the fall after we met."

Arvella's voice startled me. I was so engrossed in

the letter that I hadn't heard her come in. She stood in the doorway with a sweet smile I needed so much.

"When does your plane leave?" I asked her.

"I can't get a flight out until the afternoon," she said, "All I can do is sit and wait for any news."

She crossed over to where I was and gently took the letter from my hand. She swept the skirt of her housecoat under her legs and settled herself in the easy chair. Her eyes beckoned me to sit across from her. I was mesmerized by the mood of it all and sat near the edge of my seat. She read the letter.

My Darling Arvella, she read, *The days seem longer and longer now that we are farther and farther apart. I watch the rain outside the classroom window and I think of you. I sit at night alone in the darkness and I think of you.*

I shiver when I remember the warm and glowing times we shared together. The gathered memories, like chimes, flood my soul with melody. It is a tune of thrills, deeper than any symphony. Yet, like a hymn, it stills all worry, all foolish fears, because it hums in future years. Now, it echoes a duet. The harmony high, the melody low. And may the great Musician let it swell, some day, in fortissimo.

She laid her hand over the letter and smiled at me. I knew she wasn't in the library any more. She was seventeen again, an innocent, young schoolgirl back in that little town in northeastern Iowa, laying alone on her bed. She read on.

Reflections on a Rainy Day

by Robert Harold Schuller

Raindrops—

Those moody little raindrops
Seem to smother my window-pane.
They haunt my mind with something;

But I search for the thought in vain.

I'm sure they rest serenely
As they snooze on the fallen leaves.
Their trip has made them lazy,
And they hang on the shingled eaves.

Perhaps they're a wee bit lonesome
For their cozy bed of sky.
And now they've made their journey
They can breathe a contented sigh.

Lonesome - -

Lonesome, that's all
If she were here
I'd say, "My dear,
Lets take a moonlight walk."
I'd squeeze her hand
It's warmth is grand
And off we'd stroll and talk.

She'd smile a bit.
I love her wit
Then reach some spot of bliss.

And there we'd stop.
Her arms would drop
Around me. (It's she I miss).

- R.H.S.

"He was so exciting when I first met him. He was so sure of himself," Arvella said. "He loved the spotlight. When we were in high school, he was a senior and I was a freshman. He was in the school play." Arvella smiled as she talked. "The other actors got so upset with him because he would improvise in the middle of a performance and steal the show."

She looked up at me and said, "You know why I fell in love with him, Jim?"

I didn't have the answer.

"Because he had bigger dreams," she said. "He had bigger dreams than anyone I had ever met in my life. He used to talk about the things he was going to do. The places he was going to see, the people he was going to meet. I remember on one date, we were driving along in his car and he started telling me about the power of radio. He was fascinated by the number of people it could reach. He talked about what a great tool it could be to help people. He was... entrancing."

She looked back down at the letters in her lap. "What was so attractive about him were his dreams. He had bigger dreams. He was the most attractive man I had ever met." She paused and then smiled to herself, "He still is."

Arvella sifted through the stack of letters. She came upon an envelope that was the smallest of all. She opened the tiny flap and removed a small card. It was about the size of a Thank You note.

"This is my favorite one," she whispered. "He said he kept it in his drawer for a year before he sent it to me. This isn't really a love letter to me. It was a prayer he wrote to God."

She took a long pause. I think she wanted to be very careful that she read the words just right. She looked the letter over and said:

You be the breeze, I'll be the cloud
You be the wave, I'll be the sand
You be the wind, I'll be the feather
You be the arm, I'll be the hand.

You be the sun, I'll be the shadow
You be the hope, I'll be the dream
You be the light, I'll be the window
You be the love and I'll be the faith.

- R.H.S.

I had to catch myself, because those words caught my heart. My eyes started to mist up.

Arvella's face showed the anguish she was feeling. In the forty-one years they had been married, this was the only time he hadn't called her before going to bed. Now he was lying in an operating room halfway across the world and she was waiting to hear if he was alive or not.

*   *   *

Joop Post waited patiently with Mike and Paul while Dr. Wolbers talked. Wolbers was one of the finest brain surgeons in the Netherlands and Joop had been raised to show respect for men who had risen above others in their lives. Joop was Director of European Operations for the Ministry, but his sole experience with this hospital had been the chest x-rays they had done on him a few months earlier.

"Gentlemen, the problem is simply the brain," Dr. Wolbers explained to the three of them.

"The brain is still the one area of the body we know the least about. We are working so close to the brain that we can't be sure of anything at this time."

"Is Dr. Schuller still in a coma? Has he regained consciousness at all?" Paul asked.

"Dr. Schuller is still unconscious. Unfortunately, we won't know if there has been any brain damage until he regains consciousness," Dr. Wolbers responded. "However, his pulse and temperature are normal and his condition hasn't gotten any worse," Wolbers said.

"How much longer will the operation take?" Nason wanted to know.

"I have no way of telling at this point. You should prepare yourself for at least three to four more hours of waiting."

Four more hours? thought Nason. *It's already been almost five hours since we found him slumped over the balcony in the hotel room. And that doesn't count the fifteen hours we hadn't seen him since the night before, when he complained of a headache, and he told Paul and me to go on the dinner cruise without him. He's been bleeding for at least twenty hours now. Four more hours before we know if he's going to live or die?*

"You must excuse me now, gentlemen." Dr. Wolbers said, as he walked down the hallway.

Post, Nason and Dunn looked at each other.

"I guess we wait," said Paul.

"Should we call Arvella?" Joop asked.

"Not yet," Paul said. "I'm sure most of the family is at the house with her by now. We should wait until we know more."

Mike Nason looked around for a fresh pot of coffee.

*　　　　*　　　　*

Most of the family had arrived by the time Arvella had to leave.

Gretchen and I stood in the front hallway and said goodbye to her. Her son, Robert Anthony, put Arvella's luggage into the trunk of the car. Sheila stood next to her mother and kissed her good-bye.

"Don't worry, Mom. When Dad comes home, the Crystal Cathedral Congregation will give him a standing ovation."

"If I bring him home in a casket," Arvella said, "I hope they give him the same standing ovation."

I'll never forget those words. If I bring him home

in a casket. She was stronger than all of us. To have lived through what she had with Schuller for the last forty years, she had to have that incredible strength. It seemed to flow so naturally from her.

We stood at the window and watched the car pull away. I felt Arvella's loneliness.

It was a long way to Amsterdam.

And it was a long way home to Alton, Iowa.

- 2 -

Black Death

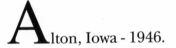lton, Iowa - 1946.

It first appeared as just a black speck on the horizon. To see it clearly was hard because the hot air rising from the summer valley, filled with rows and rows of new corn fields, made everything in the distance appear to stretch and wave. The black speck on the horizon looked like one of those old science-fiction movies, when the spaceship landed in *The Day The Earth Stood Still*.

The speck grew larger and larger the longer you looked at it. It left a trail of dust behind it so you knew it was moving. Then, as it grew larger, it took on a shape and a form. It was more than a speck now. It grew bigger and bigger. It seemed to have a sinister purpose to it, because it stayed right on the long, hilly, country road that wandered off to the west. Dead on it.

You could almost see all the way to Alton from the window of the top floor of the tiny Schuller farmhouse. There wasn't much at all to the little Dutch town of Alton, Iowa in those days. The war hadn't really changed the colony of immigrant farmers at all. Nearly all the young men had come home safe and sound. The graduating class of sixteen at Newkirk High last spring, had been a record. The new "Life" magazines had arrived at the general store earlier that week. The cover price had been raised from ten cents to fifteen cents. Another sign of something the government was calling peace and prosperity. Donna Reed was on the June 10th cover and there was an article inside about how Bing Crosby, Gary Cooper and Spencer Tracy reigned as the top movie stars of the day. There was some mention of a young cowboy star named John Wayne as well, but no one paid that much attention.

The weekly town meeting would be held in the little white Dutch church at the end of Main Street as usual on Sunday night at six-thirty. The whole town of Alton really wasn't much bigger than the little Schuller farm up the road.

Jennie Schuller busied herself in the kitchen working over her wood-burning stove. Her special apple pie was just about ready to be pulled from the black iron monster and put out to cool on the sunny window sill. It seemed like she did more baking now with the kids all grown up and gone, than she did when all five of them lived there. Jennie wiped her hands on her thin, yellow apron and grabbed a dish towel to open the hot, stove door. She looked inside the black oven, checked the state of affairs and slowly slid the fresh pie out to meet the world. She double-checked the smell, gingerly inspected the crust and satisfied, hummed as she rested the pie on its new home in the sun.

She looked out the small kitchen window to watch her husband, Tony, inspect the foot-high rows of corn. The stalks engulfed the farm and neatly stretched down the rolling valley towards Alton. *He was still a handsome man at sixty-five,* she thought, *and the gentlest she had ever known.* His hair had gone completely white now and he had picked up a pronounced limp about three years ago. His hands were still tough and strong though, not leathery like some of the men in the valley.

They had done all right, Jennie thought. Having lost his parents when he was twelve, never really affected him all that much. They had been married forty-three years now. Good ones, too. He never complained. Didn't see much sense in it, he said. He made his plan and set about getting after it. He'd done mighty good for himself with just a sixth-grade education. He'd come a long way from shucking corn for a nickel a bushel, to the 160 acres that was theirs. Three more years and that bank in Orange City would be all paid off. Sure, they'd been late once or twice. But the bank always got its money. Tony Schuller was a good, dependable man. He had never even raised his voice to her in over forty years.

The Great Depression had come and gone. They made it through that. The drought had come and gone. They made it through that. The war had ended one year ago. Both their boys were alive and in one piece. She thanked the good Lord every day for that. All three girls were married and gone now, starting families of their own already. Only young Harold was left to worry about. *Robert,* she corrected herself. *He liked to be called Robert now.* He would be home from that faraway college in Michigan for the summer any minute now. She glanced out at the sun sneaking behind a blackening cloud. *The bus is late again,* she thought.

She scouted out the amber valley below and tried

to catch a glimpse of the bus. It always started out as a black speck on the horizon.

Tony Schuller looked over the farm that he had built with his own, two hands over the last fifteen years. The main farmhouse was tiny, even though it was two stories high. White clapboard badly in need of paint, wrapped around the outside of the farmhouse. The out-buildings weren't as fancy. The red Dutch barn stood about fifty feet from the main house and was almost four times as big. Tony was proud of that barn. The red roof peak was the first thing you saw when you started up the long hill to their place and you could almost see the whole barn from the top of the general store down in Alton. That was a full two miles away. Off to the west side of the barn was the hogpen. He had almost two hundred squirming, squealing hogs in those pens now. A good sign of a prospering corn-hog farm in Sioux County, Iowa.

Their water well was between the house and the barn, next to the full-grown box elder. The outhouse leaned over to one side behind the door to the kitchen in the back. The Schuller farm wasn't much to look at, but it was their home. And it was almost paid for. *Just give me three more years, Lord, three more good years and I'll have that mortgage paid off.* Tony often prayed standing in the corn fields.

The black speck had grown into the shape of a dusty yellow bus that wound it's way toward the Schuller farm. The dusty face of the bus screeched, squealed and jerked itself to a halt. Dust from the road spit up and a rusty door pried itself open.

Nineteen-year-old Robert Harold Schuller stepped down off the bus. He wore his only black suit of clothes. He carried an old, beaten up suitcase that had a belt tied around it, to keep it from coming apart. Inside the case were the only other two pairs of pants he owned and three clean white shirts. He didn't need any of his farm clothes at college, so he had left those at home. That was ten months ago. Ten months. The bus ride had taken sixteen hours. *He never slept well on buses,* he thought to himself. He had three dollars left to his name and he hadn't eaten since he left Michigan. But it was worth it. He was home.

Schuller was tall and stocky, with short groomed hair. The white cotton shirt, hung well over his broad shoulders, tapering down his six-foot-three build. The school dress-shoes he wore felt out of place standing in the gravel stone road. He tightened his grip on the battered suitcase and stepped away from the bus. The thin metal door slammed shut. The rear tires spewed chunks of gravel into the air and the dusty, yellow bus disappeared on down the road.

Schuller stood before the one-lane road that led up to the only home he had ever known. A black-striped goldfinch perched on a nearby fence post. The little bird chirped its welcome, snapped its tiny head to and fro and flitted off to find a new adventure. The air was still and quiet. Schuller was alone.

He drank in a long deep breath of fresh summer air. *No more toilets to clean, no more long, lonely hours,* he thought. Just three months of being home with the ones he loved.

Schuller looked up the hill and saw the peak of the red barn. The top of that barn looked so good. He started the long walk. He wanted to savor every step. He wanted to remember every detail.

"Bull Schuller!" bellowed out from behind him.

Schuller turned around. A fresh-faced, tow-headed teenager jerked his head out of a red '38 Ford farm truck.

"Hey, Bull Schuller! Just get off the boat?" sparked the teen-ager.

"What do you mean?" asked Schuller. He checked himself over.

"Don't you ever get tired of wearing those same old black pants?"

Lucas Johanson, Schuller thought, *always razzing me about wanting to be a Minister.* Schuller had picked up the nickname 'Bull' on his trip to California country last summer. Schuller and three college buddies had all jumped in a black Pontiac and headed out across Minnesota. They made it all the way to California before the Pontiac gave out. Schuller picked up the name 'Bull' because he was the frontman for the bunch and had to talk pastors and music halls into hiring them for a meal or a place to sleep for the night. (They had called themselves the Arcadian Four.)

"What's the matter with my pants?" Schuller asked, brushing himself off.

Lucas hung out over the red hood. "Listen, we're all going over to Orange City tomorrow night. John DeHaan is back. You know him. Good guy. Fought in Germany. Boy, has he got some stories! He's got a little sister named Arvella. I've got her all picked out for you, Schuller. She's still in High School over in Newkirk, but just keep your mouth shut this time and you won't scare this one away."

"Thanks, Lucas. You're really building up my self-confidence."

"No sandbaggers, Schuller," Lucas warned him. "Don't make me shanghai you like the last time."

"Luke, I just got home. Let me get settled in," Schuller pleaded. "Why don't you stop by in a couple of days? Maybe we can do a little fishing."

"Fishing?" Lucas was shocked. "I'm talking about girls and you're talking about fishing? You're out there, Schuller. Way out there."

Lucas slid back into the cab and fired the truck up. He popped a smile at Schuller through the dirty side window and sped away. Schuller watched the tailpipe of the Ford disappear. The sound was gone in another second. All that was left was the still country air and the chirping of the birds.

GOLIATH

Schuller turned and walked up the hill.

Sundancer tasted the new pasture grass. It was good to be off the barn feed again. He liked the short, green grass much better than the corn and dry hay feed in the musty barn. He liked the warm, open air and the fresh smell of the corn fields.

His ears perked up at the shrill piping of the goldfinch. They stood at sharp points while the sound whistled through them. Sundancer slowly raised his long neck and struck a proud lookout. He chewed slowly, sharpened his eyes and looked around for signs of adventure.

He stood tall and firm. His coat had thinned from the winter and he had shed twenty pounds. He was ready for the feel of the heavy saddle on his back again. He was ready to feel the bit in his mouth and the wind whistling through his mane. He wanted to try out the grass down at the river, where his master lay beside the water and watched the clouds drift by.

Sundancer wasn't one of those shiny, bold-looking stallions that had come for the horse show last month. He didn't have the fancy, glistening buckles on his harness. But he seemed proud of who he was. His legs were good and strong. His hoofs were sure and shod. He was full grown and he belonged to a good master.

The goldfinch shrilled again. Sundancer took a sharper look around and spied the black speck just as it disappeared over the last hill. Sundancer saw his young master walking up the road.

Schuller saw the tips of Sundancer's ears before the rest of the auburn-stained stallion. He smiled broadly. Memories of the long, cool afternoons spent fishing down at the Floyd River, the dark, starry nights and the soft, rich ground beneath his back flooded through him.

Sundancer vaulted across the short grazing pasture. He was at full gallop and only pulled up when he was within five feet of the fencing. He bounced and jerked his head.

Schuller reached across the fence rail and smoothed his hand down the stallion's neck.

"Good boy, Sundancer, good boy." Schuller looked the horse over, checking for any signs of winter abuse. His eyes never missed even the tiniest detail when it came to Sundancer.

"Did you miss me? I sure missed you."

Sundancer reached his huge, stocky head over the fence and nuzzled Schuller's ear. Schuller stroked the stallion's bony nose. "Here, I saved this one for you." He pulled a bit of sugar from his pocket and fed it to Sundancer.

"Looks like you made it home for supper," a gentle voice rasped out.

Schuller turned around and grasped the warm, open hand of his father, Tony Schuller.

"Yes sir, I sure did."

They stood there in silence, looking each other over. They never really had that much to say to one another. Usually, it was a matter of his father doing most of the talking and Schuller doing most of the listening. And, believe you me, Tony Schuller wasn't known around Alton for his talking.

"Well," said Tony. "We better get on up to supper."

Supper, thought Schuller. How different a world it was at school in Michigan. There, dinner was the last meal of the day. It was when you sat at a long table in a big room crowded with dozens of serious young men, dressed in black pants and white shirts. Dinner meant the last meal before long hours of reading and memorizing. Here, dinner was the mid-day meal served to close family members around a small table in a tiny kitchen. It was the biggest meal of the day after morning chores and had to last through the long, hot afternoons.

What a different world Iowa was, thought Schuller.

"Looks like the crop is going to be good this summer," he said to his father.

"Yes," Tony proudly agreed. His gaze drifted over the farm.

They walked up to the house in silence.

Jennie Schuller smoothed the last crease from the blue-flowered tablecloth. She heard the front, screen door open. *Two people,* she thought, counting the time it took before the door slapped closed again. She smiled secretly and opened the top cupboard. She wanted the special plates for her son's first day home.

"Jennie, look who's here," Tony said.

Jennie Schuller hugged her big son. He was now a full foot taller than she was, she noticed. Her arms could no longer reach all the way around him. *He wasn't missing any meals at school,* she thought.

"Started smoking at school again?" she asked. She noticed a strange new odor in his shirt. It was the only habit Tony had that she couldn't stand. Her oldest boy, Henry, had picked it up before the War. Jennie was desperately trying to break young Harold's habit. *Bob,* she corrected herself.

"I'm afraid I have," Schuller said. "Been trying to quit, but it's not that easy." He was ashamed to tell her that he had fallen to smoking the leftover butts he found in the trashcans in the halls. So far, no one had seen him. He was careful to do it after the other janitors had left. He was too proud to bum cigarettes off the other students. Asking people for charity twisted his stomach. And he was much too proud to ask her for more money.

"While you're home, would you please smoke outside?" she asked gracefully.

"Yes, mother." Schuller answered, but the gnawing feeling for a cigarette never left him.

Tony finished washing his hands and took his regular place at the table. Schuller let the cold faucet spray wash over his hands a little longer than usual. He was looking at the apple pie balanced on the window sill.

"That's for later," cautioned Jennie. "After your chores are done."

Chores. What a welcome word, thought Schuller as he sat down next to his father. No more studying, no more working with numbers. Just simple, routine chores. Lots of time to dream.

Jennie put plates mounded with steaming ham, potatoes and corn in front of them. She sat down and watched as her son prayed the Dutch dinner prayer. *He's a dreamer,* she thought. He spent every waking moment thinking about faraway places. He had fifteen different ideas buzzing around in his head all at once. He still talked about traveling those two thousand miles last summer and seeing the Pacific Ocean. What everyone else in Alton had called a foolish lark, was one of the greatest memories young Harold had. He had seen the Pacific Ocean!

Tony had never even seen Chicago.

Jennie prayed a special prayer for her youngest son. She hoped the Lord would treat him good.

An hour after dinner, found Schuller loading cobs of corn into the feeder bins. He stayed on the dry side of the hog pens. He thought about going in there as a boy, wading through the slop and muck to fill up his basket with the chewed up corn cobs.

The winter had been especially bitter then. The snow was deeper than usual and the wind bit right through his corduroy jacket. Twice a day he would go into the hog pens and fill up his basket.

He remembered all the trees around the house. Tony had said the trees were too valuable to cut down to use for heating wood. "We need them for protection from the wind in the winter and for shade from the hot sun in the summer. We can't afford to cut down the trees just to heat the house."

GOLIATH

The Great Depression was on. There was no money. Nobody had any money. Certainly no money to buy coal. Corn cobs would burn well enough. Corn cobs could heat the tiny two-story farmhouse where the seven of them lived.

So twice a day he went to the hog pens to fill up his basket. He was seven years old. He lifted the wire latch off the gate and went in. The hogs scurried away, squealing and squirming. He reached down into the muck of hog excrement and picked up each corn cob with his small, bare hands. Each corn cob was important. Each one mattered.

Most days he could fill his basket without going into the thick of the hogs. But some days, the hogs were stubborn and wanted to have their fun with him. On those days, he had to fight for the corn cobs. He had to fight the dirty, smelly hogs for every single corn cob covered with the slippery goo.

But every day, twice a day, he filled up his basket.

They had two wood burning stoves in the house. One was in the living room for heat. They had cut little slots in the ceiling to let the heat drift up to the tiny bedrooms above, where they slept. The other stove was in the kitchen. They used that one for cooking. It was young Harold's job to make sure both stoves were kept well stocked with corn cob fuel.

He could almost taste the smell of those burning corn cobs in his mouth to this day.

The second push on the well handle filled the shiny, tin bucket to overflowing. Schuller was careful not to let any of the water spill out. He carried the full bucket over to the bright, yellow rosebushes by the porch. He gave each one a healthy drink. All of his father's prize rosebushes were in full bloom now. Blazing reds, yellows, pinks and burgundies set off the small, white farmhouse. The roses added a special beauty to the farm. They were the envy of every family in the valley.

"Not too much on that one," Tony called out. "She's been having a little trouble lately. I want to bring her along a little slower."

Schuller stopped the flow of water into the dark, black soil. He dunked his hand deep into the shiny pail and carefully flicked little droplets onto the delicate rose petals. Schuller knew how to treat a rosebush. He knew how to talk to them the way his father did.

Cultivating the cornfields was another chore that Schuller liked. It was a silent communion he shared with his father and the land. Slow and sure, that's how you did it. They had a tractor-driven cultivator the same as the other farms, but he always liked to do a hands-on, stalk-by-stalk inspection. That was the best way.

That way you didn't take chances. You couldn't afford to when you only had one crop. There was too much to lose.

Schuller and his father both raised their heads at the sharp clanging of the iron triangle on the porch. It was the dinner bell. Jennie rang it one more time and smiled out at the both of them. She turned and went in. They both straightened up and stretched their backs. Schuller brushed his hands off on his overalls the same way his dad did.

"That's enough for today," Tony said across the rows of corn stalks. "We'll get the rest tomorrow."

They walked toward each other until they were both inside the same furrow and turned toward the house.

Schuller barely tasted the light supper because his mouth watered for that apple pie on the counter. He wiped the thick plate clean with his last scrap of bread and drained his glass of milk. He wanted to leave plenty of room for that apple pie.

Tony looked out the tiny kitchen window. His forehead furrowed when he saw the western skies. "Looks like we got some rain clouds forming," he said. "Maybe hail. We best get outside and get the rosebushes covered."

Schuller scooped a piece of apple pie into his mouth as his father stepped out the back door. He dropped his plate into the sink and followed Tony out. In a minute, they both came out of the barn carrying two buckets in one hand and a wooden box in the other.

"I'll take care of the ones around the back," Schuller declared as he headed toward the house.

"Better hurry," Tony warned. "That hail will be here any minute."

Schuller double-timed around the back of the house. He covered the two rosebushes by the porch with the buckets and hustled on to catch the roses out by the box elder tree. Halfway there, he stopped dead in his tracks.

The sky had turned jet black.

Schuller stood frozen. The air stilled. A terror struck through him then and there as he realized his whole world had just changed. He was surrounded by something frightening and terrible. Something big and black and destructive was coming toward him. And he had no idea what it was.

"Get your mother, Son! Get her right now!" his father yelled at him.

"GET HER NOW!" shouted Tony. He bolted past Schuller in a running hop-step. "That's a twister coming!" he yelled. "We've got to get out of here!"

Schuller dropped the wooden box. It plunked against the ground. Giant, black clouds whipped in the skies above. They churned and thundered in a frenzy and started to move down across the valley. A strong wind whacked the gate against the fence post. The wind swept the buckets off the rosebushes and danced them across the yard.

In the pasture, Sundancer bucked and whinnied. Schuller shot a glance toward him. He waved a 'Get out!' 'Run!' to Sundancer with both arms and turned and sprinted toward the house. He called hoarsely for his

Mother to get out of the house. The darkening wind drowned his voice. It began to bend the box elder tree.

The wind turned into a fury, banging the wooden gate back and forth against the fence. The pigs squealed and scattered, desperately searching for safety. Tony had disappeared into the darkness of the barn. Schuller ran faster, toward the house for his mother.

Lightning cracked and bolted across the skies. The dark clouds formed a huge lump across the western horizon. Angry black clouds swelled and puffed and stretched. Then the lowest cloud stretched out and fell to the ground like a whipcord. It hung there suspended in the swimming darkness, swaying and slithering like a giant snake getting ready to strike.

Schuller flung open the front door. He saw Jennie's expectant, questioning face. "Come on! We've got to get out of here!" he shouted to her. "We've got to go, Now!"

The window crashed in! Shards of glass bounced off the walls and flew, to slice into Jennie's face. She turned away just in time.

"Come on!" shouted Schuller. He kept the front door pried open with his back. The wind shot around behind him and tried to force it closed. They would be trapped in the house!

Jennie ran toward the open doorway, keeping her hands close to her face to shield it from the sharp, flying glass. Schuller threw his arm around her and they raced out the door. The front door banged shut behind them and they flung themselves off the porch into the howling wind.

They looked down the valley as they fought their way across the front yard. It was terrifying. The storm had shaped itself into a black funnel, fifty feet wide and it was moving down the valley. It was thousands of feet long and kept whipsawing back and forth across the little road that led to their farm. It was coming straight for them.

The sound of Tony's old farm truck which was

revved up, blasted out of the barn. Tony was behind the wheel. He reached over and flung open the passenger door. Schuller and Jennie jumped in. Tony stomped the pedal to the floor and they found themselves slipping and sliding down the gravel driveway toward the road.

Rain slashed down in big, angry drops. At the bottom of the hill, Tony made a sharp right turn and headed due west, straight into the path of the black tornado. It was the only thing he could do. It was the only road away from the farm.

They drove through the rain at ninety miles an hour. Tony squinted through the flapping windshield wipers. Schuller kept his arm around his mother, hoping she couldn't see the terrified look on his face.

The spinning, black monster, twirled down the road toward them, jumping off here and there to slap the ground and then rise up again. A farmhouse exploded into the air, not a hundred yards from them. They had to get to the crossroads up ahead and turn right to get to safe ground. They were racing into the face of a giant, black tornado.

Tony kept the gas pedal pressed to the floor. His knuckles went white against the steering wheel. Jennie and her son braced themselves against the dashboard and Tony whipped the truck into a desperate, slashing right turn. The truck slid into the crossroads up on two wheels, careened around the turn and bounced back down. He had cheated the Goliath of three victims.

The truck sped down the dark country road.

They watched the devastation from a high hill. Their clothes whipped in the wind. The terrible force of it all, shattered their senses.

The monster showed no mercy. It danced and skipped across the valley. Houses *exploded!* with terrific force right off their foundations. Trees bent until they could bend no more and finally yielded to the terrible force of the roaring black tornado.

Eighty-foot, full grown oaks were bowled over and yanked out of the ground like dandelions. Branches crashed through the sides of houses and barns. Dark wind howled through the gaping holes. Windows blasted out, spitting glass all over the once-neat farmyards. The swirling wind sucked the pieces up into the sky and they were gone. Just like that. Gone.

The tornado whipped down the valley. Jennie Schuller turned away. She couldn't watch any more. She couldn't bear to see it. Tony leaned on his cane and put his arm around her. She slipped her arm around him and they held each other together with their hope.

Suddenly, the air stilled and the funnel collapsed back into the sky. The sky opened up and the storm was gone.

Gone. The Goliath was gone.

They made their way back home, looking closely at the other farms along the way. They counted eight farms completely destroyed. Most of the destruction had occurred away from their farm. They turned down the crossroads and headed home. There were a few broken tree branches lying about, but no real damage. The Maas place was still standing. Their hogs were scattered about the barnyard, but all the buildings were still up. Even the big window in the front of the house was in one piece. There wasn't even a crack in it.

Their spirits began to rise. They each took a deep breath and turned up the hill that led to their farm.

They couldn't see the top of the barn. The top of the red barn was gone. Even the Dutch hip roof was gone.

"It's gone, Jennie," he said gravely. "We've lost the barn."

Jennie reached over and squeezed his hand.

He pushed down a little on the gas pedal and forced the old truck further up the hill. The truck crested the hill and they all stared at the ghastly scene that was spread out before them.

Every building was gone. The structures had been sheared clean off, right at their foundations. All that was left were the stark-white, cement walls. There was hardly any rubble. It had all been sucked up into the sky and scattered across the valley. Over two hundred trees were gone, yanked up by their roots. Not even a stump had been left behind. Electric lines were strung over dead pigs across the driveway, babies still trying to nurse from their lifeless mothers.

Tony's bony hands gripped the steering wheel, strangling it with his anguish until his veins swelled and turned purple under the white hairs of his hands. At last he let go and pounded the wheel with his fists, shouting, "Jennie, it's gone! It's all gone! Forty years of work and it's all gone!"

He stepped out of the truck and walked slowly toward the ragged foundation of the house. He leaned heavily on his cane with each step. He stepped over the snaking electrical wires, walking around the empty yard where minutes earlier their home had stood.

"It's gone, Jennie!" Tony whispered. "It's all gone."

Jennie's heart was too pained to answer.

The ground was black. The rich farm soil had been completely turned over by the tornado. Every month-old corn stalk had been killed. Ripped out and buried by the giant storm. Their entire summer crop was completely destroyed. The fences were broken and twisted. The fields were scarred and barren.

Schuller stepped out of the truck and looked around. *Where's Sundancer?*

He turned around and a nameless horror crashed through his heart. There in the grass beyond the broken fencing, lay Sundancer. A fourteen-foot, two-by-four had been driven straight through him. The proud, gentle stallion was dead, staked to the black ground by the tornado.

Tears ran freely down Schuller's cheeks. He fell to his knees and cried. He was surrounded by a world of death. Black Death.

*   *   *

They spent that night outside Orange City, at his sister's house. Tony and Jennie slept in the extra bedroom and Schuller took the couch. He started to close his eyes many times, but sleep was slow in coming. Finally, when the house was completely quiet, he looked up into the darkness. He felt the presence of his father standing over him.

"Harold?" the old man asked in the darkness.

"Yes sir?" answered the stocky Schuller.

"Get a good night's rest. Tomorrow we start over," said his father.

"Start over?" Schuller asked. It didn't make sense. "With what? There's nothing left."

There was a moment in the darkness when Schuller wasn't sure if his father was still there or not. There was a long moment of silence before he heard his father's voice again.

"Never look at what you have lost. Always look at what you have left."

Schuller heard his father's footsteps leave the tiny living room. He had gone off to bed.

Never look at what you have lost, Schuller repeated to himself, *Always look at what you have left.*

*   *   *

They drove into Orange City the next day and bought an old, broken-down, four-story house for fifty dollars. They took it apart board by board, shingle by shingle. Schuller and his father climbed to the top of the four-story roof and removed the shingles one by one.

They saved every nail and every shingle.

"Building your own home is good for the soul," Schuller said as he handed down the shingles.

"What's that, son?" shouted up Tony.

"Nothing," Schuller answered. "Just quoting Thoreau."

Tony climbed up the tall ladder to get the last load of shingles.

"'The mass of men lead lives of quiet desperation," Tony said to Schuller. "Thoreau said that, too."

Schuller shook his head. Thoreau did say that.

They removed the sheeting and framing members one by one. They took out all the nails with crowbars and straightened out each one. They removed every strip of oak flooring.

Schuller remembered that Henry David Thoreau wrote how a man building his own house was good for the soul. How building your own home from scratch had become a lost art.

After three weeks of back-breaking work, the father and son team had removed piles of shingles. They had boxes and boxes of nails. They had stacks of two-by-fours. They had sheeting, two-by-sixes, two-by-tens and they had good oak flooring.

They pulled out the foundation, which was cinder block walls, with a chain and a tractor. They chipped out each cinder block and saved it for their new home. They loaded up the wagons with their supplies and hitched it to the tractor and pulled it ten miles home to the farm.

They replanted the corn fields. They started over with a borrowed horse and a plow that his father had made on the anvil.

"See that red flag up there on the hill?" Tony asked Schuller. Schuller was hitched to the harness of the plow behind the workhorse.

Schuller looked over the mane of the big plow

horse. He saw a stake about three feet high, sticking out of the top of the small hill. It was about two hundred yards off. Schuller squinted to see the bright red cloth waving in the breeze atop the stake.

"Yes sir, I see it," answered Schuller.

"Keep your eye on that flag, son. Never let your sight drift from it," his father instructed. "And you'll plough a straight furrow. Never take your eye off that flag."

"Yes, sir."

Schuller slapped the leather harness gently against the borrowed horse's back and they began plowing.

Nine farms were destroyed by the Black Death that summer. The Schuller farm was the only one to be rebuilt.

Schuller sat on the roof of the newly built farmhouse at the end of the summer. His Dad handed him another bundle of shingles and he nailed them home. In the distance, he heard the shrill call of a bird. He heard a bird singing.

"Look!" Jennie called.

Schuller and Tony looked down from the peak of the roof. They saw Jennie standing there, staring up at them. A smile stretched across her face.

She cradled an armful of bright, red roses.

They were just beginning to bloom.

- 3 -

Age of Innocence

Dating is for the birds, wrote the young seminary student.

"You finished doodling over there yet, Billy?" asked Robert Schuller across the tiny dormitory room. "I could use some help looking up these Bible verses."

"Give it up, Schuller," Billy groaned back. "You're the only guy I know who keeps studying after finals are over. You've got two more years to finish that paper. Who cares about a thesis on John Calvin, anyway?"

Billy kept doodling. He was a freckle-faced, All-American looking, young man who was glad school was finally out for the summer.

Schuller kept referencing. A long thirty seconds hung in the room.

"Are you writing a Dear John letter or getting one?" Schuller finally asked. He jotted down another verse number.

"What Dear John letter?" Billy growled, then added, "What do you know about it anyway? Just 'cause you've been stringing along the same girl for two years doesn't make you an expert, you know."

Schuller looked up from his notes. Spread open in front of him was the leather-bound Bible he'd brought from Iowa, the voluminous Concordance overdue from the Library and the oversized Volume I of John Calvin's *The Institutes of the Christian Religion*. The corners of the books overlapped one another so they could all fit on the small table-top that was Schuller's desk. A notebook crammed with Scripture references lay in his lap.

"You'll meet somebody else, Billy," Schuller said.

"Yeah? When?"

"It could happen at any time. It's only 1948. Practically the whole century is still left." Schuller reached up and pulled down Volume II from the makeshift bookshelf over his head. He flipped open the heavy book. "You're a Forties kind of guy," Schuller told Billy. "You'll probably meet her in church."

"Sure. I've been going to church for eighteen years. I've struck out every time I've been up to bat. Girls hang around you because they figure it's the only way to shut you up."

He's right, Schuller thought, *I'm not doing much better. Sure, I've got a steady girl, but I'm not seriously thinking about spending the rest of my life with her.*

The sudden blaring of a car horn had them both gawking out the tiny dormitory window.

There, out on the boulevard, a tan and white Dodge Sportsman roadster shot by. The top was down and it was filled with celebrating seniors. Three girls smiled and waved from their backseat perch.

"They must be from Hope," Billy said after the

Dodge made a sharp right. "Boy, they never had girls like that at Hope College when we were there."

"We were just there last year," Schuller reminded him.

Billy watched for a minute. "Well, they must be importing them from Indiana now."

Schuller flipped another page and made another note.

"At least you're going to be close to home during the summer service assignment. I'm heading for the wilds of Nebraska, for heavens sake," Billy moaned.

"What about Minnesota?" Schuller reminded him. "Come June, I've got to report to Minnesota."

"What's wrong with Minnesota?" Billy wanted to know. "Blond haired, blue-eyed Anita Martin lives in Minnesota," Billy told him. "Nobody lives in Nebraska."

"You'll meet somebody," Schuller assured him. "You'll meet somebody."

*   *   *

"What do you think of young Schuller's progress?" asked the assistant dean.

President Mulder looked down at the contents of the open file on his desk. The tab on the file bore the name "SCHULLER, ROBERT HAROLD". Mulder took a long pause that had been carefully developed over forty years of academic life. Mulder was the archetype of a Seminary President - staunch, stuffed and unyielding. The heavy cabinetry that filled his office, glowed from the same dark brown stain that his suit has been dyed with. Mulder looked down at the file over his thin, narrow glasses.

"His reputation as a prankster precedes him, I dare say," the assistant said. "He's made some good grades here this year, better than he did in undergraduate. But I'm not convinced he's changed all that much from his work at Hope College."

Mulder looked up at the assistant. "We still haven't found out who hung the dead chicken in my office, have we?"

"Uh, no sir, we haven't." The young assistant could barely contain himself. *It was by far the greatest stunt ever pulled around this place,* he thought. He almost split a gut over that one. The eggs had to be the world's first, too. And they didn't have a clue as to who did it. Probably never would.

"Where is he assigned for service this summer?" muttered Mulder.

"Iowa for the first month, sir," the assistant stammered. "Close to his parents' farm. He'll be there about a month and then on to Minnesota for the rest of the summer. He'll be delivering sermons in a different church each Sunday." The assistant meekly unclasped his hands from behind him and pointed at the papers in the file. "It - it's all right there, sir."

Mulder pawed the corners of the sheets of paper, one by one. He took his time. "Yes, I see it is....I see it is."

Mulder carefully read down the first assignment sheet. His stubby finger rubbed hard over the paper's surface.

"Newkirk, eh? Well, we'll see how he does in Newkirk."

*   *   *

"Now hold still for a minute or I'll stick you with this pin," Arvella DeHaan instructed her fidgeting sixteen-year-old sister.

"Can't you hurry it up?" needled Winny. "I'll be late for the birthday party."

"I'm fixing it for you as fast as I can," Arvella countered.

"Do you think Johnny Goertzen will be there? I

hope he is. I want to look good for Johnny. He's the living end."

"Who's Johnny Goertzen?"

"Who's Johnny Goertzen? Only the best-looking boy in all of Newkirk High, that's all!" Winny answered. "How could anyone in the whole world not know who Johnny Goertzen is? I mean, really, 'Vella, you better get your nose out of those music sheets or you're going to end up an old maid."

"I'm hardly an old maid," Arvella said quietly. She had three long pinning needles in her mouth and two more between her fingers. She wasn't taking any chances with a sixteen-year-old girl who'd just gone boy-crazy. "Eighteen is hardly an old maid." Arvella added.

"In Iowa it is," corrected her younger sister. Winny shifted her weight on the twelve inch stool that she stood on. She smoothed down the white pleated skirt and examined the fit in the full-length mirror that was fastened to the back of her bedroom door. "Do you think I should wear the yellow dress instead? Yellow is so fashionable this season."

"Yellow?" asked Arvella. She had to catch herself from swallowing a pin.

"No, I don't think so," Winny said to her backside in the mirror. She turned a little to see how the pleats looked in motion. "This white one will do just fine. But I think I might go with a red belt. Yes, a red belt. With a big buckle," she decided as she stepped off the stool. Her skirt pulled right out of Arvella's hands.

"Winny, please," said Arvella. "Do you want me to fix your dress or not?"

"Oh, that's all right, 'Vella," said Winny's reflection in the dressing table mirror. "I'm sure I can manage." Winny ran her brush through her hair for the tenth time. "You go on. I'm sure you want to get down to church for some last minute practice."

Arvella scooped up the pins and left the room. *I*

couldn't have been like that at sixteen, she thought to herself. *Could I?*

The little white church stood at the end of Main Street in Newkirk, Iowa. Across the street was the General Store and the local country school. Across from that was a big open cornfield.

The church held almost two hundred people. It was one of the largest in the county, unless you wanted to drive all the way to Sioux City. That was forty-five miles southwest.

The town members had built the little white church with their own hands one hot summer. The floor was good, solid oak from Missouri. The windows were all hand-glazed and kept clean by Martin Wanders, a loyal parishioner since 1917. His family had taken care of the church ever since it was built. Martin even made sure the old worn bell in the steeple was cleaned and oiled every Sunday.

Arvella DeHaan braced herself against the wooden steps. She pulled open the big oak door that was the front of the church. Her left arm was filled with music books and hymnals. Her purse hung over her right shoulder and she didn't want to spill anything. Not there in plain view of the whole town where everybody could see everything.

She carefully opened the door about halfway, just enough to slip herself in. Her soft brown shoes barely made a sound as she walked across the vestibule. She stopped at the second set of doors and peeked in. The afternoon sun streamed across the empty pews. There wasn't a single soul inside.

Good, thought Arvella. *Nobody here, yet.*

She marched down the center aisle and walked right up to the altar. She softly placed her music sheets on the rail of the organ, swept her spring dress under her and sat down. Outside, the sound of chirping robins came through the windows. One was definitely calling for another and their sweet melody drifted through the open windows. Arvella lifted the cover on the organ. She didn't want it to bang open like it had before when she was sixteen and had attracted the attention of the whole congregation.

The cover slid into its hiding place. Arvella's fingers pushed down into the keys and began to play.

Robert Schuller mounted the steps of the little church. Even outside, he could hear the music through the windows. It was deep and compelling. It beckoned him inside. He felt himself drawn in.

He looked into the church and saw the lone figure playing the organ. *That was where the music came from.* He watched her fingers move gently across the keys. She was so engrossed in her playing that she didn't hear him when he came up behind her.

"Oh," said the startled Arvella.

She turned and looked at him.

"Sorry. I didn't mean to - - -." Suddenly, for the first time in his life, Schuller was speechless.

Arvella looked at him. There wasn't anything remarkable about him. He was tall. His voice was deep and strong. He looked dark, but it was hard to tell in the dim afternoon light. Yet, there was something different about him.

"I'm Robert Schuller," he finally eeked out. Schuller was totally captivated by her. "I - I'm the visiting minister here this week," he went on. "You must be Arvella."

"How did you know that?" Arvella asked.

"The kid outside mowing the lawn told me," Schuller said.

"Oh, I see," Arvella answered shyly. "Well, I suppose you'll want to go over the hymns for this Sunday?" she asked.

"Sunday?" Schuller caught himself staring at her. He was watching the light from the window dance off her hair. "Oh, the hymns. Yes, well, I - I'd like to go over the hymns. If you wouldn't mind."

"I wouldn't mind at all," she said as she lowered her eyes.

That evening, Robert Schuller tried to steady his hand as he wrote. He gripped the pen a little more tightly and watched the black lines flow onto the paper.

Dear Bill, he started out. He stopped, thought a moment, and went on.

I met the girl I'm going to marry.

*   *   *

"My sermon this evening," droned Robert Schuller over the pensive, crowded church, "concerns 'The Five Wives and The Five Foolish Virgins.'"

The Five Virgins? thought Arvella. *He's got to be kidding.* She sat in the front pew of the little church in Ashton, Iowa. She really felt awkward this far north of Newkirk. Not only had he brought her all the way up here for Sunday night services, but he had sat her right next to his mother. *Some first date,* thought Arvella.

"Our text," Schuller went on, "is from the book of Matthew, Chapter Twenty-Five." He turned the pages of the heavy pulpit Bible slowly. He wanted the congregation to find the place in their own Bibles so they could read along with him. He cleared his throat and read to them in a deep, dramatic voice.

"Then shall the kingdom of heaven be likened unto ten virgins, which took their lamps, and went forth to meet the bridegroom. And five of them were wise and five of them were foolish. They that were foolish took their lamps, and took no oil with them: But the wise took oil in their vessels with their lamps."

"While the bridegroom tarried, they all slumbered and slept. And at midnight there was a cry made. 'Behold, the bridegroom cometh; go ye out to meet him.' Then all those virgins arose, and trimmed their lamps. And the foolish said unto the wise, Give us of your oil: for our lamps are gone out."

"But the wise answered, saying, Not so; lest there not be enough for us and you; but go ye rather to them that sell, and buy for yourselves."

"And while they went to buy, the bridegroom came; and they that were ready went in with him to the marriage: and the door was shut. Afterward came also the other virgins, saying, Lord, Lord, open to us. But he answered and said, 'Verily I say unto you, I know you not.' "

"Watch therefore, for ye know neither the day nor the hour when the Son of man cometh." Schuller slowly closed his oversized Bible and looked up piously at the congregation.

Arvella felt the heavy weight of his stare. She looked at his mother out of the corner of her right eye. Jennie sat beaming proudly. She looked at his father out of the corner of her left eye. A smirk started to appear on his lips. Tony glanced towards Arvella. She dropped her eyes and hid herself in her Bible. *This isn't exactly what I had in mind,* she thought. *A movie would have been just fine. Or even a coke and chicken dinner at the O.K. Cafe in downtown Alton. But church with his mother and father for our first date? What's he learning at seminary school?*

Schuller's voice boomed on inside the dimly lit church.

"Hardly a week passes when a minister doesn't hear a confession that goes something like this: 'Reverend, I want to live a good life. I know what is right and wrong. My problem is that I haven't got the power to resist temptation.' Well, it's not easy. Wendall Phillips said it, 'Christianity is a battle, not a dream.' Also, a New

Testament writer once wrote, 'Happy is the man who endures temptation for when he is tried, he shall receive the crown of life, which God has promised to those who love Him.' Let me suggest to you today some simple steps on how to overcome temptation."

Schuller deepened his voice, pounding on the word Temptation.

Turn down dates with men who wear black pants, thought Arvella. *That's one way to resist temptation.*

"My first suggestion is this," Schuller boomed, "You must sincerely want to overcome your temptation. You can live right if you really want to. No one will ever conquer temptation, unless he has the will. If you sincerely seek help, help is available. Which leads us to simple step #2."

"Learn to say, No!" Schuller scolded. "It will be worth more to you than a dozen foreign languages. When you are tempted, just remember this one word - NO!"

Schuller pounded his fist on the heavy oak pulpit emphatically. "Force your lips to say it! Say it aloud! Repeat it over and over! When Emerson was confronted with the Fugitive Slave Law in 1850, he said with a reverent profanity, 'I will not obey it! So help me God!' "

HELL, FIRE AND BRIMSTONE! Boy, he really gets into it, Arvella thought. *Preach it, brother, preach it!* She found herself caught up in the emotion of Schuller's voice. She had never seen such a fist-pounding, animated sermon before.

Still, there was something different about him, she thought.

*　　　　　　*　　　　　　*

"Are you sure your parents are asleep?"
"Sure," she told him. "It's fine. Come on in."
Schuller followed Arvella through the back door

into her father's house. The kitchen was dark. The yard
light from outside, cast deep shadows across the bare floor.

"I enjoyed your sermon this evening," she
whispered. She moved past the breakfast table toward
him. He stood against the refrigerator and watched her
take her coat off.

"People always need to be reminded of the power
of temptation," he said.

"Which one are you looking for?" she asked. "A
wise wife or a foolish virgin?"

"Are those my only choices?"

"Depends." She moved closer to him in the
darkness.

Schuller's heart started to pound. "Depends on
what?" he whispered to her. He had forgotten all about
her parents upstairs.

"You know my father is just upstairs," she said. She
gently stroked his cheek with her slender finger.

"Asleep, I hope," he answered. Their lips were only
inches apart. His arms fell around her and slowly pulled
her closer to him. He felt the soft warmth of her as their
bodies touched.

"So do I," she said.

She whispered the words softly against his lips. She
closed her eyes as he gently pressed his lips against hers.

Their lips parted. She looked up into his eyes.

"I guess I didn't learn much from your sermon
tonight about saying no," she whispered.

Neither did I, he thought. Their lips melted back
together.

The grandfather clock in the dining room struck
the midnight hour.

Schuller caught his breath and opened the door
behind him. "I have to leave for Minnesota tomorrow," he
told her.

"I know," she whispered softly.

"Can I write to you?" he asked expectantly.

"I'd like that," she said. "I'd like that very much."

She stood in the doorway and watched him disappear into the night.

*   *   *

The first letter came three days later. It was postmarked Minnesota.

> *Dearest Arvella,*
>
> *"Rise up, my love, my fair one,*
> *And come away.*
> *For lo, the winter is past,*
> *The rain is over and gone.*
> *The flowers appear on the earth;*
> *The time of singing has come.*
> *And the voice of the turtledove*
> *Is heard in our land."*
> *   - The Song of Solomon 2:10-12*
>
> *   All my love, Robert*

*   *   *

"Another letter to Arvella DeHaan?" smiled Billy. "What's that make so far this semester, twenty?"

Schuller didn't answer. He thought hard about the next line he wanted to write. *Lonesome, that's all...If she were here, I'd say my dear...Lets take a moonlight walk....*

Billy looked over Schuller's shoulder. "Ooh, pretty strong stuff, Schuller. Lonesome, huh?" he wisecracked.

"At least I have somebody to write to," Schuller said.

"Well, with the money you're spending on stamps, I could be taking two girls out," Billy snapped back.

"Sure," Schuller said, "If one was desperate and the other was hopeful."

"Yeah, yeah, yeah," Billy chuckled as he plopped back onto his bunk.

*   *   *

"Arvella, there's another letter for you here from Michigan." Her mother smiled as she handed her the letter. "Don't they have girls in Holland, Michigan?"

Dearest Arvella,

When the night is past
And the dawning of the new day
        is about to break
With fresh hopes and dreams,
Then you will hear the singing of the birds.

When storm clouds break
To drift away
Leaving bright patches of blue
With golden shafts of sunlight
On flower and leaf,
Sparkling with fresh drops of diamond rain,
Then you will hear the singing of the birds.

Yes, there are those times and places
        when the cold winter ends.
Springtime returns.
The dark night of the soul
Is dissolved into a happy daybreak.
The storm is over.
Then you will hear the singing of the birds.

- R.H.S

"Arvella?" her mother called. "Arvella, what's the matter?" Stella DeHaan looked at her daughter across the kitchen. Arvella's face was stunned. She was still in a state of shock. Or was it excitement?

81

Stella repeated the question. "Is everything all right?"

Arvella held the letter away from her face. She looked at her mother with a blank stare. Stella started to move toward Arvella.

"What is it, Arvella? What does it mean?"

Arvella looked at her.

"I think he's coming to see me."

*   *   *

"I can't believe you're doing this, Schuller. I just can't believe it."

Billy's face was frozen in shock.

"Mulder will kill you if he finds out."

Schuller kept packing his old, beat-up, brown suitcase. He prayed the leather belt would hold it together for one more trip.

"What Mulder doesn't know, won't hurt him," Schuller groaned as he jammed the case closed.

"Sit on this for a minute, will you?" Bob asked his roommate.

Billy jammed his full weight down on the case. All one hundred and forty-five pounds of him. Schuller slipped the oversized belt around the bulging box, threaded the tongue of the belt through the suitcase handle and cinched it tight.

"Mulder won't be back until Tuesday," Schuller grunted. "It's only Friday. That gives us four days to get there and get back. We'll make it."

Schuller pulled the bound suitcase off the lower bunkbed and hid it under his desk.

"How'd you talk Warren into driving you all the way to Iowa?" Billy asked.

"Took about two minutes to talk Warren into taking me to Iowa."

"Oh, yeah. I forgot. Mulder's not exactly at the top

of his hit parade." Billy watched his roommate prowl around the room. Schuller made a quick check of the place, making sure he hadn't forgotten anything. It was like watching a tiger trapped in a cage.

"What's it feel like?" Billy smirked.

Schuller smiled back. "Feels great," he said.

"Let me see it again." It was Billy's fourth request.

Schuller reached deep into his pocket and pulled out the small velvet box. A gold band shone brightly around the black, velvet box where the two halves came together. He opened the box with one finger and the diamond sparkled. Billy's eyes widened.

"Everything you had, huh?" Billy noted.

"And then some," Schuller added. "If Warren hadn't offered to stake me for the gas, I'd be the world's first to mail an engagement ring, asking a girl to marry me."

"Yeah," Billy agreed, "The world's first bonehead."

Billy caught the look on Schuller's face. Inside, he kicked himself for that last crack. He knew how hard it was for Schuller to ask people for money.

The doorknob turned and the door burst open.

"Are you ready?" Warren said. "I just saw Mulder's car pull away from his office." Warren's imposing figure filled the doorway. His voice was anxious. "I'm all gassed up. Let's go."

"I'm as ready as I'll ever be," Schuller said. He snapped the jewelry box shut and grabbed his suitcase from under the desk. "Let's go."

Warren raced down the hall and Robert Schuller ran after him.

"Hey, Bob," Billy yelled. Schuller turned and looked at Billy.

"How do you know?" Billy asked. "How do you know for sure?"

Schuller looked at him for a minute. He knew that Billy had laid himself open for a real zinger. But then

Schuller's face softened.

"You don't." Schuller said. "You just know what's in your heart. No guarantees, Billy." Schuller paused. "You take a chance."

Schuller winked a quick good-bye, turned and ran after Warren.

He never looked back.

*   *   *

Lou DeHaan had just finished lunch when he heard the doorbell ring.

"I'll get it, Stella," he said to his wife. She was clearing the table.

Lou walked through the house to the front door. Behind the curtains, he could see the outline of a tall, dark figure. The outline was fidgeting. Lou pulled open the front door.

"Well, Reverend Schuller," he said somewhat surprised. "I didn't expect to see you here, today."

"How are you, sir?" the young seminary student asked respectfully.

"Fine. I'm just fine," Lou said as he stepped back from the doorway. Schuller stepped inside the house.

"Actually, sir, I've come to see Arvella," he said.

Lou raised an eyebrow. "Arvella's not here."

"Not here?" asked Schuller. Disappointment rose in his voice.

"No, she isn't." Lou noticed the lines of fatigue in Schuller's face. He probed Schuller for what he really wanted. "Stella, where's Arvella?" he shouted at the kitchen.

"She's down at the church, Lou," Stella's voice called back.

Schuller moved back towards the door. "Thank you," he said, "I have to be going now, sir. I'm a little pressed for time."

Lou left the door open. He watched Schuller get in Warren's car and drive towards town.

He's got it bad, Lou smiled.

*   *   *

The music filled the little, white Dutch church. Arvella sat poised at the organ. She was lost in the music that filled the church. Schuller's presence startled her.

"What are you doing here?" Arvella asked in surprise.

"I need to talk to you." he said. "But not here. Would you like to take a walk?"

"Why?" Arvella asked. "Aren't you supposed to be in school? Bob, you shouldn't be here right now, you're supposed to be in school."

"Arvella, would you please be quiet just long enough for me to ask you what I've come this far to ask?"

"Yes, Bob. Lets go for a walk."

"Thank you," he said with a deep breath.

She didn't take her eyes off him for even a minute as she picked up her things and walked out of the church with him.

*   *   *

He took her down to the banks of the Floyd River. The river was the most beautiful spot Schuller knew in Alton. He had spent many a boyhood day there, watching the billowy-white clouds, float by.

The deep, blue waters crept softly by the grassy shores of the river.

Arvella wore a simple, white country dress. Her hair waved in the breeze. She was prettier than the wildflowers that she held. He took her by the hand and led her to a fallen oak tree by the river's edge.

Schuller's heart pounded in his chest. He thought

85

it would be easier than this. He hadn't been this nervous since the night he went out on his first date. He tried to put the words together in his head, but nothing seemed just right. It wasn't good enough for Arvella. He'd gone through this scene a hundred times on the drive down. How she would look, what he would say, how he would be in complete control of his emotions. He had a calm, romantic answer for every possible word she would say to him.

He would tell her how important she was, how much he needed her, how much he wanted her, how much he loved her. How much he loved her. Why was that so important?

"Bob," Arvella broke in. She caught him daydreaming. "You said you had something to tell me?"

"The river's beautiful this time of year," stumbled out of his mouth. "Do - don't you think it's beautiful?"

"Yes, it's very lovely," she agreed softly. "Did you come all the way from Michigan to see the river?"

"No," Schuller said, "I came all the way from Michigan to see you."

This is it, she thought. *This has to be it.*

"I've done a lot of thinking and praying about this," he said.

I can't believe this is finally happening. He's going to ask me to marry him.

"The first day I saw you, I wrote my best friend that I had met the girl I was going to marry." His eyes began to mist up. He tried desperately to hold back the tears. For once in his life, he wanted it to be just like in the movies. He wanted it to be perfect for her.

"Arvella, I love you. I have since the first moment I saw you. Will you be my wife?"

Arvella's heart was in her throat. Tears filled her eyes. She gathered her strength, looked up into his eyes and replied, "It would be an honor to be your wife."

Schuller reached into his pocket, took out the

diamond ring that had taken his last penny to buy, and slipped it on her finger. Arvella let the tears flow over her smooth cheeks.

Schuller put his arms around her, pulled her tightly into him and kissed her. It was a long, gentle kiss.

"I love you, Arvella."

Arvella's slender hand gently stroked his cheek. She softly wiped a tear from his eye.

"I love you, too, Bob. I always will."

*   *   *

"Just because you thought I wasn't returning until Tuesday, doesn't make it right, does it, Mr. Schuller?" President Mulder bellowed the word 'Schuller' when he turned his back on the two seminary students.

"No sir," answered Schuller. Both he and Warren had their heads lowered. At least they looked sorrier that way.

"We expect our third-year students to set an example for the lower classmen," President Mulder went on. "Ditching class is no example."

"Yes sir." they answered, almost in unison this time.

Saturday, thought Warren. *How could he come back on Saturday? He wasn't supposed to be back until Tuesday. What's the world coming to when you can't even depend on a President to keep a commitment?*

"The Board and I are still working out your punishment," Mulder went on. "Until we do, you two will remain confined to your dormitory rooms. All of your privileges have been revoked for an indefinite time period, pending a complete review of your records."

There goes my date Saturday night, thought Warren. He watched the tips of Mulder's shiny, black shoes dig themselves deeper and deeper into the plush red carpet.

The eggs, remembered Warren. *I bet he found out about the eggs.* Warren felt the hairs on his neck raise up. *It had to be the eggs.* He felt his palms start to sweat. *Naw,* Warren assured himself, *he couldn't still be mad about that. That was two years ago.*

"Do you have anything to say for yourselves, gentlemen?" Mulder finally asked. He had taken his time walking around to the back of his desk. Mulder's narrow eyes bored into the young men's expectant faces. "Well?"

Schuller opened his mouth to speak. Warren clenched his teeth and waited for what was destined to be another Schuller World's First. A desperate silence hung in the air between the lowly seminary students and the President.

"No, sir," Schuller said, lowering his eyes. "Nothing to say."

Warren couldn't believe it. Schuller was speechless.

*   *   *

Three weeks passed. During the first week, Mulder gathered the entire student body together for the sole purpose of making examples out of Schuller and Warren. Mulder went to agonizing lengths to scold the entire student body with his anger and disappointment over the two delinquents. In his opinion, it was the worst atrocity committed to date at Western Theological Seminary. The only thing left to do was let the deed be carved in stone on the courthouse steps, a scarlet letter for all to see.

Twice, Schuller requested a private audience with Mulder to make amends. At least to lay off of Warren. He was just doing a lonesome buddy a favor.

Mulder refused both times. They were going to suffer as long as he wanted them to.

In the third week, Schuller stood up in front of the gathering of the student body. It was his turn to lead the chapel service. The men before him bowed their heads in prayer.

Schuller glanced at Warren and stepped up to

address the student body, he looked directly into President Mulder's eyes.

Bob, don't make it any worse than it already is, prayed Warren.

Schuller stood at attention and began the opening prayer.

"Dear Lord," Schuller prayed, "Today, we pray for Your blessings upon this chapel service, and ask your forgiveness of our transgressions, as we forgive those who fail us."

Schuller raised his head. He opened his eyes and looked straight at Mulder. "When we bury the hatchet Lord, may we not keep the handle above the ground. Amen."

A resounding 'AMEN' echoed through the chapel and their period of penance was over.

*   *   *

The sounds of wedding bells hung in the air as they pulled up to a country church in South Dakota. It was June, 1950, just one week before Schuller and Arvella were to be married. The long trip was tough, so close to their wedding. But after all, Warren was getting married. The church was filled with friends from school and hundreds of people Arvella had never seen.

"Bob!" Warren beamed. "Great to see you, old buddy, how ya' doin'? How ya' like the monkey suit?" Warren did a quick spin around, to show off his shiny black tuxedo.

"You look great!" Schuller said cheerfully.

"Ohhhh, and Arvella DeHaan! I haven't seen you since we ditched school."

"You know, Bob wrote after your first date and said he was going to marry you!"

"Ohhhh he did, did he!" she said as she cast a teasing look at her bridegroom.

"Yeah, Billy showed me the letter."

Warren turned back to Bob and said, "We need to get moving. You're a groomsman, so you're up front with me in the wedding party." His attention slowly turned to Arvella as he continued, Sooo uhhh.."

Bob quickly chimed in and said, "Will you be all right sitting here by yourself?"

"I'll be fine. You two go on ahead," she said as she watched the two friends head for the altar office.

The aroma of spring flowers, in full bloom, filled the air as the guests slowly began to file in around her. As the organ music softly played, the church reminded her of her home in Newkirk. Arvella's mind drifted. She thought of her big day to come. Would the day be as nice, the flowers so beautiful, the..."

"Hello, mind if I sit down?"

Startled, she looked up to see a handsome young stranger standing next to her. He checked to see how big the diamond was on her ring.

"No, not at all. Please," she said as she watched him pass in front of her.

"Are you alone?" he said.

"No, my fiance is in the wedding party, so I'm just on my own for the day," she said with a smile.

"Me, too!" he said. "My girlfriend is the maid of honor, so it looks like we're in the same boat." She looked around the church. "Beautiful decorations, don't you think?"

"Oh yea, I love going to church weddings." he said. "You said you're engaged. Are you getting married soon?" he asked.

"Yes, next week as a matter of fact." she said, anxious to talk about her big day.

The organ music began to swell as the procession began its march. As the groomsmen appeared from the office near the front, Schuller spotted Arvella talking to the tall stranger.

The rage boiled up inside him. *Who's that?! I can't believe it! I leave her alone for two minutes and - - - WHO IS THAT!! The blood started to pound in Schuller's ears. I bring her all the way to South Dakota so she can sit there with him? I'm up here! I'm up here!* Schuller screamed to himself. *Why is she being so friendly to that guy?* His mind raced with questions as he watched his bride-to-be, laugh with the handsome young stranger.

The drive home was three hours of cold silence.

Schuller wouldn't say a word or even cast a glance toward Arvella. *What did I do?* she thought. *What does he expect of me? I don't even know Warren that well.* She went over the whole wedding again and again in her mind. She repeated every word she had said, every move she had made. *Why doesn't he say something?* she thought. *Anything. Just say something,* she pleaded.

Schuller drove on through the night. The headlights sliced the lonely, country road. Schuller's eyes were fixed on the dark countryside ahead. But all he kept seeing was the tall, handsome, young stranger.

It was 11:30 by the time they reached Newkirk. They drove straight to the DeHaan farmhouse. A single light had been left on outside the front door for Arvella. Everyone had gone to bed an hour ago. The whole house was quiet.

Schuller stopped the car at the front porch. The sound of gravel crunching under the tires, broke the dark silence. Schuller slowly shifted into neutral, pulled out the parking brake and shut off the engine. He was still looking out into the night.

The minutes passed like hours as they sat there in silence. Schuller's hands kneaded the steering wheel as the words formed on his lips. Arvella turned ever so slightly toward him. Her full attention focused on his eyes.

"I know I'm ready to surrender myself to the Lord,

but I don't know if I'm ready to surrender myself to you," Schuller said quietly.

Arvella smoothed the white pleats of her dress into her lap. She picked up her purse, opened her door and stepped out onto the gravel drive. She turned to him polite as you please and shouted, "Well, the wedding's next week, buster, so make up your mind!!"

She slammed the door in his face! And she stormed off into the house. *What have I done now?* Schuller thought to himself. *I am sure!*

*   *   *

"Where are we off to?" Arvella asked eagerly. She smiled and brushed the rice out of her hair as she got into what was now, their car. "Where are we going for the honeymoon?" she asked happily.

Schuller smiled and waved at the crowd that stood outside Newkirk Reformed Church. The mid-day, June sun shone brightly behind him. It was a perfect day for a wedding. Bits of rice bounced off the blue Chevy's hood as he climbed into the driver's seat.

"Where are we going?" repeated his bride.

Schuller looked at her. He was dumfounded. "Don't you know?"

"No, I don't know," Arvella answered. She looked at him playfully for a minute and then the realization came over her. "Don't *you* know where we're going?"

"..... North?" Bob suggested.

Rice bounced off the windshield.

"North?" Arvella repeated.

Schuller paused. The wheels spun in his head. "......North- - West? Chicago?"

"Are you saying you didn't make *any plans at all* for our honeymoon?"

"Well, Joseph didn't make any reservations when he took Mary to Bethlehem. And she was pregnant."

92

Arvella leaned back into her seat and shook her head. "Does that mean we're sleeping in a stable tonight, Bob?" She let the words hang between them for a minute, then she broke out laughing.

Schuller started to laugh, too. What else could he do? He was too ashamed to tell her he only had four hundred dollars to his name. That money had to take care of the honeymoon and get them to Chicago. He had a job waiting in Chicago. He didn't have the heart to tell her he didn't have the money to plan for a honeymoon.

He beeped the horn for the crowd, waved, and turned North away from the little white church. The two dozen tin cans that Billy had tied to the bumper, rattled behind them all the way out of Newkirk.

- 4 -

Into The Garden

They came to California in 1955. It was just another gray, winter day when they left Chicago.

Pastor Schuller loaded the light blue Chevy sedan with everything they owned. Arvella, of course, would sit up front. Three year-old Sheila could squeeze in between them. Arvella would have to hold Bobby most of the way. He was only six months old. Schuller had the seven hundred dollars from their savings account in his front pocket, the five hundred from the church in his wallet and a trailer full of used furniture. His new job was waiting in a town in California, called Garden Grove.

"Can I ride back here, Mommy?" Sheila said as she climbed into the back seat. Will it be alright?"

Arvella shifted Bobby off her hip. "Ask your father, sweetheart."

Sheila sat down in the back seat. She put her Raggedy Anne doll down beside her and peeked out the back window. The two big men helping them load their furniture closed the door to the trailer.

"That's the last piece, Bob," Arvella called. "Did you check the house?"

"Yes," Schuller said. "That's everything. Are you ready?"

They looked at the frozen grounds of the Ivanhoe Reformed Church. It was the last time they would see the red brick buildings and brown spindly trees. Everything in California would be sunshine and orange groves. The last four and a half years had shot by. He was still dirt-poor, but things would be different in California. There just wasn't much for a young man in the Chicago suburbs. California was the place to be.

Schuller thought about the blue Pacific Ocean. He hadn't seen it since the road trip with Warren and Billy back in '45. That was almost ten years ago. He was only eighteen then. Now he was twenty-seven.

*   *   *

They made it as far as Alton, Iowa the first day. Route 30 East, was pretty quiet. The road was dry for February, but all the county ditches were filled with freshly plowed snow. The sun stayed behind the clouds the whole way there.

Sheila colored and little Bobby slept until they pulled into Alton. It was almost supper time and he woke up cranky and hungry.

Schuller stretched his tired muscles the minute he got out of the car. The air was crisp and cold. In a few hours they would be warm from a home-cooked meal and bedded down for the night. It was the last time they would see Iowa for at least a year.

*   *   *

"Well, I suppose I could take about four hundred down now and you could owe me the rest at, oh, let's say, about thirty-eight dollars a month until you get it paid off."

Howard Duven rubbed his hand over the richly polished organ as he finished saying, "until you get it paid off." Arvella watched her husband for a response. She wanted the new organ. She never had a real organ or piano she could call her own and this one that they were looking at in the music store was just perfect.

"That's the best you can do for an old friend?" Schuller bargained.

"Bob, I'm making fifty dollars on this. That's the best I can do, even for a church."

Schuller looked at the richly polished organ. He extended his hand to Duven. "It's a deal, Howard. Can you get it to California at the same time we arrive?"

Duven scratched his head. "When are you planning to get there?"

"Well, it's Tuesday, now," said Schuller. "Pulling that trailer and with kids, we make about three hundred miles a day." Schuller looked out the store window at their blue Chevy sedan. "About a week should do it. We're leaving first thing in the morning."

Duven scratched his head one last time. "Wednesday? Let's see. That'd be the fifteenth of Feb'wary?" Duven jotted down figures on a yellow sales pad. He crossed out the last mark and said, "Sure. I can do that."

Arvella squeezed her husband's hand with delight. She had an organ to play for their first Sunday service in California. She would be able to help out. She would be able to do her part.

99

They made it to Kansas City that next day. U.S. Highway 75 South was dry and clear into Carthage, Missouri where they picked up Route 66. That would take them all the way to California.

Schuller stopped in Carthage to fill the Chevy. Sheila sprang out of the back seat to investigate another filling station restroom and report back her findings. Her Raggedy Anne doll never left her side.

They went on to Amarillo the next day. Traffic was light through the Panhandle and they stayed the night. Schuller hoped they could make it halfway through New Mexico by lunch tomorrow.

"Is this Abba - kurky, Daddy?" Sheila asked.

"Albuquerque, honey, Albuquerque" Schuller said. "I didn't think there would be so much snow this far south," he added to Arvella.

"Is that the Red Queen, Mommy?" Sheila pointed at the mean-looking woman in her picture book.

"Yes, honey. That's her."

Sheila sat in Arvella's lap in the front seat. She pointed at the *Alice in Wonderland* storybook. The Disney movie had come out three years ago, but there was no money to go to movies in Chicago. She had bought Sheila the book for Christmas instead.

"What's the Red Queen saying, Mommy?" Sheila wanted to know.

"Well, let's see," she said. "Alice tells the Red Queen, 'One can't believe in impossible things' and the Red Queen answers, 'I dare say, you haven't had much practice. When I was your age, I always did it for half an hour a day. Why, sometimes I believed in as many as six impossible things before I even had breakfast.' "

Arvella turned the page. Across the seat, Schuller listened intently to the reading.

"What are all those teacups, Mommy?" Sheila asked.

"The Queen is having a tea party. See? Everyone is sitting at the table and Alice is pouring the tea. There's the Mad Hatter, and Tweedle-Dee and Tweedle-Dum," Arvella pointed.

"They're the fat ones, right, Mommy?"

A sharp twinge of pain reminded Schuller about his diet. He saw a mental image of himself, as both of the fat characters from the storybook. He made a note to keep away from the sweets on this trip.

"That's right, honey," Arvella smiled. She knew what her husband was thinking without even having to look over at him. "They're the fat ones."

"I'm going to have a tea party as soon as we get to California. I'm going to invite all my new friends and serve them tea. Just like the Red Queen and Alice are doing," finished Sheila.

Arvella shuddered as her mind's eye saw smashed and cracked teacups all over the backyard.

"We'll see, honey. We'll see."

"More coffee, sir?" the waitress asked.

Schuller slowly looked up at her. She had distracted him from the white napkin. "Yes, please," Schuller said and she filled his cup with steaming black coffee. "Do you know how the roads are up ahead?" he asked.

"The truckers say it's clear all the way into Needles. How far are you going?"

"We're trying to make it to Arizona tonight," he answered. "And then to California tomorrow." He said 'tomorrow' with a big sigh. He was sure she had never been out of New Mexico.

The southern range of the snow-capped Rocky Mountains, sparkled in the coffee shop window. Schuller started to realize how far California was from Iowa. They were only halfway there and he was already feeling homesick. They had almost a thousand more miles to go.

"There has to be an empty hall somewhere in that

town we can start with," Schuller said to Arvella. She held Bobby on her knee, while Sheila colored on her Big Chief tablet.

Schuller looked down at the white napkin. He turned it over, took out a black pen and listed ten numbers down the side.

1. Rent a school building.
2. Rent a Mortuary Chapel.
3. Rent a Masonic Temple.
4. Rent an Elks Hall.
5. Rent a Seventh Day Adventist Church.
6. Rent a Jewish Synagogue.
7. Rent a community club building.
8. Rent an acre of ground and pitch a tent.
9. Rent a drive-in theater.
10. Rent an empty warehouse.

Arvella looked at the list. "Where are we going to get the money?" she wanted to know.

Schuller folded the napkin, put it in his pocket and paid the lunch bill. He planned to keep the napkin there in his pocket all the way to California. "You don't need money," he said. "What you need are ideas. If you have the right ideas, you'll get the money you need."

*   *   *

They arrived in Garden Grove on a bright, sunny day. It was February 27, 1955. Schuller pulled the Chevy into the driveway of the little house that the Reformed Church had provided. It was just another enticement to get a young minister and his family to start a new church. It was a tiny, one story tract home. The floors were brown asphalt. The windows were dirty and bare.

I guess this will do for a start, Schuller thought. He was too tired from the last twelve hours of driving to argue. All he wanted was a good night's sleep.

"Do you know how many members of the Dutch Reformed Church there are in Orange County, California?" Schuller asked at breakfast the next day.

"No, dear, how many are there?" Arvella answered. She was keeping one eye on Sheila and the other on Bobby.

"Two," Schuller said dejectedly. "Can you believe it? Two families and they live thirty miles away. Do you know how many families that leaves to start a church with?"

"No, dear, how many?" Arvella caught Sheila's glass just before it spilled off the table.

Schuller knew his wife hadn't heard a word he said.

Arvella set Sheila's glass upright and gave her a stern look. She looked up at her silent husband. "How many?" she smiled.

Schuller stared a big fat zero at her.

Arvella looked down at the kids, around the bare kitchen and back at him. She kept smiling and held up the finger 'One'.

*   *   *

"No, I'm sorry. It's against the law in California to rent government-owned buildings for religious purposes," said the civil servant.

*   *   *

"No, I'm sorry. I've already rented my Mortuary for Sundays," said the Mortician morosely. "The Baptists have it."

*   *   *

Schuller hung up the phone. "Well, that's it," he

said to Arvella. The late afternoon sun streamed through the kitchen window. Schuller looked at the cracked, black wall phone. "That's eight out of eight on my list. There isn't even a Jewish synagogue or an Elks Club in the whole county."

"What's next on the list?" Arvella asked. She rinsed out the ragged washcloth and wiped down the linoleum countertop.

Schuller chuckled to himself. "A drive-in theater." He started to cross it off the list.

"What are you doing?" Arvella asked.

"Nobody's going to come to listen to me preach in a drive-in," Schuller said despondently. That just leaves a community club building. I don't even know if there is one."

"What's wrong with a drive-in?" Arvella asked. "We passed that big theater on the way to the house yesterday. Here, look." Arvella flipped open the afternoon paper and pointed to the movie ads. A box in the lower corner showed a re-run of "From Here To Eternity" and "Shane" for the Saturday dusk-to-dawn show.

Schuller looked it over. "Well, I guess anything's worth a try."

*   *   *

"Can I help you with something?"

Schuller turned around. A middle-aged man wearing a plaid, green shirt hulked over him.

"Hello, I'm Robert Schuller," he said to the man in the plaid shirt. It wasn't the first time that he felt out of place in his black Dutch pants.

"Norman Miner," the man replied as he shook Schuller's hand.

Schuller got right to the point. "I'm a minister, new to the area, and I'm looking for a place to hold Sunday services."

"Well," Norman scratched his head. "My snack bar doesn't have any chairs so I don't think I can be of much help."

"Actually, I was thinking more about the roof," Schuller said.

"The roof? I'm sorry. You've lost me now."

"I want to stand on the roof of that snack bar," Schuller explained, "and the people who come will sit in their cars out here and listen to me through their car speakers." He lifted the silver metal speaker box off its post and motioned to the wavy gravel parking lot.

Norman scratched his head again. "You're going to stand up there and talk to the people down here through these speakers?" he said.

Schuller smiled as seriously as he could. "That's right."

"You'll have to get a microphone that will work with my sound system."

"How much will that cost?" Schuller said.

"I don't know, but I'll have to charge you rent."

"We're a small church. We can't afford much."

"Well, it will cost me at least ten bucks to have my sound man come out and open the place up on Sunday and turn on the power." Norman scratched his head one last time.

"You can have the place for ten bucks."

"Thank you very much!" Schuller said as he vigorously shook Norman's hand, "I'd like to start in three weeks."

Norman couldn't help but be amused by the young Dutchman and his black pants. "Why so long?"

"Well, I have to round up a few people."

Norman Miner squinted his eyes at Schuller. "How many people do you have in your church?"

Schuller stared up at him and glanced around the empty drive-in. Not finding anyone, he looked back at Miner. "Counting you?"

Norman smiled. He liked this brash young man. "Sure, counting me."

Schuller held up two fingers.

*   *   *

"Orange County's newest Protestant church will hold its first services on Sunday, March 27, 1955. Worship in the shadows of rising mountains, surrounded by colorful orange groves and tall eucalyptus trees. Worship as you are...in the family car."

Schuller finished typing the advertisement on his old Smith-Corona typewriter. *Kind of catchy*, he thought to himself. He leaned back in his chair to give the ad one last look.

"Bob," Arvella walked up behind him and began to rub the hard day's work out of his shoulders. "How's it coming?"

Schuller quickly took stock of his preparations for the church service just one week away.

"I built a wooden cross that we can lean up behind me, on the snack bar roof. We've got that old trailer to pull the organ over to the drive-in. We've got the microphone, the brochures are finished, and I've finished painting the sign to put on the highway to announce our services."

"So why do you look so worried? You've done all you can."

Arvella's hand slid up his neck to rub out the tension. "You've got the biggest pulpit in the world when you stand out there on that snack bar roof."

"I'm just not sure anybody's going to come," Schuller said quietly. His voice was filled with anxiety. "I don't know if the people in Garden Grove are ready for a Dutch preacher from Iowa. In many ways, it's like a different country out here."

Arvella silently stepped around her husband and

slid into his lap. Her hands gently wrapped around his neck. "Why don't you do what you did last week? Go out and ring some doorbells? You know, get to know the community?"

"Going door to door, asking people to come to church has given me a new appreciation for the Fuller brush man," Schuller chuckled. "I'm not sure anyone I talked to last week will even come."

"I'll come," Arvella whispered.

Schuller let go of a deep breath. He looked into her eyes as his hands folded around her waist. "I love you, Arvella," he said quietly. His lips softly pressed against hers.

*   *   *

"If you have faith as a grain of mustard seed," Schuller spoke into the microphone. He stopped himself from pounding on the pulpit because he was afraid the microphone would fall off.

A grand total of forty-six cars spread out in front of the snack bar. There might as well have been none. The Orange Drive-In had space for 1700 cars. His door-to-door campaign last week had attracted a grand total of sixteen families.

"You can say to your mountain, Move!" Schuller boomed, "and nothing will be impossible to you!" He jerked his foot loose from the hot, sticky tar paper roof. He thought about how many more doors he could pound on in the next week.

Not bad, not bad, thought Norman Miner looking out the snack bar window. *There are more cars here than I thought there'd be. Actually, maybe he isn't all that crazy. This could work.*

*   *   *

"Good Morning, sir," Schuller said, "My name is

Robert Schuller. I'm the Pastor at the new Garden Grove Community Church."

"So?" responded the man standing inside the doorway.

This was the tenth door Schuller had pounded on. He was trying to cover at least sixty more before sundown. It was already three o'clock on Saturday.

"I'd like to invite you to come to our church service tomorrow morning."

"You're another one of those Christian hypocrites, aren't you?"

"Pardon me?" said Schuller.

"Hypocrites, you know, you stand up there and preach and pass the hat. Meanwhile you live your lives completely different during the week. All you Christians are hypocrites. The whole bunch of you. Just like the rest of the country."

"There's a lot of truth to that." Schuller admitted. "But there are a lot of ministers who are not hypocrites. They work their hearts out. Do you really believe there are that many hypocrites in church?" Schuller asked the man.

"Yes, I do."

"Then why don't you come to church? One more won't make any difference."

The door slammed in Schuller's face.

*   *   *

"Yes?" asked the well-dressed man who stood in the doorway. "May I help you?"

"I certainly hope so," answered Schuller from the clean porch. "My name is Robert Schuller. I'm the Pastor at the new Garden Grove Community Church and I'd like to invite you to come to church this Sunday."

"You're a Pastor?"

"Yes, I am." Schuller looked at him carefully. The man was obviously successful. Well-dressed, well-mannered. "I'm the Pastor at Garden Grove Community Church," Schuller repeated. "Do you go to church now?"

"No," the man told Schuller. His eyes wandered away as he spoke. "No, I don't. I stopped going to church many years ago."

"Would you mind if I asked why?" Bob said.

The man stepped back, and without a word, invited the young pastor into his home. Schuller slowly followed the man inside. He wasn't sure how much of a chance he might be taking.

The room was well furnished. Beautiful drapes, expensive furniture, marble statues and books. The living room was graced by a hand-carved mahogany table. Schuller noticed a copy of *The Power of Positive Thinking* by Norman Vincent Peale lying on it.

"I haven't been to church in, oh, I guess it's been almost fifteen years now," he said. "Well, except for that one time about six years ago." He looked away from Schuller. "We were back visiting my parents. I went to church with my mother. But that was the last time," he paused. "That was the last time I went. Just before my mother died."

Schuller's feet welcomed the softness of the thick, plush carpet.

"I'm not a sinner, you know." The man had turned around. "I work hard. I work hard every day to take care of my family. My own business provides jobs for sixty people. Built it up from scratch with my own two hands."

He looked into Schuller's eyes. "I'm not a sinner."

Schuller kept listening.

"Just because I don't go to church anymore, doesn't make me a sinner. I do my part. I work hard."

The man sat down. He looked tired. "I don't feel safe in church," he said. "I don't feel needed there."

"Come to our church," Schuller said. "We need people like you."

"Do you have a program for teenagers?" he asked.

"I have two teenagers."

"If you help us start one, we will," Schuller said.

The man smiled and shook the young pastor's hand.

Outside, Schuller held up another finger.

*   *   *

"Going to the drive-in this week-end?" Schuller called into the garage as he approached.

Scooter Frazier pulled his head out from under the hood of his new Chevy Bel Aire convertible. He squinted into the sunlight outside the dark garage, to see who was talking to him. The voice had a funny, thick accent that he didn't recognize.

Frazier wiped the grease from his hands with a yellow rag and stepped into the sunlight. "I was thinking about it."

Frazier looked over the tall stranger standing in the driveway.

"And who are you?"

"My name is Robert Schuller, I'm the new pastor holding services over at the drive-in theater."

"Oh, yeah, I heard about you," Frazier said. *Pastor, hum?* Frazier thought about the homework assignment that his professor had given to him.

"Do you know anything about the story of Moby Dick?" Frazier said quickly.

Schuller thought for a minute. "I know a little bit about Moby Dick, but I know more about the book of Jonah."

Frazier's eyes widened. "Do you want to talk about whales?"

"Sure, why not." Schuller laughed. This was turning out to be the best house call of the day.

- 5 -

To Hell and Back

"**M**r. Frazier?" Professor Michaels asked. "Mi - -ster Fra- -zier - -?"

Scooter Frazier lifted his head up from his copy of Moby Dick. Frazier was a curly-headed, lanky boy. He wore faded jeans, a striped shirt open at the collar, and sneakers. Orange sneakers.

Frazier was famous for the art of reading by osmosis. He would put his head down on the desk and cover it with an open book. He claimed the words seeped into his brain from the open pages. Frazier had majored in psychiatry. Some day, he hoped to have a practice in Beverly Hills. Most of the 200,000 people who lived in Orange County spent all day in orange groves and bean fields. They didn't need psychiatrists.

"Mr. Frazier," continued Michaels, "Would you summarize what we've read so far?"

Frazier looked sheepishly around the classroom. Mary Lou popped a four-inch, pink bubble at him and went on chewing vigorously. Professor Michaels walked around the full classroom and re-read the passage.

> "*I saw the opening maw of hell,*
> *With endless pains and sorrows there;*
> *Which none but they that feel can tell —*
> *Oh, I was plunging into despair.*
>
> *In black distress, I called my God,*
> *When I could scarce believe him mine,*
> *He bowed his ear to my complaints —*
> *No more the whale did me confine.*"

"Well, Mr. Frazier?" challenged Professor Michaels.

"He's having a nightmare," Frazier said with a yawn.

The entire class broke up in laughter.

"A nightmare?" asked Michaels.

"Sure," quipped Frazier. "He's running from something. Or somebody. He's hiding out in the darkest corner he can find. Took a room without a view."

"A room without a view?" asked Michaels.

"You know, no window. Gone underground. He doesn't want to bunk with anybody." The class looked at Frazier with blank stares.

"He's afraid somebody might see," he told them. "So he hides out down below. He doesn't want to face the music." Frazier struck a finger across a passage in Moby Dick.

"Jonah sleeps his hideous sleep," he read. "He sees no black sky and raging sea, feels not the raging timbers, and little hears he or heeds the far rush of the mighty whale, which even now with open mouth is cleaving the seas after him. Terrors upon terrors run shouting through his soul. In all his cringing attitudes, the God-fugitive is now too plainly known, since he but too well knew the darkness of his deserts."

Professor Michaels smiled. *At least somebody still cared about great literature.*

Scooter Frazier chewed the point off his pencil. *Good thing I spent an hour talking to a door-to-door preacher about The Book of Jonah. Thanks a lot Pastor!"*

"He's having a nightmare," Frazier repeated to the professor.

*   *   *

"Arvella! Arvella!" Schuller shouted through the house. "Arvella!"

Arvella ran down the narrow hallway. "What is it, Bob?"

"Look, look," Schuller said, almost shouting. He waved a half-read letter in her face. An envelope stamped Marble Collegiate Church, lay ripped open on the kitchen floor.

Arvella took the letter from Bob.

"Dear Bob," it started, "Would be happy to accept your offer to preach in your church. Tell me when and I'll be there. Yours truly, Norman Vincent Peale."

Arvella looked up from the letter. She couldn't believe it. Norman Vincent Peale was coming from New York to preach in a drive-in. "Does he know our church is a drive-in?" she asked.

Schuller didn't answer. He was busy rummaging through the drawer of his writing desk. He pulled out a handwritten reply, found the same pen he used to write the invitation and signed it.

"You already wrote the acceptance letter?" asked Arvella in surprise.

"Sure," Schuller said. He was surprised she would ask such an obvious question.

Schuller slipped the letter into a pre-addressed, stamped envelope, and looked up. "What do you think a full-page ad in the Los Angeles Times costs?" He moved before Arvella could answer, stopping when the door was half-open. "I'm going to the post office," he said, "and to the newspapers. I'll be back." The door was half-closed when he popped his head back in. "Do we know anyone at the L.A. Times?"

*　　　*　　　*

"If Jesus Himself were standing here today talking to you, do you know what He would tell you?"

Norman Vincent Peale's words echoed through the drive-in.

Schuller barely heard Peale's voice. He was busy gaping at the sea of cars that crammed the Orange Drive-In. *There must be over four thousand people out there*, Schuller thought. Every space in front was filled with a Chevy or Ford station wagon. Pontiac convertibles with white tops scattered the back rows. There were even a couple of the new '57 T-Birds here today.

They had jammed the freeways for two hours this morning. Now it was eleven o'clock, already eighty-five degrees and they were still trying to get in. *I knew the ads in the Los Angeles Times would help, but the Women's Section of the Times? That was a stroke of genius!*

"What do you think Jesus would say to you?" Schuller heard Peale repeat. "Do you think He would tell you what a bunch of miserable sinners you are?"

You bet he would, Schuller thought. *There's a bunch of them here today. That's for sure.*

"No, He wouldn't," Peale said. "He wouldn't call you a bunch of miserable sinners."

Schuller was stunned. *What is he talking about? Of course, they're sinners. Otherwise, what am I doing here? Of course, they're sinners.*

"Jesus never called you sinners. He never called one of you out there a sinner." Peale pried his foot loose from the tar-papered roof of the snack bar. He held up a black Bible. "Look it up. Look it up in the Bible. You won't find it anywhere, because Jesus never called one person a sinner."

Schuller squirmed in his seat. *What is he talking about? What is this? That's no way to start a sermon. You're supposed to spend the first twenty minutes making people feel guilty. Then you spend the last five minutes telling them about how Jesus saves. How He died on the cross to save them, the miserable sinners. What does he mean, Jesus never called them sinners? Of course, He called them sinners!*

"You are the light of the world," Peale said. "Let your light so shine that everyone may see your good works."

The words echoed through the air. Scooter Frazier turned up the volume on his car speaker a little. He wanted to hear every word.

Schuller sat through the rest of Peale's sermon. But all he could think about was how he would show Peale that Jesus did call them sinners. He would spend the rest of the day reading through the Bible if he had to. He would find the words.

The cars poured out of the drive-in. Scooter Fraizer turned left on the service road to head for the beach. He looked up at the marquee. "Norman Vincent Peale" it said. "To Hell And Back" showed in red letters underneath.

Frazier chuckled. No one had taken down the lettering for last night's movie in all the excitement. There were a little over a hundred people at last night's showing of the Audie Murphy war saga. Over four thousand came to see a soft-spoken preacher from New York City.

Schuller shook Peale's hand. "I owe you a debt that

I will never be able to repay."

Peale looked deep into the young pastor's eyes. "Bob, you're a dreamer. And that's a great thing to be today - a dreamer." Peale held onto Schuller's hand. "Great dreams come with great problems. Be ready for that."

Schuller thought about looking up the words in the Bible.

Schuller looked up from the Bible. *It's not here,* he thought. *Dr. Peale was right. Jesus treated people positively. You have to build people up in order to help them Making them feel guilty doesn't do them any good. They already feel guilty.*

That's why they won't come to church, Schuller thought. *They need self-esteem. They want to feel good about themselves.*

Schuller opened the drawer of his tiny writing desk. He looked through the scattered papers, trying to find a clean piece to put his thoughts down on. Suddenly, he pulled his hand out of the drawer. He was holding the white napkin from Albuquerque on which he had written down his ten possibilities for church sites.

He looked at the list. *Possibilities,* he thought. *Self-esteem and possibilities. That's what people need more than anything else. People aren't any different no matter where you go,* he realized. *We all have the same basic needs.*

*   *   *

"Some of you out here today think you don't need religion. You don't have religion, never have had it, don't need it, don't want it. You think you have all the answers."

Schuller paused and looked out at the drive-in crowd. "Some of your answers may be wrong," he said.

I know some of mine have been, Schuller thought to himself.

Schuller was on his second sermon of the day. He

was halfway through the eleven o'clock service at the drive-in. He had finished up the 9:30 morning service at the Chapel, loaded the organ on the trailer and sped down Chapman Avenue, four miles to the drive-in. There wasn't time to unload the organ anymore, so Arvella played right there on the trailer.

Nobody seemed to mind. The drive-in following had grown to four hundred since last summer. That was twice the number of people attending the Chapel on Seacrest and Chapman.

The home office of the Reformed Church gave Schuller four thousand dollars to buy land with and build a traditional church. He had found a two acre site near the parsonage and bought it. The bank loaned him the seventy thousand dollars he needed for construction and they had quickly built a 300 seat chapel.

But people kept coming to the drive-in. In fact, so many came, that Schuller delivered two sermons each Sunday, one in each location.

"If you have faith as a tiny grain of mustard seed, you can say to your mountain, Move! And nothing will be impossible to you. Faith holds the key. And faith is nothing more than thinking about your possibilities. That's what God wants for you in this life. That's why Jesus never called you sinners. He wants you to discover the possibilities life holds for you."

Norman Miner checked the power feeds to the microphone. He wanted to make sure that the people sitting in their cars could hear every word of this.

*　　　　*　　　　*

"People want the Bible, Schuller, not Possibility Thinking," the assistant minister said. "Go back to your drive-in church! Leave the Chapel to me."

This isn't happening to me, Schuller thought. *It's a nightmare.* The months and years of standing on that snack bar roof in the blistering summer heat and the drenching winter rains. The days and nights of walking, down street after street, knocking on door after door - it all came flooding back. He had built it, and now it looked like his dream would be lost.

Schuller looked his assistant in the eye. "I'm not leaving."

Schuller stood towering over the shorter man. He still resented the fact that the Board Members had hired the young assistant while he and Arvella were on vacation. It made matters worse that the assistant delivered the second sermon at the Chapel while Schuller was out at the drive-in. Not to mention the secret meetings.

The young man shrugged. "I'm not going to waste time talking about it. The people in this Chapel don't want things to change. They like it here. They don't want to move to your walk-in, drive-in church. Nothing you can say will change their minds."

Schuller exploded into a fury! "Nothing - - - You think - - - Why you - - - I built this Church! I built it from nothing! I built it!" Schuller's angry voice turned into a deep, bullish roar. "You came here selling plastic pots and pans! You gave nothing, you came here only to take! *I* started this church! *I* went out and rounded up the the members - - *I* pounded on the doors."

Now the fury was out of Schuller. He was not bellowing at the younger minister anymore. "I personally made the down payment on the organ. I hauled it back and forth, on that broken-down trailer. I was the one who stood out in the rain all those times. I was the one who stood out in that hot, blistering sun all those Sundays on that tar-paper roof. I was the one." Now Schuller was close enough to the smirking, younger man to grab him by the scruff of his neck and lift him bodily off the office floor, so he could stick his face right into the young challenger's.

But he didn't. Schuller didn't grab the assistant by his shirt.

Schuller stepped back. His voice became quiet. "I'm the President of this Corporation *and* the Chairman of The Board of this Church." Schuller turned his back to the younger man. He turned away and looked out the window, signaling that the meeting was over.

"We'll see who's the President of what and who's the Chairman of what," the younger man said to Schuller's back.

As he turned and left the room, he closed the heavy, oak door with a loud, resounding *slam!*

*   *   *

Schuller hardly said a word all through dinner. He finished cleaning his plate and went immediately into the study. Arvella spent an extra hour cleaning up the small kitchen and putting the children to bed. After she was finished, she went into the study. She found Bob sitting at his desk, with only a single lamp to light the room.

Arvella walked in slowly. Bob's eyes were transfixed on a spot somewhere on the wall. He barely acknowledged her presence in the room. The room was quiet.

"Bob," she began with her soft country voice.

Schuller shifted in his chair, turned away and looked out into the night.

"Bob, what's wrong?" Arvella said to him.

Schuller slowly turned to her. He took a long time saying it.

"I'm afraid," he said.

Arvella let her silence ask the questions.

"I'm afraid of failing," Schuller answered her. "I've always been afraid of failing. Ever since I can remember, I've been afraid of failing."

"I don't know what to do," Schuller went on. "I don't even know what to say anymore. Where's the justice in this? I try and I try. I work and I work. For what? They hold secret meetings behind my back. I try to tell them, I try to make them understand. But they don't. None of them do."

Arvella sat down in the empty chair across from Bob. She listened.

"Where is my God now, Arvella?" Schuller said. "Where is his mercy and justice now? Sometimes I wake up at night and think I'm going to flip out and loose my mind. Sometimes I think I'm going mad, Arvella. Where is *my* salvation, where is *my* comfort?"

"I lie awake at night in the darkness and pray for a heart attack," he confessed. "Did you know that? I want to die every morning that I go down to that church." He hung his head in shame. "Do you know how hard I pray that a truck or bus will slam into me on the way and end all the pain and heartache for me?" he asked her. " Do you know how hard I pray for that?"

Arvella's lip quivered. The tears began to well up in her eyes as she sat there unable to help the man she loved so much. If only she could lash out at them, the way they had lashed out at him. If only she could wave a magic wand and make everything all right again. If only she could remove the shadow of Goliath, the attacker, the enemy.

"It's going be all right, Bob," she comforted him.

Schuller raised his head.

"I wish I could believe that," he sighed.

*   *   *

"We have three options," Schuller told the full church. A hundred members had turned up to decide the fate of the little Chapel at Seacrest and Chapman.

"One," Schuller said, "Drop the drive-in ministry and let the sick and the handicapped, the old and the infirm go home and listen on the radio like they do all across America. Two, divide the two churches, each with its own pastor. I will resign from both churches to eliminate any conflicts. Three, merge both churches into one. This would be a new, creative development called a 'walk-in, drive-in church.' "

"In my opinion," Schuller said, "this little church we are attending will never be able to expand. It will always be a medium-sized church in an ever-growing town. It will be like shooting elephants with a .22 rifle," he warned.

"Where are you going to get the money?" was the first question. "Where are you going to get the money to buy the land, not to mention the buildings, for this walk-in, drive-in church that you're talking about?" The words were tinged with sarcasm.

"Our job is to be great thinkers for God," Schuller replied. "We must trust God. God is not a pauper."

Schuller let this settle into the crowd for a minute. Then he said,"The question isn't,'What will it cost?' The question is, 'Will it help people?' "

They sat and listened in silence.

"If this will help people, then it will surely help this ministry. I am sure that God will find a solution to the financial concerns, if we give Him a chance.

Schuller looked at them for a minute. Then he sat down.

"God does not belong in a drive-in theater," one woman spoke up."That's only one step away from pitching a tent. In this new walk-in, drive-in church of yours, will we have a roof over our heads? There's no roof over your head out at the drive-in theater. There are no pews for people to sit in. There are no classrooms for Sunday Schools. The children have to thumb-tack their papers to picnic tables so the wind doesn't blow them away."

"Just who are you trying to impress, Schuller?" she asked.

"I'm trying to impress people who don't go to

church," Schuller answered in a hurt whisper. "I'm trying to make an impression on the non-religious American who is riding by on the freeway."

Schuller took a deep breath and blurted out, "I'm trying to get the attention of the person in this world who is too busy running around in the rat race, who is frustrated sitting in traffic, and the person who is looking for a better way, for themselves and their family. That's who I'm trying to impress. The person who's too busy to look for God in the little things in life. The flowers, the water, the trees. I'm trying to help the person who is caught up in the noise and stress of today's world. I'm trying to help that person find God. That's who I'm trying to impress," he said.

"Are you trying to impress Christians?"

"I'm not trying to impress the Christians or the Methodists or the Catholics or the Jewish or the Lutherans or even the Baptists. They have churches to go to. What do I have to offer them? I'm trying to help people who don't have a place to go to church. Because they're physically or emotionally handicapped. Because they can't find a place made especially for them. I'm trying to help those who don't or can't go to church. I'm trying to inspire people."

You're doing a pretty good job of it right now, thought Arvella.

*   *   *

The morning paper lay on the front steps of the parsonage. Schuller opened the door to get it. There, stacked on his doorstep, were the resignations of half of the Church Board and a little less than half of the members of the Chapel. One hundred and fifty in all.

Schuller brushed back his graying hair. He was thirty-one years old. The grayed hair would always remind him of this dark time. The vote the night before had been

52 to 48 in favor of his walk-in, drive-in idea.

Now all he had to do was find the money somewhere.

He still owed Howard Duven five hundred dollars for the organ.

"And I thought they were with me." Bob sighed.

"Great ideas never die, Bob," Arvella said. "People may quit on the idea, but the idea seldom, if ever, quits by itself." She touched his arm. "Have a little faith, Bob. Have a little faith."

- 6 -

For Rosie

I t all started with a phone call.

"You don't know me, Reverend, but my name is Warren Gray," were the first words Schuller heard over the phone. It had been late in the day in the summer of '56.

"My wife and I have been coming to your church since that first Sunday in the drive-in theater." Warren Gray said, in a gravelly voice. "We live twenty-one miles from the theater. I know it's a long way, but could you come out and see us?"

Schuller remembered the day as if it were yesterday. Arvella was washing the dishes in the tiny sink. He had asked five-year-old Sheila if she would help her

Mother dry tonight, because Daddy had an important meeting to go to and he wouldn't be back until later. And would she help Mommy watch little Bobby while Daddy was gone? Three year-old boys needed watching, Schuller reminded his little girl.

Sheila said she would be glad to help out. Arvella rolled her eyes. *Thanks.*

Warren Gray was waiting for Schuller out on the front porch. Schuller pulled his car into the small ranch. The layout reminded him of his father's farm, back in Iowa. The tiny ranch house needed another coat of paint. He knew, without asking, that there was probably no money for painting before the winter. It would have to wait until next spring.

Schuller stopped his '53 blue Chevy sedan in front of the porch. He stepped out of the car and noticed the old green Buick with patches of white, the same one he had seen parked in the back row of the drive-in on so many Sundays. He had always wondered who drove that old Buick. The Buick usually pulled in just as Schuller started the service and always left before he made his rounds afterwards. The Buick was always parked in the same spot in the back row.

Schuller stepped up onto the porch and met Warren Gray. He was a tall, gangly man wearing a sweat-stained, cotton shirt and denim rancher jeans. His face and hands had been tanned by the sun during the countless days of toiling in the open fields. His skin was a worn, brown color and was leathered from long, hard use. The rancher was well into his sixties, Schuller noted, maybe even his seventies. But there was a strength and sternness about him that impressed the young pastor.

The rancher took off his old felt hat with a gentle respect and shook Schuller's hand. The grip was warm and firm.

"Before you meet my wife," he said, "I should tell you that she can't walk and she can't talk. You see, she had a stroke some years ago. She can only grunt a little, cry a little, and smile faintly. Her mind is good, though. And her spirit is strong."

"We never miss church," he went on. "I'm old, but I'm still strong. I lift Rosie up, put her in the front seat of the car and we go out there to your drive-in church every Sunday and listen to you talk about faith."

The old rancher looked at the young pastor with smiling eyes and said, "It's wonderful." Then his face took on a kind of pleading look. "We want to join your church."

Schuller gathered all the strength and respect he could into his voice and said, "You and your wife are more than welcome at our church."

The old rancher beckoned Schuller into the small ranch house. The screen door creaked open. He held it open wide and Schuller walked in.

Inside, there was Rosie, sitting in her chair. Her chin was slumped on her chest. Her eyes stared straight out from under a head unable to turn. Her mouth hung open. She looked drugged and dazed. The young pastor walked over to her. A spark in her eye indicated that she recognized him.

"Hello, Rosie," he said. "I'm Reverend Schuller."

Schuller saw a faint smile try to cross Rosie's lips.

"Do you want to join the church, Rosie?" he asked.

Her lips opened slightly. Her eyes lifted to meet his and tears slid slowly down her cheeks. From the paralyzed lips that struggled vainly to pronounce words, she managed a long sustained mumble. It was more like a child's gurgling.

Rosie and Warren Gray were baptized two weeks later at the drive-in theater.

That was two years ago. But the scene in that ranch house, when he had first met Rosie Gray, was still fresh in young Schuller's mind. He thought about how fast two years could go by as he picked up the phone to call Warren Gray.

The click-clack dialing of the black wall phone echoed off the hard, linoleum counter tops in the Schuller kitchen. Schuller needed to raise another eighteen thousand dollars in cash within three months if they were to close on the ten acres of land that he had found for the new walk-in, drive-in church. He had already cashed in his life insurance policy, borrowed money from his father, asked both his uncles to send what they could spare and asked his brother Henry for a loan. All told, he had raised almost three thousand dollars from inside the family. Added to the thousand dollars that the church had put up, Schuller needed another fifteen thousand before the close of business on Friday, April 18.

Black Friday, Schuller thought.

He click-clacked off another number.

"If you're serious about your plan," the Realtor had told Schuller over the phone last week, "I know where you can buy ten good acres of land for sixty-six thousand dollars. You can put nineteen thousand down in cash and pay off the mortgage at four hundred dollars a month for fifteen years."

Schuller let the Realtor wait for a minute.

"How much would the mortgage and interest rate be?" Schuller finally asked.

"That's a mortgage of forty-one thousand dollars with an interest rate of about eight percent annually," the answer came back.

Sixty-six thousand dollars just for the land! thought Schuller. *That's almost as much as we paid for the land and the chapel on Seacrest. I suppose we will get some money when we sell the Chapel, but it won't be much. We'll have to raise almost twenty thousand in cash just to close the deal.* Schuller thought about his $300 a month salary, that he still took thirty-eight dollars from each month to pay for the organ he had bought three years ago. He still had eight months to go on that loan.

"If you're interested," the Realtor said, "we can open a 120-day escrow today with only $1,000."

"I'll have to submit it to the Board for approval," Schuller said. "Can you wait a week until I can call a Board meeting?"

"Well, I'll do what I can with the seller, but don't wait too long. This is a real bargain at only sixty-six thousand, especially in that location."

"Thank you," Schuller said, "I'll let you know our decision within a week. Good-bye."

Schuller listened to another number click-clack off to Warren Gray.

The Realtor was right. The Disneyland Park that had opened just three years ago was really attracting the crowds. Disneyland was only two miles from the ten acres being offered for sale on the corner of Chapman and Lewis. Hotels and new apartment buildings were popping up all over the place. Just behind the property, they had broken ground on a seventy-five house subdivision.

Eighteen thousand dollars. I could buy a brand new house in that subdivision for eighteen thousand dollars. He looked around the sparse kitchen Arvella had to cook in.

He click-clacked off the last number on the black wall phone.

Schuller had never even seen $18,000 all in one place at one time, in his whole life. The most that had ever filled the collection plate, was three thousand dollars and that was when Norman Vincent Peale himself had come and talked to almost four thousand people. Schuller figured he knew a grand total of maybe twenty people he could ask for money. And he sure wasn't any Norman Vincent Peale.

The phone rang for a second time at the other end. Schuller was about to hang up when he heard, "Hello?"

It was the gravelly voice of Warren Gray.

"Hello?" he asked again when Schuller didn't respond.

"Hello, Warren?" Schuller started meekly. "It's Bob Schuller."

"Oh, hello, Reverend Schuller," the old rancher replied. "How are you tonight?"

"Oh, fine, just fine, thank you."

Silence hung in the air.

"Reverend Schuller?" Warren finally said, "Are you there?"

"Yes, I'm here, Warren," the young Pastor eeked into the phone. "Listen, Warren, I'm calling about our project to buy the ten acres of ground for the new walk-in, drive-in church. I'm in charge of the fund-raising and I've been sitting here trying to kind of set a schedule about how much we need and our time frame and all and - - - ." Bob switched the phone from one ear to the other as he fumbled for more words. "And, well, we've got a thousand dollars that the church authorized to open the escrow with. Now that's a one hundred and twenty day escrow, Warren. We have to close by April 18th or, well, I guess we fall out of escrow."

Schuller had almost run every word together with the next. Arvella peeked into the kitchen where her husband could see her and mouthed 'Slow down.' She added wide open eyes and a signal of hands pushing toward the floor to illustrate her point.

"Reverend Schuller?" Warren Gray said.

"Yes?" Schuller responded.

"I wasn't quite able to catch all of that. Could you back up and go over that one more time a little slower?"

"Certainly, Warren. Where would you like me to start?" Schuller wiped a handful of sweat from his brow. He was sure he hadn't had this much trouble asking for his first date.

There was silence again from Warren Gray's side. The old rancher was trying to digest what he heard.

"Are you asking me to help you call people and ask them for money, Reverend ?"

"No," said Schuller emphatically. *That's my job,* Schuller thought. *I'm just not very good at it.* "No, Warren, we've got the fund-raising well in hand."

"Just ask him," Arvella whispered from behind. "Ask him."

Schuller hung on the phone, hoping, praying for a thunderbolt to strike the phone lines down so that the agony would be over.

"I can give two thousand dollars," Warren Gray said through the silence.

Schuller's eyes grew as big as golf balls. His feet almost jumped off the floor.

"Two thousand dollars!?" he exclaimed. "That would be wonderful, Warren. Just wonderful!"

"Do you want me to bring the money over tonight?"

"No, no," Schuller said excitedly, "Just stay where you are. I'll come out and get it."

Schuller grinned from ear to ear. *Two Thousand Dollars! On my first call!* Schuller's grin faded as he saw the seriousness in Arvella's face. The next words came out in a calm, pastoral tone.

"Uh - Warren, just whenever you get down this way in the next week or so would be fine." Schuller looked to Arvella to see if that would be fine. She nodded that it would be.

"Okay, Reverend. I'll bring 'er to you this week."

"Thank you, Warren. Thank you very much. Good-bye."

Schuller hung up the phone. His palms were still sweaty.

Seven-year old Sheila stood in the doorway. She rolled her eyes at her father. Some salesman.

*　　　　　*　　　　　*

135

"How are we doing, Bob?"

It was the end of March. Ninety out of the one hundred and twenty days had passed. Arvella asked the question at the dinner table.

"I'm thinking about writing a book called 'ONE THOUSAND AND ONE WAYS TO SAY NO!' " Schuller moved a carrot around on his plate. "I think I can raise more money that way." he added. "I never really thought it was going to be this hard."

"How about doing what you did when we came out here?" Arvella asked. "You know, write down ten different ways to do something and go through each one until you've exhausted all the possibilities?" Arvella was enthusiastic with her suggestion.

Schuller's face took on a sheepish look. "I passed number ten last Tuesday, he said. Then he added, "Last month."

"Oh," Arvella muttered.

*   *   *

Schuller heartily munched down the last bit of potato on his plate. He hadn't been this proud of himself since Arvella had said "Yes", out on the banks of the Floyd River, nine years ago.

They had made it. They had the money. Fifteen thousand was already in the bank and the rest would be here tomorrow. He had three good pledges of a thousand dollars each, to cover the last three thousand dollars. Friday's closing was two days away. It looked like Goliath had been defeated

Maybe I'll just go to closing tomorrow, a day early, he thought. *Take Arvella and the kids to the beach on Friday.*

He'd made it. It was either put up or shut up and he'd come through. Eighteen thousand dollars! He had raised eighteen thousand dollars!

He hadn't failed.

         *   *   *

Schuller hung up the phone slowly. He wasn't quite sure what to do next.

The first pledge had fallen through. "Changed my mind," were the words. "I don't think a walk-in, drive-in church is a good place to put my money," he'd said.

Changed my mind. Where am I going to find another thousand dollars in twenty-four hours? thought Schuller. *I better check on those other two pledges in person.*

"My daughter just got married," the second man said. "Do you have any idea how much that costs? It just about wiped me out. I'd like to help you out, Pastor, but I just can't do it right now. My wife hasn't even balanced the checkbook and - - ."

- - And now Schuller was two thousand dollars short.

"Come back in a month, Reverend." the third man said. "I'm flat broke right now. Come back in a month."

I don't have a month, Schuller thought, lying in bed. He hadn't slept all night. *I have twelve hours to come up with the money. Twelve hours.*

"It's not that I didn't come through with the money," Schuller said over the phone. "It's losing the land, Norman. You know we'll never get a chance to buy ten acres this close to the freeway again for sixty thousand dollars."

"I know, Bob," Norman Miner said into the snack bar phone. He knew that another ten acres just across the street from the Lewis property had gone into escrow at $120,000, double what Schuller was paying.

The population of Orange County had tripled in the last three years. And with the announcement of the opening of the new Santa Ana and Garden Grove Freeways, the Lewis property would be smack in the center of Orange County. Land prices were going up daily.

"Have you got any ideas at all, Norman?"

"I'm sorry, Bob, I don't. I don't know a soul who you can call. I'd give you the money myself if I had it."

"I know you would, Norman. Thanks."

Schuller only had one more name. He knew one more possibility in downtown Santa Ana. If that came through, he would be only four blocks from the escrow office. He could still make it.

"Hello?" came Arvella's cheery voice.

She checked her watch. It was two o'clock.

"Arvella, we lost it."

He's at a pay phone, she thought. She could tell from the screaming rush of traffic in the background.

"I did everything I could," Schuller went on, "I tried everybody, but it's no good. I lost it."

"What about Warren Gray?"

"I can't ask Warren. He's already given two thousand dollars. Besides, he just came home from his cancer surgery yesterday. I can't ask him to give twice."

"Call Warren Gray, Bob," Arvella said. "Call Warren Gray."

"Arvella, I just can't do it."

"You have to call him anyway and tell him you're going to give him his money back. Call Warren Gray, Bob."

Schuller watched the traffic stream by him on Main Street in Santa Ana.

"Call Warren Gray, Bob."

The private nurse picked up the ranch phone on the second ring.

"Just a minute," she said, "I'll see if he's able to come to the phone."

Schuller waited for what seemed like an eternity.

"Reverend Schuller?"

"Warren? Listen. I have some good news for you. I'm going to be able to give you back the two thousand dollars that you gave me to build the church. You can use it to pay your medical bills."

"Why? I don't understand."

"Well, escrow closes today and we're three thousand dollars short."

Silence fell on the other end of the line.

"Bob, where are you?"

"I'm in a phone booth on Main Street in Santa Ana."

"Do you know where the Bank of America building is, in downtown Santa Ana?"

"Sure. It's right down the street."

"Meet me there in an hour."

The phone clicked dead in Schuller's ear.

Warren Gray walked down the steps of the Bank of America. He was ashen-faced. His hair was uncombed. There was a look of fierce determination in his eyes.

The old rancher walked straight up to Schuller. He held a bulging white envelope in his right hand. He clutched his old rancher's hat in his left hand. Gone was the friendly smile, gone was the pain of the hospital rooms. He walked right up to Schuller and stared him straight in the eye.

"Build your church, Bob," Warren Gray said, "Build the biggest and most beautiful church that you can dream of."

He put the envelope into Schuller's hand. Inside was three thousand dollars, in fresh, new bills.

"For Rosie," he said.

Schuller looked at the money in his hand. He shook Warren's hand hard and looked into the old man's weathered face. "You're a good man, Warren Gray."

Warren put his sweat-stained hat back on, nodded, and walked off. He climbed into the old green Buick and drove away. Schuller stood there until the Buick's tail lights had disappeared down Main Street.

It was 3:30 p.m. One more hour and the escrow office would be closed. Schuller still had to go to the bank and withdraw the fifteen thousand he had deposited in the church's account. Then make it over to the escrow office.

At 4:25 p.m, Schuller pushed open the wooden front door of the Orange County Land & Title Company. He put eighteen thousand dollars into escrow and closed on the ten acres at the corner of Lewis and Chapman Streets. They owned the ground.

The fall would be a good time to break ground, Schuller thought, as he signed the last closing document. *The summer heat would be off and the skies would still be clear. Yes, we could make September. We made the 120-day escrow. We could break ground by early September.*

Ground breaking took place on the morning of September 10th, 1958. It was a beautiful day. Everyone turned out for the historical moment, to celebrate the victory. They were full of smiles and hearty congratulations. Everyone except Rosie.

Rosie Gray died on September 8th, two days before the ground-breaking.

- 7 -

Ladders of Love

Death is like a dream, wrote Robert Schuller.

Arvella softly placed her hand on her husband's shoulder. *He's worn out,* she thought. *He's way past tired this time.* She had never seen him so exhausted before.

Robert Schuller was thirty-three years old.

"How's it coming?" Arvella finally asked. Her voice was a whisper.

Schuller stared down at the words on the paper. It was eleven-thirty at night. The only lights on in the house, were the ones over the kitchen stove, the lamp in the living room, and the tiny lamp that he used at his desk. The kids had been put to bed hours ago.

Bobby had decided that he wouldn't go to sleep again without his Davy Crockett hat and cowboy boots where he could see them. *Strange companions for a five-year-old,* thought Arvella. Sheila wanted to know why everyone was so sad tonight. *You can't hide much from eight-year-old girls,* Arvella thought.

Arvella noticed the waste can was overflowing with crumpled balls of paper. *Not good enough,* she could hear Bob thinking as he wadded the sheets of paper into his hands and tossed them aside. She always tried to leave him alone when he did his writing late at night.

He normally stayed up until two or three in the morning, writing. And that was just for the regular Sunday morning services. This was something special. This was something he had never done before. He was writing the eulogy for Rosie Gray.

Arvella looked over Bob's shoulder as he read through the words he had written. She knew that he felt her presence next to him, but she was sure that the words she just asked, had not yet registered. He was too deeply involved with the paper in front of him.

"Honey?" Arvella began again.

"Hhmm..?" Bob answered as he struck out another sentence.

"That's for Rosie, isn't it?"

Bob reached his left hand across his chest and caressed Arvella's arm. "I want it to be the best I can do. She deserves the best."

Bob turned and lifted his head, so Arvella could see him. His cheeks were reddened with tears.

Arvella squeezed his hand and wiped a tear away from her own eye. She squeezed all the love and encouragement she could into his hand and said, "You'll do a great job, Bob. I know you will."

A welcome smile flashed across Bob's lips.

"Do you have a kiss for me tonight?" Arvella smiled.

"I'm going to bed now."

Bob stood up, took his wife into his arms and kissed her. *What would I ever do if I lost you,* he thought as he felt her warmth flow through him. *What would I ever do?*

*　　　*　　　*

The wind blew gently through the leaves of the big, tall, oak tree that stood silent watch over the small gravesite. The oak tried to offer a safe haven from the late summer sun, but it was no use. An early fall was taking its toll on the oak's long limbs. There were more leaves spread across the grassy hilltop, than there were on the branches of the aging tree. Winter was on its way. The early morning dew would soon be frosty. Time was moving on for the frail oak tree.

"Death is like a dream," began Robert Schuller.

He stood at the head of Rosie's grave. Her casket stretched out before him. The sun was at his back and he could see his shadow reach out to where Rosie's feet would be. The freshly cut sides of the grave fell away to darkness.

Warren Gray stood beside Schuller. He wore a clean black suit and a dark gray tie. Polished, black, boot tips pointed out from under his trouser cuffs. He clutched his sun-bleached rancher's hat in his wrinkled hands. The hat brim was streaked with reddish-tan stains.

"Death is like a dream," repeated Robert Schuller. "When you live right, when you make your life stand for something, when you make a difference with the life the Lord has given you, death is not the end. It is the beginning. It is the beginning of a beautiful, everlasting dream."

The words brought a smile to his lips. It had taken him until four in the morning to get the flow just right. His head was still a little smokey from the three hours sleep he had finally gotten. But Robert Schuller was happy. Rosie's eulogy was as perfect as he could get it.

145

The young Pastor paused and looked up from the grave. He saw a spark of warmth in Warren Gray's old, tired face. Schuller shared the warmth deep in his own heart. His eyes drifted from Warren to the faces of the crowd.

A few hundred people gathered around the final resting site of Rosie Gray. The families of many church members had come to pay their respects. They stood in silent, awed reverence at the passing of the woman who meant so much to them. The same woman who couldn't walk. The same woman who couldn't even say her own name.

Robert Schuller felt he had to speak for Rosie today.

"The sun sets and night-time falls," Schuller went on. "And in the morning, the sun rises again to a beautiful, new dawn." Schuller raised his voice to the crowd now. "The dream of a beautiful new day begins with each new sunrise. Every end is a new beginning."

He let the words hang in the air and then repeated them. "Every end is a new beginning."

"Rosie Gray's life mattered. She made a difference. She made a difference to everyone here today."

Schuller paused again. He felt the wind brush his graying hair across his forehead. He looked down at Rosie's casket. Rows of fresh flowers surrounded the open grave. The sun sparkled on the petals of each and every blooming flower there. The wind gently brushed the petals against each other.

"Rosie's life is not a candle being blown out," Schuller went on, "but a wonderful new sun rising over the mountains. Rosie is not gone from us. She lives on in each of our hearts. Look into your hearts. Listen for a minute. Be still and listen. Can't you hear Rosie?"

Schuller looked out over the group. Everyone was smiling.

"Rosie's dream for us is just beginning. Her love

146

will always be with us. Her love will always be in our hearts." A tear appeared on Robert Schuller's cheek. Warren Gray saw that tear.

"Rosie Gray made a difference," Schuller said. "She made a difference in my life. She taught me the true meaning of love."

"God bless you, Rosie."

He blessed Rosie's body and they lowered her into the earth. Each member of the crowd passed by and paid their last respects.

Schuller walked away from the grave-site with Warren Gray. They heard the first echo of dirt fall onto the wooden surface. The sound drifted away into the sunlight. Schuller walked with Warren down the grassy hill.

"She was a good woman, Bob," Warren choked. "You know pastor, I don't think Rosie would have made it as long as she did without you standing on that snack bar roof every Sunday."

"She was a great lady, Warren. One of the greatest." Schuller put his arm around Warren and helped him down the hill.

The old oak stood silent watch over Rosie.

*   *   *

The new homes lined the street like identical nutcrackers under the Christmas tree. Simply designed, affordable, and ready to occupy. At this point, Schuller and Arvella had reached a milestone in their lives. Home ownership. Not a home provided for them by the church, but a first time, home-buyers dream. A brand new home, never before occupied.

With it, however, was the arduous task of landscaping the barren yard. As they stood on the front porch, the front yard stretched out in front of them. It was divided at the street by the neighborhood sidewalk.

"Bob, what did you want to do with that four foot wide piece of ground between the street, and the sidewalk?" said Arvella curiously.

"Well, I imagine we'll put some grass in," he said, wondering what she had in mind.

"What about bricks!"

"Bricks?! Why bricks?" he questioned.

"Well, we will be entertaining a lot, and folks can get out of their car, step on the bricks, and walk up the sidewalk, right to the front door!" she said.

"Hmmm," he said, shaking his head approvingly. "That's not a bad idea. I'll go down this afternoon and check out the price of bricks!"

"Oh, you can't do that!" she said sharply.

"Why not?"

"First you have to take out about ten inches of dirt, replace it with sand, and put the bricks on the sand." she instructed.

"What for?! That sounds like a lot of work!"

"Bob, the mud will seep through the bricks if you don't, and it will end up a big mess."

Schuller's mind began to calculate the hours it would take to excavate ten inches of soil, four feet wide by eighty feet long. Quickly he said, "Well, I think our house might look out of place if we put bricks there."

Ready for such a response, Arvella said, "Bob, you will never have to mow it!"

That got his attention.

"You will never have to weed it!"

The job was looking easier all the time.

"You will never have to edge it!"

His interest was peaked as he said, "Okay! You sold me! I'll do it!"

By the time Sunday rolled around, Schuller had lost his enthusiasm for the project. It would just be too much work. After all, he had a church to run. He didn't have the time it would take to do the job. As he, Arvella, and the kids drove home from church, the question came up once again.

"Your sermon was very motivational this morning, Bob!"

"Really?" he said, surprised. "What did you like about it?"

"Here, I wrote them down," she said, as she reached into her purse.

"Here it is. 'There is no gain without pain', I like that one!" she said smiling.

His face beamed from his wife's approval.

"Or this one, 'Inch by inch, anything is a cinch!' That one is great!" she said.

"Wow, you really listened this morning didn't you? he laughed.

"But the one I like best is, 'Beginning is half done!'" She paused, slowly turned her eyes to his, and said, "So when are you going to start on the bricks in the front yard?"

The smile left Schuller's face as he realized that he'd been had!

Dressed in a pair of grubby overalls, Schuller pushed his wheelbarrow to the edge of the front lawn. The job looked impossible. But slowly, he began to shovel out the soil. After filling his wheelbarrow with its first load of dirt, their only neighbor on the street pulled his car up next to the curb.

"Hey, Bob, what are you doing!" he said, enjoying watching the local pastor do some hard labor.

"Digging out the dirt so I can put in some bricks for a walkway!"

Then the question of the day floated out of his neighbors mouth as he said, "What are you going to do with all that dirt?!"

What am I going to do with the dirt? he thought. Then he remembered a house he had seen next door to the church. Quickly he said, "I'm going to make a mound in the back yard, and put a palm tree in it!"

"I don't know," his neighbor said sarcastically. "That's going to be an awfully big mound!"

"I'm a possibility thinker, I always think big!" Schuller fired back proudly.

The negative thinking neighbor smiled broadly, and as he pulled away he said, "It's going to take you a month of Sundays to dig out all of that dirt!" And with that, he was gone.

Faced with impossible odds, Robert Schuller found a new enthusiasm to finish the project. With vigor and energy, he dug out the next four shovel fulls of dirt. But with the hot California sun beating down, and the sweat on his brow, that enthusiasm began to subside. He laid down his shovel, looked up to the sky and said, "Dear God in heaven, there has got to be an easier way than this!"

The words had hardly left his mouth, when he heard the rumble of a truck coming down the street. As it slowly came to a stop, Schuller noticed that painted on the door was a sign that read, 'Roy Thayer, Excavation and Dirt Hauling.' Schuller couldn't believe his eyes. Roy Thayer was the head usher in his church.

"Good morning pastor," Roy said with a husky, yet cheery voice.

"Roy, what in the world are you doing here?"

"Well to tell you the truth, I'm lost. Maybe you can help..." Roy cut himself short at seeing Robert Schuller in his grubbies, holding a shovel. Pushing his hat off of his forehead, Roy asked, "What are you doing?"

Schuller lightly chuckled, motioned to the ground and said, "Well, I'm digging out some dirt so I can put a few bricks in."

Shaking his head in disapproval, Roy said, "It's

going to take you a long time doing it that way Pastor!" At that, Roy began climbing out of his truck. He quickly sized up the project, and said, "Why don't you let me do it for you, I've got my skip loader here. I'll have it done in no time!"

Tempted by the offer, Schuller hesitated and then said, "Much as I'd like to Roy, I can't afford this kind of equipment."

Roy smiled gently as he realized Schuller's predicament. Slowly he reached down, scooped up a handful of dirt and said, "This is mighty good dirt, Pastor. Used to be an orange grove here if I remember right."

Seeing an opportunity to cash in on Roy's services, Schuller said quickly, "Great Dirt! Full of fertilizer!"

"Yeah, tough to find dirt like this around here." Roy said.

It was like manna from heaven. The perfect opportunity to finish the job quickly, and painlessly. Quietly he turned to Roy and said, "What are you getting for dirt these days, Roy?"

Roy looked at him as he removed his hat, then turned to the task at hand. Scratching his head, he said, "Tell you what, Pastor, I'll do the whole job, if I can have the dirt for free!"

"It's a deal!" Schuller said excitedly.

Two hours later, Robert Schuller was pacing back and forth in an empty hole. Ten inches deep, four feet wide, eighty feet long.

Arvella walked out on to the front porch. She saw her husband's endless pacing and said, "Bob, are you okay?"

Without lifting an eye, he shook his head in bewilderment and said, "Yea, I'm, just walking off my amazement!"

"Well, sweep the dirt off the curb, lunch is almost ready!" she said.

Schuller began to sweep off the curb. He could see

the car turn the corner, it was his neighbor coming home for lunch. He could see the look of amazement as his neighbor spied the empty hole. As he climbed out of his car, the shock was still on his face.

Schuller called out to him and said, "Church is on Sunday, at 10:45 a.m."

His neighbor slowly raised his hand in acknowledgement, his jaw still hanging wide open. He never missed a Sunday the rest of the year!

*   *   *

Who do you want to impress?

Schuller could not get the words out of his mind. *The unchurched people of this county, of course. But how can I get them to church? We won't have the uniqueness of the drive-in theater to lean on.* Schuller always kept his primary mission in mind. A mission station for those who would not normally attend a church. And the first question he would ask is, "How do we get them to come?"

Schuller contemplated the question as he stood in his back yard. Thinking almost prayerfully as he watched Sheila and Jeanne chase each other around the yard with water pistols. Mesmerized by their melodic laughter, he began to feel nature envelope his mind. The scent of blossoming flowers. The warm California sun. The majesty of the tall, oak trees reaching heavenward. His thoughts turned to his second family, the church.

"Arvella!" Schuller called into the house.

The answer came from a nearby window as she said, "Bob, I'm in the kitchen."

"Wasn't man created to live in a garden?"

"No!" she said.

No? he thought to himself. His train of thought was broken by such a negative answer. Frustrated, he said, "Why not?"

"There are too many bugs, we would all get eaten

152

alive by mosquitoes!" She said teasingly.

"I'm serious. After all, God first placed Adam and Eve in the tranquil setting of the Garden of Eden," came Schuller's reply.

The retort came from the kitchen. "I suppose you're right, but God also gave man a mind so he could create glass windows to keep out the weather, and screens to enjoy the beauty, and still keep the bugs out."

He knew she was teasing him, but she did have a point. There were many Sundays at the drive-in, when an indoor church would have been better. Preaching in the rain was not as fun as singing in it!

"I'm meeting with the architect this afternoon, I don't think he has screen doors in mind for the new church!" Schuller said cheerfully. He gathered Sheila and Jeanne in his arms.

"Daddy, what's a arch-ti-teched?" said Jeanne curiously.

"Well, he's a man who draws buildings, and then other men come and build them."

"Ohhh," she said.

Sheila chimed in quickly, "Who's our architect?"

"He's the best architect in the whole wide world. A nice man named Richard Neutra! Is that okay with you?"

Jeanne thought for a minute and said, "O.K. with me!"

"Me too!" said Sheila. And with that, they were off chasing across the yard.

Robert Schuller and Richard Neutra, stood alone together on the recently purchased ten acre plot of ground.

"What do you have in mind, Bob?" asked Richard.

Excited to give his input to such a famed architect, Schuller quickly said, "We can have a whole panorama. Scripture, creation, the prophets, the whole lot, in stained-glass! We can portray the life of Christ, the dreams of the end times, and something about the modern church in mission!"

Neutra looked puzzled at this response. It was not the one he expected from a pastor who had started his church on the roof of a drive-in theater snack bar. He turned to Schuller, and said warmly, "That's fine if it's just for your own religious people, but what will you do with all of the non-religious people who come in here? I'm Jewish, but I don't practice the Jewish faith. And when I go into a place that surrounds me with stained-glass windows, I feel threatened. I feel like people are shouting sermons at me. Who is it you really want to impress?"

There it was again, Schuller thought, *who do I really want to impress?*

"Well, I suppose I don't want to impress the religious people. They have already accepted the message before they come to me."

"Build a structure that follows your mission, Bob!" Neutra said.

"You're right," Schuller exclaimed. "We'll make it comfortable for people of all faiths or no faith to come to a church service! The world's first walk-in, drive-in church!"

*   *   *

A shining sea of windows filled the newly completed church with the morning sun. It was a spectacular building. A long rectangular sanctuary, with one whole side a solid glass wall, floor to ceiling with windows. The windows revealed a garden, with twelve dancing water fountains, and beyond that, the drive-in church facility. The stage hovered between the first and second story. A mechanical glass door separated the stage from the balcony, allowing Robert Schuller to step outside and address the drive-in congregation directly. The drive-in was equipped with a system which allowed cars to tune in to the message on their car radio.

The day had arrived. Dedication Sunday was November 5, 1961. The battles that had been waged to build the church, somehow managed to escape Bob's memory system, as thousands filled the auditorium, drive-in lot, and outdoor garden. As the new pipe organ majestically played the opening hymn, Schuller sat on the platform, drinking in the sweet fragrance of success.

As he turned to see his mentor, Norman Vincent Peale, sitting next to him, he remembered his six years of struggle in the drive-in theater.

Glancing to the front row, he saw his family: Arvella, Sheila, Bobby, and their youngest daughter Jeanne. Schuller remembered the support and love they all gave to him.

Schuller turned to look at the drive-in parking lot; he could see the old rancher, tipping his hat in approval at the new church. Suddenly, the memory of Rosie's funeral came rushing back. The words of an old rancher echoed in his ear, "You made a difference Bob. You made a difference!"

With a tear of joy in his eye, he walked to the platform, and said, "This is the day that the Lord has made. Let us rejoice, and be glad in it!"

*   *   *

A cascade of sunlight gently cast its golden beams across her face. It reminded him of the first time he had seen her. A blushing young school girl, excited and ready for life. He loved the morning most of all. The world seemed fresh, new, hopeful of the new day. As she lay in silent slumber, he watched her from his chair across the room. His heart was filled with love anew. Marriage was more than a commitment. It was a passionate burning, deep within the heart. It was the love of a lifetime only the brave dare find. It was the new life growing inside of her. *Would it be a boy?* he thought to himself.

A little brother for Sheila, Bobby, and Jeanne?

"I love you," he said softly to her. "Both of you!"

She stirred, and gently rolled over into the light.

Her eyes, kissed by the sun, opened to meet his. A soft and tender smile appeared on her lips. She could read his mind. He was a poet of expression, transparent to those he loved the most.

"How long have you been sitting there?" she said.

"Not long," he said. "How do you feel? Any morning sickness?"

"No, just hunger. I think I'm over the worst of the morning sickness!" she replied.

He smiled, pleased with her energy, and optimism.

"How about some fresh orange juice?" he began, when suddenly, he was interrupted by the telephone.

"Now who could be calling at this hour?" he said.

"I'll get it, Bob, I don't want to wait for that orange juice!" she said with a smile.

"Bob!!" she said with sudden alarm.

Sensing her anxiety, he rushed down the hall to the bedroom.

"What is it, Arvella?!"

Her face was pale, her eyes tense with emotion.

"It's your mother. Your dad has pneumonia." She stopped, not wanting to repeat the words that came from the Doctor's mouth.

"The Doctors...are not sure...he's going to make it." The words cut like a knife into his heart. Fear gripped his chest as his eyes welled up with emotion.

"Bob, she needs you to be with her, your Dad needs you!"

His mind began to cloud over, like a fog rolling into shore from the blue Pacific. All of life's possibilities were beginning to vanish as he suddenly faced death.

"I have to get there in time Arvella!" he said

anxiously. "Dear God, let me get to him in time!"

The sky was blacker then a hundred moonless nights as the lonely jet streaked across the sky. Out into the cold, he stared silently through the tiny window, his mind lost somewhere between fantasy and reality. It seemed like a dream, this thing called life. Its beauty lay in the changes in its color, texture, and rhythm. But in the changes also lay fear, tragedy, and death. Goliath.

His wandering mind slowly began a prayerful journey into his sub-conscious. That place we seldom reach for, but seem always able to find where we last left it.

"Harold, are you studying?"

"Yes, momma!" he says sheepishly as he scurries across the room back to his book.

"You will never make it to seminary if you don't study!"

A gentle smile cracks his lips at the boyhood memory.

"Sit up straight, Harold." His dad ordered in a quiet whisper. "Church is no place for messing around." Young Harold's head hung low at the scolding. As the church choir finished their song, he found himself staring at a large, white, Dutch peppermint laying in his fathers open palm, and a nickel to put in the offering plate. With quiet excitement he looked up to see his Fathers gentle grin forming at the corners of his mouth.

Thirty years later, thirty thousand feet in the air, and I can still taste that peppermint, he thought to himself.

His mind continued to race through the years.

"Son, you start sifting through that rubble over there for nails. Pull them out of boards, or anywhere you can find them. We will rebuild this place ourselves if we have to."

"Dad?"

"Yes, son?"

"Have you ever seen anything like this? I mean, nine buildings wiped clean by a tornado. Our house, our barn, everything?"

"No, son, I haven't. But God will provide Harold, God will Provide."

He never gave up, he thought to himself. Goliath had come many times in his life. A tornado wiping out the family farm. The Great Depression with the foreclosure of the neighboring farms. None of it seemed to matter to Tony Schuller. The simple man of faith just moved each mountain as it appeared.

"Ladies and Gentlemen, the captain has turned on the seat belt sign for our descent into Sioux City..."

"Dear God, Dad needs you now more then ever. Father, I give him to you." A gentle peace washed his soul as the plane slowly made its way toward earth.

A long narrow hospital corridor lay before him. He had made the same walk many times before, in many different hospitals, living out the life of a church pastor. But this one was different.

"Dad?" He called quietly into the dimly-lit room.

"Who's there?"

"It's me, Dad, Harold."

As he approached the bed, he saw his father's face.

A tall man of stature lay in solitude. His eyes still had a sparkle. Without a sound, Bob leaned over his father, and for the first time in his life, gently kissed him on both cheeks. Tony's elderly hands slowly began to wrap around his son's back as Schuller pressed his cheek to his father's. A lifetime passed in the midst of a hug. The simple touch of a father and his son. The tears from Schuller's eyes gently washing away their years of physical separation. In silence they held each other, their touch conveying the magic of the moment.

Schuller appeared in the hospital lobby to see his mother sitting quietly in a corner chair.

"Mom?"

His mother rose to embrace him. Whispering in his ear she said, "I'm going to miss him when he goes."

With his hands on her shoulders, he gently pushed her back. Looking into her eyes he smiled and said, "Why, you always said that he was too quiet. That he never said anything."

She smiled broadly at his comforting remark and said, "But I always knew he was there."

Anthony Schuller died just a few days later.

   *   *   *

"Dad?" asked young Bob.

Schuller looked up from the kitchen table. His seventeen year old son towered over him. His arms were full of school books. The pants he wore were his nicest pair of slacks. He was the style and image of Southern California.

"Yes, son?" Schuller answered.

"I was wondering if I could borrow the car tonight. Cecil and I want to spend some time at the library."

"Sure," Schuller said. "The keys are on my dresser."

"Great," Bob answered, and sped down the hallway. He was back in a minute and headed out the door. "See you guys later," he shouted.

Schuller sat there with a quizzical look on his face.

Bob had told the truth about one thing. He did go to the library. He was there just long enough to drop off some books in the return chute and speed off to his girlfriend's house. Studying was the last thing on his mind.

"Cecil," said Schuller into the phone.

"Oh, Hi, Dr. Schuller."

"How are you tonight, Cecil?"

"Oh, I'm okay, Dr. Schuller. How are you?"

"Tremendous, Cecil. I feel tremendous." Schuller said, "How was the library?"

"The library? What library?"

"You were studying at the library with my son, Bob, tonight weren't you?"

Cecil paused for a minute. "No," he answered. "I didn't go to the library tonight, Dr. Schuller. I'm studying at home by myself."

"Thank you, Cecil. That's what I thought," Schuller said.

Bob's car pulled into the driveway. The headlights lit up the darkness. He pulled into the garage and blinked the lights off.

Bob was careful to close the door very gently. He was two hours later than he had told them he would be. *They're asleep by now,* he thought. *I can sneak in without them knowing what time I came home. By breakfast, this will all be forgotten.*

Bob opened the front door. There in the entryway, stood Schuller. He sipped from a blue and white teacup out of Arvella's Dutch collection. The teacup was from a collection of cups that only the adults were allowed to use.

The teacups in the china cabinet, Arvella's precious collection, were special. They had been given to her by her mother and were never to be removed from the china cabinet.

"Where have you been, Robert?" Schuller asked his son. Bob pressed the door shut.

"Oh, I've been studying hard," he stammered. "My brain is exhausted. I've got to hit the sack now." Bob tried to dodge past his father to his bedroom down the hall.

"Where have you been studying?" asked Schuller.

"Oh, boy, that library," the teenager evaded. "It's a

great place to study, I tell ya. It - - It's the place to go."

"And I suppose you were studying there with Cecil?"

"Oh, yeah, yeah. Cecil and I were just cramming for finals. We made a lot of progress there."

With those words still hanging in the air, Schuller took his teacup and smashed it down on the tile floor in the entryway. The pieces flew in every direction.

Three tiny pieces glanced off the young teenager's face.

"Robert," Schuller said, when all the pieces had settled, "My trust in you now holds as much water as that teacup."

And he walked away.

He turned, walked down the hall, and turned out the lights.

Young Robert A. Schuller stood there in the darkness.

He swept up all the pieces he could find with a little whisk broom and headed for the trash can. Before he put them in the trash can, he thought, *Well, maybe I can put this thing back together.* So for the next two or three weeks, the young teenager, working with model airplane glue, did his best to put that cup back together.

It had cracks all through the whole thing. You could see the glue had dried and dripped down all around the cup, but if it had to, it could hold some water. And he gave it back to his Dad.

"I trusted you," Schuller told him. "I believed what you told me. I believed. I didn't have to see you at the library. I didn't have to go down there and look for you. I believed in you. I had faith in what you told me. And do you know why?" Schuller asked.

"No. Why?" asked the young Robert A.

"Because I love you. You're my son and I love you. No matter what happens, no matter what I say, no matter what you say, no matter how much we hurt each other, I'll still love you. No matter what, my love for you will always be there."

Schuller went over to the family Bible. "Look," he said to his son. "Look at what was written almost two thousand years ago." Schuller read from the family Bible. "Heaven and earth may pass away, but my words shall not pass away."

Schuller looked right at his son. "God's word is love. That's why this book has lasted longer than any other book in history. The word Bible means book, Robert. God's word means love. For love to work, you have to have faith. That means you have to believe in something that you can't see."

Robert Anthony listened to every word.

"You can't see love, can you?" Schuller went on. "You can't hold it in your hand and look at it, can you? You can't take a picture of it, can you?"

Robert Anthony shook his head no.

"But you can feel it, can't you? You can feel your heart being broken, can't you? You can feel the love your mother and I have for you, can't you?"

Robert Anthony nodded yes.

"Do you believe that love exists? Do you have faith in it?" Schuller asked.

"Yes," answered his son.

"Then you believe in God."

"You can't have love without faith. You have to believe it to see it." Schuller continued.

"Heaven and earth may pass away, but My words shall not pass away. Only love lasts. My love will not pass away. It will last forever. That's the message of God. That my mission, to spread that word, to tell people that they are loved. That it's okay for them to feel good about themselves, that it's okay for them to believe in love. That's it's okay for them to have faith. And my job is to help them find the love that their God has for them, to help them strengthen their faith so that they can enjoy as great a love as they can handle in this life."

"The Beatles sing about love. 'All you need is love,' they say. You need faith, too. You need faith when you can't find love. Faith gives you hope. And you need these three things - faith, hope and love."

Schuller took the teacup and put it into the china cabinet. He found a special place for it next to Arvella's Precious Teacups.

- 8 -

Bigger Dreams

Anaheim stadium towered before him. Schuller walked with his family toward the massive home of the California Angels. Turning slightly, he could see the church campus. There it was, standing on the horizon. The Tower of Hope, with a lighted cross on top, standing 90 feet tall. It was the latest addition to the growing church complex. They had dedicated the Tower last spring. It was the tallest building in the county that year. A beacon to the world, a message that someone out there cares. The year was 1969.

Quickly he turned back toward the stadium to continue his journey. *All these thousands of people coming to hear one man,* he thought to himself. Suddenly, before him stood the reason why. A tractor trailer filled with broadcast equipment, the nerve center which sent electronic signals to the far corners of the earth. How often he had watched Billy Graham on television.

"Arvella, look at this!"

Diverting her attention from young Jeanne, she said, "Look at what?"

"This communications trailer, it's the ultimate drive-in theater."

Uh, oh! she thought to herself. *I've seen that look before.* She remembered their early days of dating.

Bob had always been fascinated with the opportunities that radio provided. The ability to reach millions with a message of hope.

"Just think of it Arvella, all we would be doing is replacing the snack bar roof with a camera, and the family car with the family couch."

Arvella turned to face her husband. She could see his mind running in overdrive at the possibilities that lay before them.

"Hello, Mr. Chairrrmaaan." Arvella said.

Receiving the message loud and clear, Schuller's daydream ended abruptly. She continued, "You have work to do. They didn't put you in charge of the Orange County Billy Graham Crusade for nothing!"

Schuller quickly glanced down at his watch and said, "Oh my goodness, I'm late!" and started off toward the V.I.P. trailer.

"Hey, where's my kiss!" Arvella called after him.

Looking back, he could see his wife facing him with her lips pointed skyward. He chuckled lightly as he dashed back to oblige her request. He quickly kissed her and said, "I should be home around 10:30 p.m."

"I love you, too!" she said and he dashed toward the stadium entrance.

The office trailer was simple and tastefully decorated.

There were several desks, with two doors leading to offices at one end. As Schuller entered the trailer, he was quickly spotted by an elderly woman.

"Pastor Schuller, Come in! Dr. Graham is waiting to see you. Last door on the left."

Her kind words made him feel at ease. With a simple nod of the head he said, "Thank you very much."

"Can I bring you in some coffee?" she said.

Without hesitation he said, "Oh, yes please, thank you very much."

Smiling broadly she said, "Coming right up!"

"Robert Schuller, How are you!" Billy Graham said, in his well known southern drawl.

Schuller turned toward the voice at the end of the trailer to see Billy Graham standing in his office doorway. His accent and southern hospitality, seemed to bring the room to life.

"Terrific. How are you, Dr Graham!" said Schuller as he marched forward to shake his hand.

"Bob, please, call me Billy," he said with a broad smile.

"Okay, Billy."

"Well, come on in and have a seat, Bob. You know, I have to tell you that you have done a terrific job getting support for this crusade." Schuller's heart leapt for joy at the adulation he was receiving from this great minister.

"A five night crusade in a stadium this size, is a tall order, but you have really pulled together the support of the local churches for this one."

"It was a pleasure and an honor to chair the Orange County committee for your organization. Besides, with all the people coming to know the Lord at this event, our local churches will probably be receiving a lot of new members!"

"Praise God for that, Bob! Now, what can I do for you?"

Schuller thought for a minute and then said, "Well

Billy, you have been to our church, right?"

"Yes I have, and it's truly a beautiful place to hold services. Why?"

"Well, I was wondering what it might take to televise our Sunday church service in the local area? We are over-crowded every Sunday morning. We have over five thousand church members, and if some folks could watch at home, that might help keep our attendance down, so we don't have to build a bigger church."

The smile on Billy's face appeared to grow wider with each passing word.

Schuller continued saying, "And as you know, there are people in the hospital, or sick at home, who can't make it to Sunday church."

"Bob, that's a fantastic idea!" Billy's enthusiasm for the idea inspired Schuller. His eyes widened as Billy continued, "You have a very positive message anyway, and that's what people need to hear on television. And your campus, with the water fountains, those moving glass doors, the religious statues and all, would be a terrific backdrop!"

He's making a lot of sense, Schuller thought to himself. *This might be something to consider in the future plans of the church.*

"So, when are you going to start?!" Graham asked.

Schuller's stomach suddenly leaped into his throat. He had not expected such an enthusiastic response from Billy Graham.

"I don't know anything about television! What does it cost? How can I raise the money? And even more than that, everything you say goes onto unforgiving film. What if I make a mistake?"

Schuller took a deep breath as he spoke the next words. "I've got to tell you, I need help, I can't do it alone!"

Dr. Graham sat back in his chair and thought for a minute. He understood his colleague's hesitation. Billy clearly remembered his first experience with the television camera. Then a smile appeared on his face as he said, "I have an idea."

He leaned forward to look Bob square in the eye and said, "I'll set up a meeting between yourself and my television producer, Fred Dynart. He can give you all the information you need. Total costs, weekly budgets, airtime rentals, and all the rest. Talk with him, then give me a call and we will talk some more if you wish."

That sounds simple enough, Schuller thought to himself. *There's no commitment involved with an exploratory meeting like that.*

"Okay, Great!" Schuller said cheerfully. "Let's do it!" Dr. Graham extended his hand, and said, "I'll have Fred call your office first thing in the morning."

They shook hands cordially. Schuller said, "Thank you very much for your kind words and your time!"

The warm night air felt refreshing as Schuller left the trailer. Walking into the packed stadium parking lot, his mind was filled with excitement.

Television!

Thoughts of the church campus came to his mind. *Could it be that we haven't finished building our church for you, Lord? Physically the buildings are there, but an electronic church! The millions of people that you could touch Lord, through a television church service!*

Millions! he thought. *Listening to me?* An insecure feeling gripped him as he climbed into his car. *Me, on Television?!* His eyes quietly closed in reverence as he said, "Dear Lord, if this is your will, I need your help." And then with a slight shudder he remembered Goliath.

"Daddy!"

The welcome sound rushed to his waiting ears as Schuller walked through the front door. He dropped his briefcase off in the front hallway as two and a half year old

Gretchen fell into his waiting arms.

"Hello, sweetheart, how are you?!"

"Great, come read me a story?" She said, flashing her beautiful brown eyes at him. His heart melted like ice on a hot summer day. Arvella appeared from the kitchen as he said, "You bet, just give me a minute to change my clothes, and talk with Mommy. Is that okay with you?!"

"Yeah," came the reply as Gretchen tore off down the hallway.

"How did the meeting go with Mr. Dynart?" said Arvella as she greeted Bob with a kiss.

"All right, I suppose."

A quizzical look crossed her face as she said, "All right? That doesn't sound very positive. So, what's the problem?"

"Four hundred thousand dollars is the problem! That's the cost of renting a T.V. truck, cameras, crew, and airtime in Los Angeles for one year." He said.

"Wow! This house only cost us twenty-five thousand dollars!" She said as her head shook in disbelief.

"I can't ask the congregation for that kind of money! We just finished building the Tower, and it's not even paid for yet." he said.

As he wrapped his arm around her, they began to walk toward the kitchen. Searching for a word of comfort she said, "Have you called Dr. Graham back to discuss your meeting?"

"No, not yet." he said.

"Well, you have a few minutes before dinner, why don't you give him a call. At least thank him for arranging the meeting. I'm sure he would appreciate that!"

"Okay, I'll make the call. Then I have a date with Gretchen and her storybook before dinner!" he said. His face lit up just thinking of his second obligation.

"Hello?"

"Billy? Bob Schuller here."

"Bob, I was just thinking of you, how did the meeting go?"

He hesitated as he searched for just the right words. "Fine, just fine. Mr. Dynart was very helpful."

"You don't sound very confident."

"Well, to tell you the truth, four hundred thousand dollars is a lot of money for our church to raise right now."

"Bob, do you think that your going on television would be beneficial to people and the community?"

Schuller thought for a moment and said, "Yes, very much so. Why?"

"Well, then why don't you put out a fleece? It worked for me on my first radio program in Portland, Oregon."

"Well, I know what a fleece is, but how would I apply it in this case?"

"Well, Bob, just like Gideon did it in the Old Testament. Only update the language. For example, let's set a dollar amount for half the amount you need."

Bob replied, "Two hundred thousand."

"Right. Now, go to your congregation. Without divulging the amount, ask them what they would be willing to pledge toward the television project over the next year. If you get pledges totalling over two hundred thousand, take that as your answer from God."

"What about the other half of the money?" Schuller inquired.

"That's where your faith comes in. If God answers your fleece by having the people pledge two hundred thousand, you have to trust Him to bring forward enough viewers of your program to cover the remaining cost." A long silence fell across the wire.

"Pray about it Bob, see where the Lord leads you!"

"Thank you, Billy. Very much. You have been very encouraging, and very, very helpful."

"I'll see you soon. Say hello to Arvella for me."

"I'll do that, Billy. And thanks again."

It was a cool November day as Schuller stood in his office, atop the thirteen-story Tower of Hope. The view of the large, coastal county was breathtaking. Schuller didn't seem to notice it. His mind was preoccupied with the vote that had been cast by his congregation the previous morning. *Four thousand dollars short of the two hundred thousand dollar mark. He wasn't sure how to take the news. Sure, the practice of "putting out the fleece" was in the Old Testament. And fundamentalist churches across the country actively practiced the ritual. Schuller, however, had never experienced it in the Reformed Church practice.*

A knock at the door disrupted his thoughts.

"Come in?"

"Pastor, Mr. Dynart is in the lobby. He would like to talk to you."

"Send him in please." Bob began to head for his office door, as Fred Dynart appeared before him.

"Hello, Bob."

"Fred, its great to see you again. Please, sit down."

"So, Bob, how did it go yesterday."

With only a touch of disappointment, Bob replied, "We didn't make it. We were four thousand short."

Fred smiled broadly as he said, "Four thousand short! Is that all!"

Schuller looked puzzled as he said, "I know it's not much, but we didn't reach the goal."

"I realize that, but you must understand that some folks do not respond right away. They want to go home and talk it over. Pray about it. Let's see what the mailman brings today. You just might reach your goal yet!"

Schuller's heart skipped a beat as he realized that Fred was right. A wave of fear passed over him. *What if the fleece came through? Do I have enough faith to follow through with it?*

"Well, I suppose you're right. I guess we will just

have to wait and see."

Fred stood up and said, "I'll call you in the morning to find out the results."

The soft glow of the moon fell through the bedroom window. Restlessly he tossed back and forth, haunted by his fateful decision. Arvella's eyes suddenly opened; she sensed her husband's nightmare. She knew the problem all too well and she knew he needed to talk it through.

"Bob, are you okay?"

Schuller stared at the ceiling. "I don't know what to do," he confessed. "With the pledges that came in today from the mail, we've gone over the two hundred thousand dollar mark. Our fleece has been answered."

"What kind of a pastor am I if I don't have enough faith to follow a simple fleece?" he asked. "The Old Testament teaches it after all. Yet, how can I risk the assets of the church on such a big contract?" Schuller turned to Arvella, his eyes a window to his hurting soul. "Arvella, what should I do?"

"Do what you have done all your life, follow your heart. Ask the questions you always tell me to ask; Is anyone else doing it? Is God in it? Will it help people? Then God will guide you, if you follow your heart."

Without a sound he leaned over to kiss her good night. Deep down in his soul, he knew she was right. He turned over and slowly closed his eyes. His mind recited the simple slogan he had written years before: "When faced with a Mountain I will not quit. I will keep on striving until I climb over, find a pass through, tunnel underneath, or simply stay and turn the mountain into a gold mine, with God's help!"

He slowly drifted off to sleep. The feeling of fear gripped him once again. Goliath was drawing near.

The familiar smell of bacon and fresh coffee filled

the air. His sense of smell beckoned his eyes to open. It was a new day. As he rose into the morning sunlight, a smile came to his lips. Suddenly, the answer was crystal clear. He knew what he had to do. Putting on his robe, he quickly marched down the hallway, tears forming in his eyes with each passing step. Entering the kitchen, he spotted Arvella, enjoying a carefree morning with her children and her first cup of coffee. Then came the announcement.

"Arvella, we're going on television, and you're going to be in charge of it!" A bolt of lightning ran down her spine.

"I'm what!!!???"

"I want you to be in charge of the program!"

"You have got to be kidding! I don't know anything about television!" she said, trying to find a way out of the position.

"You'll learn. Besides, you know music. That's how we first met, and you've been the organist for years. And you know about programming a service. We've always done that together..." She interrupted him.

"I, I, Ahhhh, I can't do this Bob!"

"Sure you can! I'm going to have my hands full just getting a message together every week. Besides, Mr. Dynart will report to you and handle the technical end of things. All you have to do is learn how to program and produce!" Before she could object further, he took his cup of coffee and marched back down the hallway. A new day had begun.

Book I

Bigger Dreams

Robert Harold Schuller - 1947

Arvella DeHaan on her wedding day - June 15, 1950

Left: Robert Schuller - 1935.
Farm overalls were the dress of the

*Right: Graduation from Floyd
Independent School - 1938*

Opposite: The Schuller barn waits for the tornado.

*Above: The remains of the Schuller farmhouse after the tornado.
The house was picked up and smashed down in a nearby field.*

*The foundation of the farmhouse was all that was left. Nine farms were
completely destroyed by the tornado. Only the Schuller farm was rebuilt.*

The entire school body of Newkirk High School in Newkirk, Iowa. Robert Schuller is standing in the top row of boys, seventh in from the left. Arvella DeHaan is in the third row of girls from the bottom, second from left. The date is 1941.

185

Robert Schuller - High School Graduation, 1943. He is sixteen years old.

Arvella DeHaan - High School Graduation, 1947

The greatest of these is love.
Robert and Arvella Schuller - Wedding Day, June 15, 1950

Over the threshold and into a new life together.

Robert and Arvella Schuller spent the first five years of their marriage at a small church outside Chicago. It was quite a change from rural Iowa.

Cover girl Arvella in first Chicago snow - 1951.

Sheila Schuller with her mother and father in Chicago.

Sheila, Bobby and new baby Jeanne.

Reverend Robert Schuller discusses the Five Wives and The Five Foolish Virgins.

At the beach with Bob and Arvella

Pastor Schuller and Arvella with Sheila and Bobby - California, 1955

The Schuller's first house in California had two bedrooms, one bathroom, a one-car garage and asphalt floors.

Starting Sunday, March 27th, attend . . .

Southern California's Beautiful

DRIVE-IN CHURCH

HELD IN THE

ORANGE DRIVE-IN THEATRE

Santa Ana Freeway (Highway 101) and Chapman Avenue

*Worship in the Shadows of Rising Mountains, Surrounded by Colorful
Orange Groves and Tall Eucalyptus Trees*

Storytime for the youngsters   Outstanding choral singing
Playground nursery for children   Inspiring preaching

"Worship as you are . . . In the family car"

ADMISSION FREE . . .   FREE-WILL OFFERING

Robert Schuller on the top of the snack bar roof at the drive-in. Arvella played the organ behind him.

Every Sunday, the Schullers hitched the trailer up with the organ and hauled it to the drive-in.

The world's first Walk-in, Drive-in Church, Garden Grove, California.
Ten acres were purchased in 1958, the building was completed in 1961.

"We had a chance to buy the ten acres next to us. These ten acres are the key to 21st Century." - Robert Schuller 1967

Above and facing page: The Garden Grove Community Church Campus in 1968. The Tower of Hope (tall building with cross) was completed in 1968. The walnut grove was purchased in 1968. The Crystal Cathedral was later built on these ten acres.

Pastor Robert Schuller - 1968

Arvella Schuller - 1968

Robert Schuller with his famous fishing pole.

*At Disneyland - Arvella, Jeanne,
Carol (in red) and Gretchen.
Robert Schuller's shadow is
taking the picture.*

Just tourists.

Three coins in a fountain.
Sheila, Bobby and Jeanne

Book II

The Cathedral

- 9 -

Pandora's Box

Schuller whistled cheerfully as he rode the glass elevator up to the top of the Tower of Hope. *Zipp-a-dee do-da. Zippa-dee-aay.* He couldn't seem to get that bothersome tune out of his head this morning.

He saw the sparkle of the Pacific Ocean as he passed the eighth floor. The clear winter sky showed the outline of Catalina Island. The blue horizon seemed to stretch on forever behind the island. To the North, the white-capped Matterhorn jutted up from the center of Disneyland. It was like standing on a mountain top. The ability to see above and beyond the problems of everyday life. It was like reading the words of a great dreamer. Walt Disney had said it best with these words framed on his office wall:

"I can't believe that there are heights that cannot be scaled, by a man who knows the secret of making dreams come true." A smile beamed across Schuller's face at the the simple statement. He thought to himself, *Dreams are nothing more than believing in yourself.*

The elevator slowed at the twelfth floor. The doors opened and he stood face to face with a somber-looking church treasurer.

"Bob, we have a big problem."

Schuller walked toward his office door. "Good morning to you, too, Frank."

"Bob, I'm serious, we've got a big problem," Frank said nervously.

"Well, come on in and we'll talk about it."

Schuller's office was lined on three sides with windows. His wooden desk stood at the near end. Behind the desk was a bookcase that ran the length of the wall. Most of the shelves were empty, except for Schuller's pictures of Norman Vincent Peale and Arvella.

Schuller sat down and motioned for Frank to do the same. Frank sat in one of the small chairs in front of the desk and watched Schuller calmly as he leafed through a stack of messages on the desk. "What's the big problem?" Schuller finally asked.

"We have to put in a new transformer for the television lights," Frank told him. "Otherwise, we can't tape our first show."

Schuller crumpled a message up and tossed it aside. "Fine. Put one in."

"That's not the problem, Bob."

"What is the problem?" Schuller smiled at a note from his secretary. *Good. A wedding.*

"We need to order the transformer today or we won't have it in time to tape," Frank said.

"So? Order it today."

"I need to get ten thousand dollars to the power

company today. The deadline is four o'clock."

"How much do we have in the new television account so far?"

"Nothing!"

"Nothing? What do you mean, nothing?"

"We just have pledges. No real money has come in yet."

"What about a line of credit with the power company?"

"We tried that. They want cash."

"Can we borrow it from the bank?"

Frank rolled his eyes. "Of course not. We don't have any assets. The Church already has a mortgage."

"What about the pledges?" Schuller asked. "Will they take the pledges as collateral for a loan?"

"No. They don't consider pledges, collateral."

Schuller sat back in his chair. He had signed a contract with KTLA Television in Los Angeles to begin airing one month from today. The first program had to be taped within the next two weeks to meet the contract deadline.

"Frank, you're the Treasurer. Where are we going to find ten thousand dollars in the next six hours?!" Schuller demanded.

"I may be the Treasurer, Bob, but you're the guy with the hose that waters the money tree."

Frank got up to leave the room. He knew that Schuller would come up with some brilliant idea before he reached the door. *Why not? He always had before.*

Frank first started to worry when he reached the door and Schuller hadn't stopped him. *He always stops me before I get to the door.*

He'll come out and say something before the elevator gets here, Frank thought. He pressed the white call button.

He'll call me back. He will.

Frank quietly rode the elevator down to his office.

He'll call me later. He always calls.

Ten thousand dollars by four o'clock? Who is he kidding?
Schuller pulled his hand out of his pants pocket.
Fourteen dollars and fifty-three cents lay in his hand.
Well, it's a start.

Schuller's secretary popped the door open. "Dr.
Schuller, there's - - "

"How much money do you have on you?"

"What - How much - -?"

"How much money did you bring to work today?"
Schuller repeated.

"Not a dime," she said. She wasn't going to get
stuck buying lunch again. "I'm brown bagging my lunch
today."

"Oh. Well, never mind," he said. "What can I do for
you?"

"There's a couple here for their appointment."

Marriage counseling, he thought to himself. He
walked to the window trying to clear his head. "Please,
send them in."

She motioned for the couple to come in.

"Pastor Schuller, it's great to be able to come and
spend some time with you," the husband said cheerfully.

"I'm glad I can be here for you." Schuller said.
"Please have a seat."

They sat down. He was young and well dressed. She
wore a white spring dress with a red belt.

"So, why don't you tell me a little about yourselves,"
Schuller said when they sat down.

The couple looked at each other and grinned.
"Oh, we're not here for counseling," they both said at the
same time.

Schuller looked surprised. He sat back in his chair
and said, "You're not?"

"Oh, no, Pastor!" he said quickly. "We couldn't be
happier!"

"Well, then, what would you like to talk about?"

The couple smiled at each other. "You gave an interesting sermon on 'Giving' last week," the husband replied.

"Quite frankly, we've never done anything like this before," the wife added. "But when you challenged everyone to give ten percent of their income back to the Lord, to give back some of what He has given us, well, we thought that was a great idea."

Schuller leaned forward in his chair, "You know, if everybody had the same spirit that you do, our church would never have a money problem!"

"Exactly," the young husband responded. He reached into his pocket and pulled out a check as he said, "Pastor, last year we had a profit of one hundred thousand dollars! So we want to give you this check for ten thousand dollars. Exactly ten percent!"

Sudden shock gave way to relief as the check was laid down on his desk. He looked across at the smiling couple.

Who were they? He had never seen them before. *How did they know?*

Looking into his teary eyes, she said with delight, "Pastor, I'm sure there are things around here that never get done because you don't have the proper funds. So we want you to use that money for anything you feel is necessary!"

Without hesitation, Schuller quickly rose to hug the couple. With his eyes tightly closed he prayed, "Thank you, dear God, for this man and this woman, your special servants on earth. Bless them for their generosity and their faithfulness! Amen."

"Thank you very much," Schuller said to the couple.

"You're welcome, Dr. Schuller." The couple slowly headed for the door.

"When is the first television program going to be

taped in the church?" the man asked. "We would love to come."

"Oh," Schuller said excitedly. "The television trucks will be here in two weeks." He thought about the large television trailers he had seen only a few months ago at the Anaheim Stadium. He still couldn't believe they were coming to tape him for television. A chill of excitement ran down his spine.

"I'm sure you have your sermon all ready to go, don't you," the woman responded.

Sermon? That's right! What am I going to preach my first Sunday on television?

"Oh, Ah, I've been working on it." Schuller said sheepishly. The couple headed out the door of Schuller's office.

"We'll see you next Sunday, Dr. Schuller, Goodbye."

Frank sat in his office. It was three o'clock already. The phone hadn't rung all afternoon. Frank had chewed the ends off of six pencils already.

Ring!

"Yes." Frank snatched the phone off the hook, saying 'Yes!' before it even got to his mouth.

"Frank?" said Schuller at the other end.

"Yes?" hesitated Frank.

"What are you doing in your office?" Schuller asked. "Why aren't you down at the power company?"

"The power comp- - No, you didn't. You got the money? I don't believe it. How did you do it?"

Schuller paused, searching for just the right expression.

"Just turned on the hose."

*　　　*　　　*

Schuller scanned each of their faces for ideas. He needed ideas. He needed a name for the television show.

He needed a good name. Fred Dynart and Arvella were there to help him come up with one.

"Think big," he told them. "This is the first televised church service in California. All of Los Angeles will be watching. There are already a number of religious programs that people can watch. Fulton Sheen is on, Billy Graham is on. Our name has to be something that grabs people. It needs to be something that makes them tune us in on a Sunday morning."

"How about "The Schuller Hour?" Fred offered.

"Thanks," Schuller said, "but it doesn't convey hope. I want the name of the show to give people hope. People need to know they're going to feel better about themselves after watching this show."

"It's an hour long," Arvella said, "why don't we call it "The Hour of Hope?"

Schuller leaned back in his chair. He rolled the words off his tongue. *The Hour of Hope.* After a moment he shook his head and said, "That doesn't have any drive. It needs action."

"Maybe we should have the word 'family' in the title," Fred tried, "to let people know it's a family show."

"The Church Hour, The Religious Hour, The Schuller Hour," Fred thought aloud.

"Well, Billy Graham's Program is 'The Hour of Decision', isn't it?" Arvella asked.

"And William F. Buckley's got 'Firing Line'," Fred added.

"No," Schuller said, "That's getting away from it. The name has to say what the program is. What I want is something that tells people that this is a positive, powerful message. The name has to drive that home." Schuller thought harder. The name was so important. They didn't have any money to promote the show. Commercials and newspaper advertising were out of the question. The air time was already too expensive. The name would have to be it's own promotion.

Fred laid his head back and said, "Drive..., you want drive. You want power."

The word hit Schuller like a sledgehammer. He blurted out, "The Hour of Power," and waited for their reaction.

Arvella smiled. *He still knows how to think big.*

Fred's eyes widened. "That's it," he said. "That's it!"

"People have to know that they can have power over the difficult times in their lives. God gives it to them," Schuller said. "The Hour of Power! People want power. They need it. They need the power to live their own lives. They need to know how to do that. The name promises that."

*   *   *

"Ten seconds to opening," barked the assistant into his microphone. He readjusted his headset. "Roll tape."

The young assistant director looked into a panel of six television screens in front of him. He was used to directing football and basketball games on Sunday Morning. But a church service?

The Director barked out his signals to the waiting cameramen's ears.

"Camera four, pull in on the choir. Camera two, give me a wider shot on the water fountains," he instructed.

The television trailer buzzed with activity. The video tape operators made their final equipment check.

"Five seconds, four... three...." called out the assistant.

"Camera Two on Schuller," called out the Director.

Arvella Schuller sat quietly in the corner watching the men do their jobs. *What was a producer supposed to do, anyway?* She looked over to Fred Dynart standing behind the Director. He knew that Arvella felt out of place. He quickly flashed a signal in her direction. His lips let out a whisper.

"Arvella," he said. "Bob looks great." And gave her a thumbs up signal. He turned back to the control panel and watched Robert Schuller appear on monitor number two.

"Two...one...Cue the choir director." called out the assistant.

On the screen, Arvella could see the choir begin their opening chorus. She smiled as the church service started. *I can't believe this is happening,* she thought to herself. *We're actually going on television.* It seemed like a long way from her country church back in Newkirk, Iowa.

The assistant pointed to the waiting announcer. He was poised over his microphone, ready to give the opening lines of the program.

"From the Garden Grove Community Church, Welcome to The Hour of Power, with Robert Schuller." The announcer said it professionally, stretching out his words.

The words 'The Hour Of Power' were shown in small white letters over a color background of the church. The fountains in front of the walk-in, drive-in church, burst up as Camera One panned by. Camera Three panned the smiling faces of the choir. Camera Four looked over the audience. The church held a total of seventeen hundred people, and it was packed wall to wall. The entire congregation of the Garden Grove Community Church had wanted to be there for this big day.

Camera Two held tight on Schuller.

Schuller looked into the eye of the camera. He tried to keep calm as the red light by the lens came on. He knew that Goliath was watching his every move.

Dear Lord, please give me strength!

As the music ended, his voice echoed the words now heard weekly around the world.

"This is the day that the Lord has made. Let us

rejoice and be glad in it!"

*   *   *

"Arvella, come here. Quick! It's starting!"

Schuller shouted the words into the kitchen. "Arvella! You'll miss the opening."

"Gretchen! Stay away from the T.V., honey," Schuller said as he picked up his three-year old daughter.

Arvella wiped Gretchen's peanut butter finger prints off the screen with her wash rag.

Schuller carried Gretchen back to the couch. He put her down between Jeanne and Bobby. Carol lay on the floor, propped up on her elbows in front of the television.

"There's, Dad!" Carol shouted, "Look, Mom, there's Dad!"

"This is the day that the Lord has made...," said the robed figure on the screen.

"That camera angle is all wrong," Schuller started in. "And they need to show more of the trees and fountains. They're so beautiful."

"It looks great, Bob," Arvella told him. "Relax and enjoy the program." She watched the screen with an intense interest. There was no money in her production budget to edit the show. The program had to be perfect the day it was taped. That first program broadcast in February, 1970, was the raw footage shot just three weeks earlier.

"When's the commercial?" Carol asked, " I want to get a drink of water!"

"Sshh, honey," Arvella warned her, "Your father's trying to watch the show."

"I'm Robert Schuller, Pastor of the Garden Grove Community Church," spoke the somewhat stiff figure on the television screen. "And this is the first broadcast of our church service here in Garden Grove. We're calling it 'The Hour Of Power.'"

"You look pretty good on television," Arvella said.

"Hush," Schuller told her, "I'm trying to remember what I said."

"This broadcast is being seen all over the Los Angeles area here on KTLA this morning. I'd like to thank the owner, Gene Autry, for allowing us to buy time on his station."

Schuller clenched his fist and shook it at the screen. "That's right, Schuller," he said to himself, "Give Mr. Autry a nice endorsement."

Arvella smiled. She knew how important The Hour of Power had already become to Schuller. Even though it was their first telecast, there was a professional touch about it that was unmistakable. There was something different about it.

Schuller looked over at Arvella and winked. He moved in closer to the screen. His eyes absorbed every shot; his ears made a special note of every word they heard. He was making improvements already.

- 10 -

Camelot

A cool August breeze gently rocked the tall pine trees. The scent of summer wild flowers filled the mountain air. Arvella sat out on the cabin's balcony and looked down the valley. She noticed she was getting a little too much sun on her legs.

Schuller walked up the steep drive towards the cabin door. He gazed up at the brown, boxy cabin. It was the only flat-roofed structure in the area. *And they said the lot was unbuildable*, he thought."The side of the mountain is too steep, Schuller," they had said. Never mind that the new driveway he put in slid down the mountain after the first spring rain. A few well planted trees had taken care of that. The second driveway had held just fine.

Carol and Gretchen followed their father. They

carried a string of trout for dinner. Gretchen dragged hers along in the dirt. Schuller set his pole against the cabin.

I'm glad he's relaxing, Arvella thought. It was good to have this week off before starting the Fall schedule. Program schedules, choir music, guests - all that had been left down in Orange County. Up here at the cabin, she could forget all that and let her mind wander.

"Mom, where are you?" yelled Gretchen. It was 1975. She was seven years old.

"Upstairs on the balcony!" Arvella called back. Gretchen and Carol quickly chased up the stairs. They let the strings of fish *whap!* against the steps all the way up to their Mother.

"Look at what we caught!" cried Carol. She proudly displayed the string of fish.

"Yeah, Mom. You should have seen it. I bet we caught every fish in the whole lake!" added Gretchen.

Arvella pulled Gretchen onto her lap. "Sooo! My little fisher ladies did a great job catching dinner, huh!" Their faces beamed with excitement as she hugged them tightly.

"It was great! Dad put the worm on my hook and everything," said Gretchen. "I hate worms."

"I put it on all by myself!" said Carol.

Arvella laughed. "Oh, you two are something else!"

"We had quite a day," said Schuller from the top of the stairs. "How was yours?"

She looked back at him with a sheepish smile. "Not as eventful as yours, I see." Setting his pouch of fish down on the kitchen table, he knew immediately what kind of day his wife had. Half of the breakfast dishes were still on the table next to his pouch. The rest were in the sink and programming notes filled the main room of the cabin.

He smiled as he thought to himself of the responsibility he had given to her just six years earlier. Producing a now nationwide television program didn't always leave time for household chores. In an instant he knew what he had to do. With a kitchen as his pulpit, he announced the evening schedule.

"All right, girls. Kitchen patrol!"

Their excited faces turned blank. The sound of final pleas from the prisoners hit his waiting ears.

"Daaaad, we just got back.." said Carol. "Yeah Dad, I'm tired." Gretchen added.

Undaunted by their lack of enthusiasm for the project he said excitedly, "Gretchen, you clear the table! Carol, you grab a towel to dry with. I'm going to wash!"

Slowly the girls rose to come in from the balcony. Their feet dragged the floor as they walked. As he watched his girls move past him, he looked up at Arvella and smiled broadly. "We're going to whip this place into shape in no time!" All she could do was shake her head and grin as her husband took charge of the house.

With one graceful, sweeping move he came to kneel by her side. As he slid his arm around her shoulders, he said gallantly, "I missed you today."

"I missed you, too. Sounds like you had more fun than I did," she said. Gently he kissed her, and said, "I shall return victorious!"

Romanced by his chivalry, she said, "I married a crazy man, you know that don't you!" His eyebrow raised slightly as a grin formed at the corners of his lips.

"No, just a fool in love with the fairest of maidens," he said.

With a slight squeeze of his hand on her shoulder, he bounded back into the kitchen. Pulling an apron from the cabinet as if he were drawing a sword, he said, "Onward Christian soldiers, we have work to do!" As the sink began to fill with water, a song began to fill his heart. With a bold voice, a humorous song about role reversal began to fill the air. Sounding more like a pirate ship then a kitchen, Bob started to sing:

I am the captivated husband of a liberated wife.

Marriage to an executive has surely changed my life.
Once had lots of lovin'-Now all I have is strife.
'Cause I'm the captivated husband of a liberated wife.

Laughter began to flow freely from the balcony. "You've got to be kidding, Bob! Where on earth did that come from?"

With a boyish grin he said, "From me! 'Cause I'm creative!"

"Oh really!" she said with a grin, teasing his boastful attitude.

Tossing a towel over his shoulder, and strutting back to the sink, he turned his attention to the task at hand.

Dunking the next plate into the suds he sang:

She goes to work each morning, drives the biggest car.
She's climbing up the ladder-goin' very far.
Sits behind her office desk, in a fancy downtown store.
I'm alone with daytime T.V.-quickly that's a bore.

Gretchen and Carol quickly joined into the fun. The drudgery of work quickly faded as they called out suggested lines to the singing preacher.

"Dad, what about washing dishes!" yelled Gretchen. "And going to work every day," said Carol. "Sing that!"

"I've got it, I've got it." he said. "How about this:

In fancy clothes, she leaves the house, kisses me goodbye.
Goes to lunch in restaurants, high up in the sky.
She's left me with the house and yard, the dog, and all the
    kids.
I do all the washing-pots and pans and lids!

Giggling as they worked, the simple tune was turning into a chorus line. As Carol was drying the last of the dishes and Gretchen put them away, Schuller continued the fun by picking up a guitar.

"What about making all the money?" Gretchen said.

A chorus of laughter filled the cabin as Arvella beamed with approval. "Yeah Bob, what about making money!" His eyes rolled back as he began to search for the right words:

> She brings home the money-and a 'Honey how are you?'
> I tell her, 'Thanks', and smile, but in my heart I'm blue.
> I plan to make her happy with a special meal.
> 'Sorry dear, I'm tired tonight-food has no appeal!'

As she laughed, Arvella said, "You're starting to sound like a country and western star, singing the blues!" Bob glanced back to Arvella and said, "Well, it's always nice to have something to fall back on in life isn't it."

"Oh, no! The Robert Schuller and Gene Autry Hour!" she said excitedly.

Bob just winked and said, "Do you think he would take me?!"

"Be careful what you wish for!" She said as the song continued:

> She feels like a million-I feel like a mouse.
> She has got the power, I have got the house.
> Once I knew she needed me–but that's not true today,
> So how can I keep lovin' her, along this changin' way?

Building up to the big ending, Schuller raised his hands into the air as they all sang:

> I am the captivated husband of a liberated wife,
> Marriage to an executive has surely changed my life.
> Once had lots of lovin'-now all I have is strife,
> 'Cause I'm the captivated husband of a liberated wife!

*   *   *

The eleven o'clock service was standing room only. Seventeen hundred people filled the inside of the church.

Outside, they had set up five hundred chairs for the service and every one had been filled an hour ago.

Two thousand cars filled the parking lot. The extra ten acres to the north of the church, bought three years ago to handle the overflow, had been graded and paved. Now, even that space was full.

"There just isn't any more room, Bob," said Mike Nason.

"What do you want me to do," Schuller said in frustration, "turn them away? I hired you to solve problems. Solve this one!"

Nason looked out the window at the crowd. Schuller was right. They had a problem. A big problem. They had run out of room again.

"Bob, there are only two options. Build a bigger church or hold more services."

"We're holding three already, Mike," Schuller said.

"Well, then, there's your answer. Build a bigger church."

"I hired you to solve problems, not create them," Schuller said firmly. "There is no way that I'm getting involved in another building project. Find another way."

"The only way to keep what you have, is to keep moving ahead," Nason said. "When you started this church, you only had one member - your wife. How long did it take you to gather up a hundred members? About a year?"

Schuller nodded."That's right. About a year."

"And how long to get a thousand members?"

"About five years," Schuller said.

"And now you have over six thousand members." Nason said. He looked down on the parking lot jammed with cars. "Those thousands of people told all their friends about you. See all those people down there?" Nason pointed out the window. "They just did what you did when you were knocking on doors. You wanted people to come to church. Well, there they are!"

GOLIATH

Schuller knew he was right. *This is exactly what I wanted.* He remembered how thrilled he was the day Peale had preached at the drive-in. He remembered the two thousand cars that had jammed the Orange Drive-in sixteen years ago.

He was looking at the same sight today.

"The only way to keep what you have, is to keep moving ahead," Nason told him.

He's throwing my own sermons back at me. I hate it when they do that, Schuller thought.

Schuller stepped into the pulpit. He surveyed the crowd. The church was jammed with worshippers as the rain began to fall.

From the corner of his eye he could see a young couple slowly get up from their seat in the open air garden. The young husband's hand gently cradling his wife's side as they walked to the parking lot. Schuller's heart began to break. He knew that they had just lost their child and needed to be in church, but there just wasn't room. His fear was strangling his church. Goliath was holding him back. Deep down he knew something had to change.

- 11 -

Diggin' A Hole

ll glass.

Philip Johnson stared back at Schuller. He couldn't believe the two words that he had just heard.

"All glass?" Johnson said back to Schuller. "Do you have any idea what you're asking for?"

Schuller stood at the window of his twelfth floor office. He looked down at the parking lot that would be the foundation for the new church. He let his words bounce off the plate glass.

"Mr. Johnson, I want there to be as little as possible between the people sitting in church and nature. I want everybody to be able to see the sky and hear the birds outside. I want the sun to shine in from all angles."

Schuller turned away from the window and looked at Johnson. "The only way I know how to do that, is to make it out of all glass."

Johnson looked down at the sketches for the new church he had designed. They were spread out across the table. The famed architect looked at his design again. He had spent weeks on it. He had finally come up with a structure that would hold four thousand people, with floor to ceiling windows on three sides. The inside space rose to a fifty foot height.

"That's just not what I had in mind," Schuller said as he looked over Johnson's shoulder. "It has to be so striking that it will cause people to stop and look. It will cry out to be built."

Schuller walked around the table and faced the architect from New York.

"But, quite frankly," he said, "I'm not sure if it's even feasible. I'm not even sure I know what I'm talking about."

Johnson looked up from his drawing and adjusted his thick, black spectacles. "Reverend Schuller, architecture is too important to be left to the architects. Churches are what architecture is all about. The building should be so moving that you feel the power and the presence of God as soon as you walk in."

"Neutra had the same idea," Schuller said. "He told me, 'A building should inspire people without preaching at them.' He designed all of our buildings to bring in the beauty of nature. All I'm trying to do is tell people that God loves them. I want people to know that if they find God, they find love. I want people to know that there is love. And that they don't have to go sit in a dark, forbidding place on a Sunday morning to find God."

Schuller paced the floor. It was hard for him to say what he was feeling to the thin, white-haired architect. Finally, he just blurted it out. "If we lived in the eighteenth century, we might not have to do all this. Life was simple then. You didn't have a whole lot of choices to make. But we don't live in the eighteenth century. We live in the twentieth century. People rush by each other at a frightening pace. They seem to chase around their whole lives without ever finding what they're looking for."

"I need something big and beautiful that will make people stop and look and listen. I need something that will attract attention."

"And you want the whole thing out of glass?" Johnson asked.

"Every corner," Schuller said solemnly, "All glass."

Johnson started to roll up his plans. He knew the meeting was over. "What kind of budget do you want me to work with, Reverend Schuller?"

"We don't have any money. We borrowed the money from the bank to hire you, Mr. Johnson. So it doesn't matter what it costs. Design the most beautiful church you can dream of."

Johnson shook Schuller's hand and flew back to New York. His mind focused on the words: 'All Glass'.

*   *   *

"Ten million dollars?!" Schuller said in disbelief. He stared at the six-inch model of the all glass church Johnson had designed.

"Mr. Johnson," Schuller said, "It's beautiful. It's just what I had in mind, but ten million dollars?" Schuller started to shake his head in defeat. "I don't think we could raise one tenth of that much money."

"Well, if you just built the shell and didn't finish the basement, you could get by with about seven million."

"Seven million," Schuller said. "You say that so easy. Seven million for a shell."

"You said it didn't matter what it costs, Reverend Schuller. And this is what you asked for."

How are we ever going to raise seven million dollars? Schuller thought. *I still don't know how we're going to pay the* *bank the $200,000 we borrowed for this design.*

"Thank you, Mr Johnson. It's just what I wanted. But, to be quite honest, I have no idea how or where to get that kind of money. I'm going to have to think about this for a while."

They shook hands and Johnson left.

"It's hopeless," Schuller said to Mike Nason. "How are we going to raise that kind of money?"

"You need to think bigger, Bob. There are people out there who have the kind of money to support a project like this."

"People with millions of dollars don't give their money away," Schuller argued. "The way they stay rich is by keeping their money."

"That's really not true, Bob," Nason countered. "You can't get rich without helping a lot of people along the way. The more people you help, the richer you get." Nason walked to the window. "Look outside at the campus, Bob. Look what happened when you decided to move away from the drive-in and buy this ten acres. Remember how much trouble you had raising the $18,000 to buy this land?"

"That was almost twenty years ago, Mike. The world has changed in the last twenty years. The next ten acres cost us over a million dollars just for the land."

"You raised that money didn't you? And The Hour Of Power is costing almost five million a year. People are sending that money in."

"Almost all of that comes in small five and ten dollar donations, Mike. You know that. I haven't got the slightest idea where we're going to find seven million dollars."

Nason walked over to Schuller's desk and put a blank piece of paper in the center. He took his pen out and wrote the numbers one through five down the side and looked up at Schuller. "Practice what you preach, Bob." And he left.

Schuller sat down behind his desk. He looked down at the blank piece of paper.

This is a waste of time, he thought. Reluctantly, he wrote the words 'Raise Seven Million Dollars' on the top of the paper. Under that, he listed five ways.

1. Find seven people with $1,000,000 each.
2. Find fourteen people with $500,000 each.
3. Find seventy people with $100,000 each.
4. Find a thousand people with $7,000 each.
5. Find ten thousand people with $500 each.

I wonder how many windows are in that place, Schuller thought as he looked at the model of the glass church. *Five, six, seven, maybe ten thousand windows.* Schuller reached over for the phone.

"Marjorie," he said to his secretary. "Call Philip Johnson over at the hotel and find out how many windows he put in the new church.... Never mind why I want it. Just get me a window count. And then get Mike Nason in here. We need to find somebody with a million dollars."

Schuller hung up the phone. He started to scratch out some figures.

Let's see, he thought, *Ten thousand windows, times five hundred dollars each is five million. Is that right? Yeah, it is. Plus two one million dollar gifts...*

Schuller put his pencil down. *It just might work!*

*　　　　*　　　　*

"The first person I'd ask is John Crean."

Schuller sat in another meeting in his office. To his right sat Mike Nason. To his left sat Doug Lawson and Victor Andrews. Nason had suggested Schuller go outside and hire professional fundraisers for the million dollar donations. The windows could probably be sold over the television. Nason had said Schuller would have to personally scour the country for the seven figure gifts. Lawson and Andrews were well known throughout the country for their contacts.

Lawson was the first to suggest John Crean.

"John and Donna Crean own Fleetwood Enterprises, Bob," added Mike Nason. "They're right here in Orange County. Fleetwood is one of the largest manufacturers of mobile homes in the United States."

"They started out making window blinds in their garage in the early fifties," Lawson added. "They were selling to trailer manufacturers. They saved their money and started making the trailers themselves. Now they're one of the biggest."

"The Creans are well known for their generosity, Dr. Schuller." Victor Andrews spoke in a low, thoughtful tone. He had the aristocratic look of a man who spoke of millions of dollars easily.

Schuller looked at the suit Andrews had worn to the meeting. It was obviously tailor made and very expensive. He looked at the lines of character in Andrew's face. Schuller trusted Victor Andrews.

"And you think the Creans would be interested in donating money to build an all glass church?" Schuller asked.

"I don't know, but he's certainly worth asking." Andrews said. He gave the impression that he chose every word only after careful thought. Nason knew that Andrews had learned his mannerisms from long years of political fundraising.

"Well, I guess we should make an appointment to see John and Donna Crean, shouldn't we?" Schuller asked.

"I'll set it up," Lawson said. He smiled as he shook Schuller's hand.

*   *   *

"Gentlemen, I'd like to help you, but I just can't do

240

it right now."

John Crean's voice echoed in Schuller's head. His answer was blunt and to the point. He was kind, but the answer was still 'No.'

John Crean sat behind the desk in the Spanish style study. The dark oak beams gave the room a heavy feeling. Crean wasn't much older than Schuller, but his accomplishments spoke for themselves. Lawson had set up the appointment at the Crean Ranch in San Juan Capistrano. The estate was a rolling ranch of ninety-five acres, part of an original four-hundred-year-old Spanish Mission.

Crean was not a harsh man, but when he spoke, his tone was firm. Schuller knew that John Crean had made his decision.

"It's a beautiful building," Donna Crean said. She tried to console the look of disappointment that was evident on Schuller's face. It had taken months to set up this appointment and Schuller had drawn a big fat 'No.'

"We want to call it The Crystal Cathedral," Schuller said to Donna. He tried to sound positive, but he found himself failing again. "The design is based on a four-pointed star, the Star of Bethlehem."

"I see it's about four hundred feet long," Donna said. She ran her finger over the drawing. "And you've got three balconies inside...What's the seating capacity again, about thirty-five hundred?"

"About three thousand, actually," Schuller said. He was visibly impressed with her. She was truly interested in the design. Most other people he had shown it to thought it was just another one of his pipe dreams.

Crean smiled at Donna's interest. "Donna final-checks all of our product designs," he said. "Nothing clears the production line without Donna's approval."

Schuller smiled. He was hoping he had renewed their interest.

"It's quite a building," Donna sighed.

241

"The design was inspired by England's Crystal Palace and the amphitheater at Epidaurus, Greece," Schuller added. He was searching desperately for anything to keep the conversation going.

Donna smiled and put her hand on her husband's arm.

Schuller watched John Crean look at his wife. After all the hard work and suffering, these two people were still in love. They still cared.

"How much will it cost again?" John Crean asked Schuller.

"Seven million dollars," Schuller said. This time his answer was blunt and to the point.

"Well, I'm still not sure there's anything we can do to help, but I want to thank you for taking the time to come see us," Crean told Schuller.

John and Donna Crean saw Schuller and Lawson to the door. Schuller said a prayer before he left and Crean closed the door.

"What do you think?" Donna asked her husband.

John Crean looked into his wife's beautiful eyes. "I think that if he's crazy enough to build a church out of all glass, then we ought to be crazy enough to help him get started."

*   *   *

"Bob, telephone," Arvella called down the hallway. "It's John Crean."

"John Crean? Could it...naaaa, couldn't be that. He probably wants to come to church on Sunday. After all, it's Easter!"

As Bob reached the kitchen, Arvella was anxiously waiting by the phone.

"Hurry up, Bob," she said quietly. Her heart was racing as Schuller said, "Hello?"

"Bob, John Crean here."

"Yes, Mr. Crean, what can I do for you?"

"Well, Donna and I talked it over, and we decided to give you the million dollar gift."

Bob's heart skipped a beat. He quickly turned to Arvella, his eyes telling her the unspoken story.

"That's terrific news, may I ask what changed your minds?"

"Well, quite frankly, we prayed about it and well, we just believe in you. We feel God wants us to do this!"

Bob's voice suddenly became quiet, almost reverent as he simply said, "Thank you."

*   *   *

The next six months shot by. Crean had started a fire in Schuller. Johnson made a larger model of the structure that showed all the details. It was a lacy-webbed, table-top version. Schuller took it before the congregation and asked for pledges to raise five million dollars.

The people turned out to be as enthusiastic as he was. Things were going so good, he asked Johnson how much it would cost to finish the basement and not just build the shell.

"Around three million," Schuller was told. So the total cost was now ten million for the Crystal Cathedral, completely finished.

But nothing seemed to matter to Schuller. He was unstoppable. He had a few million dollars and he was just getting started. He knew he was on good terms with the Farmers and Merchants Bank. He'd just ask for a loan. Churches could get loans like anybody else. Schuller called the president at the corporate office in Long Beach.

"We can give you four million, Dr. Schuller," Ken Walker said. "I still remember the first five hundred dollars that you brought in to open your account, back in

'55. Our maximum loan amount is four million. If you can get the rest of the money in through donations, we'll make the construction loan."

Not to be outdone, Victor Andrews arranged for Schuller to meet with W. Clement Stone in Chicago. Stone was one of the most successful insurance salesmen in the history of the country and was known for giving away millions. Schuller walked into Stone's Chicago mansion brimming with feelings of impending success.

He walked out with a promise.

"Schuller," the mustachioed Stone had said, "If you can raise the first nine million in cash, I'll stand good for the tenth."

Schuller was all smiles the entire way back to California. Ten million dollars in a little over ten months. They were going to make it.

*   *   *

"Fifteen million dollars?!" Schuller shouted the figures out loud. "How can the costs be up to fifteen million dollars?" He looked at the stony-faced men around the table. "How can that be possible?" Schuller asked. "We haven't even done anything yet!"

"Bob," Victor Andrews said. "Construction costs are up all over in this economy. There's a building boom on right now. We just have to face that."

Schuller stopped his pacing. He didn't even feel like looking out the window anymore. He hadn't had a headache in three months. Now his head was pounding. He stared at the sheet of paper on his desk. The final bids totalled fourteen million, seven-hundred-thousand dollars. By the time he added the construction interest, it was a pretty safe bet the costs would exceed fifteen million dollars.

"Vic, I'm not blaming anyone," Schuller said, "I just don't know how we can do it. This is fifteen million dollars! We've been fundraising for a year and we've only got three million dollars in the bank."

"But we've got a four million dollar construction loan in place at Farmers and Merchants Bank," Nason said. "And we're ready to go on television and ask people to donate windows. That will surely raise a few million."

Schuller let Nason's words sink in. They boiled down to just one word. One word only. Integrity. Schuller was getting ready to go on television and ask people to give. He would ask them to donate a window for five hundred dollars. Nason was right, ten thousand, six hundred windows would add up to a lot of donations. But could he ask when he was not yet certain if he could deliver on his promise? It was a matter of Integrity.

At least we haven't gone on television yet, he thought.

But he had already asked people to give to the project; there was no turning back from that. And now he didn't know how he was going to complete it. Schuller felt the weight of Goliath begin to bear down on him.

"It's not your name out there on the letters asking for money," Schuller said to Nason. He had raised his voice to emphasize his point. "It's not your face in front of the congregation every week, promising people that you'll come through. I've raised money, a lot of money for this project. What am I supposed to do? Get up and say, 'Sorry, folks, I wasn't good enough. I couldn't make it?'"

Schuller had done his best to keep the anger out of his voice, but he couldn't help it now. To come this far, just to let his dream die, was out of the question. He looked around the room for Arvella. *What a time for her to be away editing the program,* he thought to himself.

"Bob, don't take it so personally," Nason said calmly, "This is a business decision, like any other, I - "

"This is not just another business decision!" Schuller said. "I made promises to people. I promised enough seats so that no one would have to be turned away. Every time I look out that window, I see that young couple whose son I buried, walking away because we didn't have a seat for them in this church."

"You don't get up in that pulpit every Sunday and look at those faces. None of you do. You don't have to live with it." Schuller stopped, because his words were running into each other. He looked at Mike Nason. "Do you expect me to get up in front of all those people and say, 'We made a mistake, folks. Here's your money back?' "

Vic Andrews sat calmly at the table. He had listened in silence to Schuller's tirade. He waited until the bellowing subsided and said, "Bob, I think we have to consider all of our options."

"Okay, Like what?" Schuller said.

"Giving back the money in the building fund for starters. Call John Crean and tell him the project can't be done in today's economic environment."

"What's he going to think of us, Vic?"

"He's a business man Bob, he knows the pitfalls. And he'll be glad to know you took his gift seriously enough to give it back rather then spend it on a project doomed to failure."

Schuller looked long and hard at Andrews before slumping down behind his desk. He searched his mind for another solution, but he knew Vic was right. It was easier this way. There was no way he could ever raise fifteen million dollars to build a church.

"Mike," he said, "I want you to prepare a press release telling everyone that we're cancelling the project. I'll tell Arvella tonight after dinner."

Schuller looked at Vic Andrews. "I'll give John Crean a call."

"Hello?"

"John, it's Bob Schuller."

"Bob, how are you, it's nice to hear from you!"

"Thank you. Listen, John, I have some news for you. It looks like I'm going to have to give you your million dollars back!"

Saying those last words twisted Schuller's stomach. It was admitting defeat. No matter who he blamed, no matter what excuse he came up with, it didn't change anything. He'd failed. And there was no one to help him now. Goliath had won.

"Give my million dollars back," Crean said. "Why?"

"The costs are just too high, John. The estimates are at fifteen million dollars, and I'm sure they'll be higher before we get through. We haven't raised anywhere near that amount and can't get there even with bank borrowing."

"But I thought you were going to break ground next month?" Crean said.

"There's no way we can break ground, John. Not with knowing the costs could go past fifteen million. We just won't be able to build the Cathedral."

"Dig the hole, Bob."

"What?" Schuller said. "What did you say?"

"Dig the hole," Crean repeated. "Get started. You'll find the money someplace. I'm not taking the million dollars back."

Schuller hung up the phone and looked at Arvella.

"What did he say, Bob?" she asked.

Schuller let go of a deep breath. "He said, 'dig the hole.' "

Arvella chuckled, "He's thinking like you do, Bob."

"How's that?"

"He's a possibility thinker too."

Schuller smiled. He knew she was right.

- 12 -

Carol's Story

Carol Schuller looked at the big black motorcycle and waited. It was her turn next.

She loved the summer in Iowa. She couldn't wait to feel the cool night air rush against her legs. White shorts were what all the older girls were wearing in California. She was thirteen now and had brought a new pair to show off in Iowa. She had been in shorts almost all summer back in California. Softball, horseback riding, she even wore white shorts water skiing.

Gretchen hopped off the back of the big Honda. Mark had steadied the black bike so she could get down. He was a big, good-looking kid for his age. His dark brown hair had grown a little longer for the summer. It was already starting to sneak over his ears. He could wear his hair a little longer now that he was nineteen.

"Watch your legs on the tailpipes," he warned Gretchen as she got off. "They'll burn a scar clean through your skin."

Gretchen carefully swung her left leg over the seat and stepped off the throbbing motorcycle. She listened well for an eleven year old.

"How was it?" Carol asked her sister.

"Great!" Gretchen exclaimed. "What a blast! We went all the way down to Uncle Henry's place."

Carol loved being on the back of a motorcycle. They all called her a tomboy back in California. But she didn't care. She loved horses and sports. She was a teenager now and riding on the back of a motorcycle was the most exciting thing that had happened to her during their entire vacation.

Gretchen handed Carol the helmet. She tucked her long, blonde hair up into it, tightened the strap and hopped on behind Mark.

"Ready?" he asked.

Carol eagerly nodded her head.

Mark let up on the clutch, cranked the throttle open and they sped off into the night.

*   *   *

Schuller stretched his legs out across the bed. He glanced over at the clock on the dresser. 11:00 a.m. *That means it's about five o'clock yesterday back in California,* he thought as he lay back. *Or maybe it's five o'clock tomorrow.*

He never could keep the time differences between California and the Orient straight. They had gotten into Seoul too late last night. He quickly found out his Korean hadn't improved since the last trip. If not for Ike

Eichenberger, they probably wouldn't even have gotten to the hotel last night.

Ike handled all the details on the overseas trips. Last year had been their second trip to Russia together. Schuller liked traveling with Ike. He was so easy going and likeable.

Schuller looked at the clock again. Arvella had gone sight-seeing half an hour earlier. She wouldn't be back until around two. Or did she say three? The trip from Hong Kong had messed up his sense of time.

I'll just rest this afternoon, he thought. *It's Saturday. That way I'll be fresh for tomorrow's lecture.* He dug his head into the pillow. In a minute, he was fast asleep.

*   *   *

"Hang on!" Mark yelled.

Carol grabbed his jacket tighter as he shifted the heavy bike into third. Strands of her long blonde hair whipped in the wind. Mark opened up the throttle and she felt the power of the big bike rocket them forward.

It was dark now. The moon had made the corn stalks into shadows. In the road ahead, two red taillights started to close in on them. Mark watched the car ahead of them slow down.

Probably going to turn off, he thought. He eased off on the throttle and the bike whined down. Carol slid forward on the seat. Suddenly the tailights blazed bright red. Mark knew the car had come to a complete stop.

He also knew there was no way he could stop in time.

"Hang on!" he yelled back to Carol as he gunned the bike forward. He leaned to the left to swing around the stopping car.

She heard the brakes screech. She remembered that later. But Carol never saw the headlights of the oncoming car. It just came from somewhere out of the dark.

Boom!

The bumper of the oncoming car smashed into Carol's leg. The impact slammed the motorcycle into the stopped car and flung Carol through the air. Mark went down between the bike and the car.

Carol's body slammed down ninety feet away in a shallow ditch. She lay face down beside the smelly remains of a hog yard. The blackness washed over her.

"Somebody's over here! There's somebody over here! Bring a flashlight. Hurry!"

Carol could barely make out the voices. It felt like somebody had hit her face and chest with a baseball bat. It was hard to breathe and everything started to spin. The first pain stabbed at her when she tried to lift her head. It was a cold, stabbing pain.

"Here! She's over here!"

"Good, you brought a flashlight. Shine it down there. In the ditch."

Carol saw the dirt and muck as the light searched over her.

"Dear God," she heard the voice say in horror. Then it added, "Call an ambulance!"

*　　　　　*　　　　　*

Arvella had spent some time sight-seeing that morning. The remainder of her day was spent on 'Prayer Mountain' with a Korean friend.

She thought about the events of the day as she made her way back to the hotel.

I hope Bob has gotten some rest, she thought as she rode the elevator up to their room. She knew how much this trip meant to Bob. She also knew that the burden of building the Cathedral had been weighing heavily on Bob. *I'm glad we took this trip,* thought Arvella as she reached the hotel room.

*　　　　*　　　　*

"Mark, Mark, where are you?" Carol's voice was little more than a chilled whisper.

The night air is getting colder, she thought. *That's strange. It's never this cold in the summer. I must be lying in some water. That's why it's so wet and sticky.*

"Mark," she tried again.

"I'm right here, Carol. I'm across the road." His voice was hoarse. She could hear pain in it.

"Mark, I think my leg's broken," she said. She was trying to keep from drifting in and out of consciousness.

"I know, Carol. Mine's broken, too. Just lie still." His voice was quiet now.

It seemed like an eternity before they heard the scream of the ambulance.

"Carol! Carol! Where are you?"

She could hear Mark's voice. It sounded so far away Where was she? All she could feel was the hard stretcher beneath her.

"Why can't I see her?" Mark called. His voice was much louder this time. "Is she okay? Carol!"

Carol tried to focus on the glaring ambulance lights, but it was no use. They kept going in and out, in and out. If she tried too hard, the pain would rush back again.

"Carol . . . Carol, listen to me now." The new voice was soft and calm. Experienced. She looked up and saw the masked face of a Doctor above her. His face was very serious. "We have to send you to Sioux City, Carol," he said. "It's about an hour's drive from here. Do you understand?"

She nodded the best she could. "Can I have a pain killer?" she asked. She heard the anguish in her own voice. She hoped the Doctor wouldn't notice.

"No, it's too dangerous," the Doctor said. "We can't

give you anything. You might fall asleep."

"It hurts!" she screamed. The pains had come back. They were stabbing at her now. "It hurts so much!" The pain tore through her, then throbbed, then tore again.

"Why won't you let me see my leg?" she cried.

They wheeled her into the ambulance and shut the doors.

"Carol, Carol. Don't go to sleep, now. Stay awake. I know it hurts, but you have to stay awake."

Carol blinked her eyes. Her whole left side was numb. *Why wouldn't the pain stop?* She couldn't feel anything below her hip. *Why wouldn't the tearing stop?*

"If you go to sleep, you might go into shock," the young paramedic said. He didn't dare tell her that if she went to sleep, she might not wake up again.

Carol's confused eyes stared back at the paramedic. He gently took her hand and squeezed it. "I know you can do it, Carol," he said. "It's not much further. Try to stay awake. I know you can make it."

The siren screamed on through the night.

*   *   *

"He's in Korea. He went over to speak to about 10,000 Korean Ministers.... Yes, I think so. I brought his itinerary home with me...All right. I'll try to reach him. Good-bye."

Mike Nason hung up the phone and looked down at his wife. It was hard enough to tell her what had happened. How was he going to tell Schuller?

*   *   *

"Hello?"

Schuller answered the phone on the second ring.

"Bob? It's Mike Nason."

256

Book II

The Cathedral

An early Hour Of Power broadcast. The first shows were broadcast live.

The outside of the Garden Grove Community Church as seen on television.
Dr. Schuller is standing in the top half of the screen.

Above: The original Hour Of Power shows were broadcast live using the equipment and crews from the NFL football games. *Below: The congregation inside church.*

Final microphone check for Dr. Schuller.

Dr. Schuller with Hour Of Power announcer Ed Arnold.

Dr. Schuller with his daughter Gretchen.

Camelot

The mountain cabin the Schullers called Camelot. The nameplate is visible hanging from the top left roof. The site was claimed to be unbuildable by the owner of the land. In fact the first driveway Schuller put in slid away with the first snow. The second driveway hel

Jeanne with fish.

Right: Carol (standing) with Gretchen behind her in the snow at Camelot.

Below: The Schuller family. l to r - Jeanne, Arvella, Gretchen, Sheila, Carol and Dr. Schuller. Robert A. was away at school.

Dr. Schuller announces the Crystal Cathedral. He holds up a six-inch tall model created Philip Johnson. The original announcement was made at the Anaheim Convention Center the twentieth anniversary of the Garden Grove Community Church.

Above: Dr. Schuller with Pope John Paul II in Rome. Dr. Schuller has had numerous audiences with the Pope during his ministry.

Above: Architect Philip Johnson with the original model of the Crystal Cathedral. The objective of the design was to 'tranquilize'; to awaken the senses, to uplift the spirit and allow the individual to see the heavens above.

Dr. Schuller reviews final construction plans for the Cathedral with the Contractors.

Above: Dr. Schuller asks the congregation to donate money for the 10,600 windows to be installed in the Cathedral.

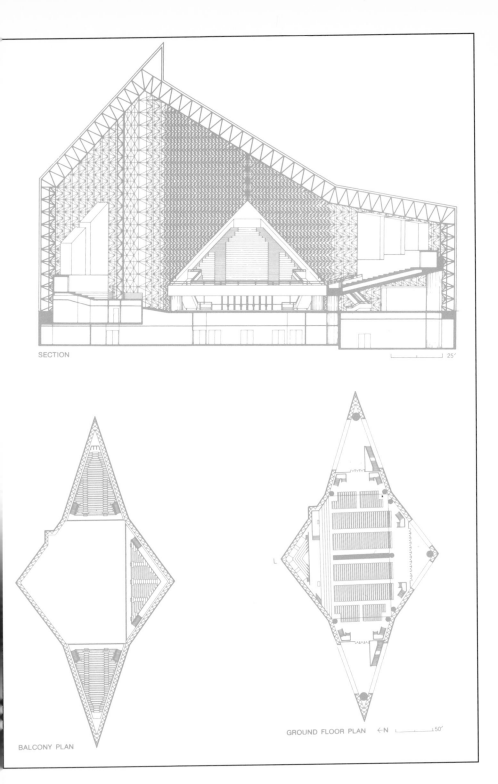

SECTION

25'

BALCONY PLAN

GROUND FLOOR PLAN   ←N   50'

267

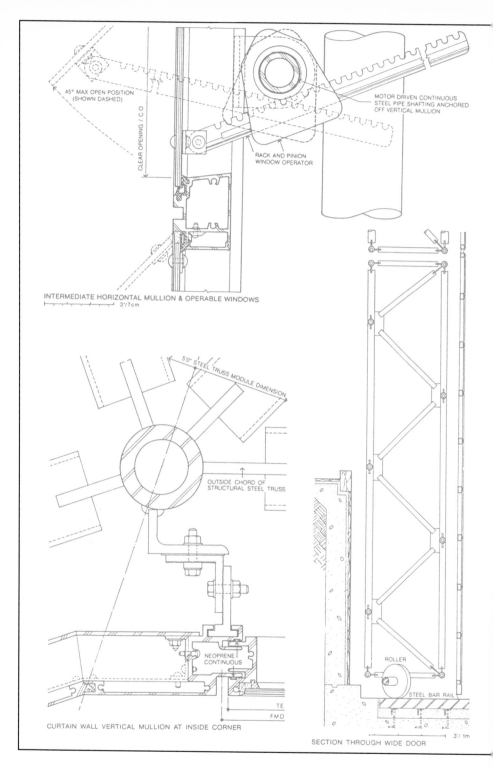

45° MAX OPEN POSITION
(SHOWN DASHED)

CLEAR OPENING / C O

MOTOR DRIVEN CONTINUOUS
STEEL PIPE SHAFTING ANCHORED
OFF VERTICAL MULLION

RACK AND PINION
WINDOW OPERATOR

INTERMEDIATE HORIZONTAL MULLION & OPERABLE WINDOWS
3"/7cm

5'0" STEEL TRUSS MODULE DIMENSION

OUTSIDE CHORD OF
STRUCTURAL STEEL TRUSS

NEOPRENE
CONTINUOUS

TE
FMD

CURTAIN WALL VERTICAL MULLION AT INSIDE CORNER

ROLLER

STEEL BAR RAIL

3'/1m

SECTION THROUGH WIDE DOOR

268

the hole, Bob." Schuller had almost decided to cancel the construction of the Cathedral a costs doubled before construction began. Long time friend and supporter John Crean "Dig the hole, Bob", when Schuller called to tell Crean he was going to cancel the project.

south balcony of the Cathedral is raised. The Tower of Hope is to the left.

The scaffolding erected to build the steel outerwork. The scaffolding collapsed, almost shutting down the project and making the Cathedral unbuildable.

The Skeleton. The steel framework of the Cathedral is completed. The Tower of Hope is in the background.

270

The ninety-foot doors of the Cathedral. The concrete platform is the altar, which is to be wrapped with marble.

The windows begin to be installed in the steel framework. A total of 10,600 windows were installed. The project had been underway almost two and one half years at this point.

Crews install the final rows of windows on the western side of the Cathedral.

Looking west at the front of the Cathedral.

Dr. Schuller and Arvella with Beverly Sills. The world famous opera singer gave one of her
public performances inside the nearly completed Cathedral in May, 1980. Her presence sol
the entire Cathedral and raised over $4.5 million dollars. Donations from the concert allow
the Crystal Cathedral to be dedicated completely debt-free.

A bird's-eye view of the nearly completed Crystal Cathedral. The design is based on a four-pointed star. The Cathedral measures 415 long, 207 feet wide and 128 feet high at its apex, totally enclosed in glass.

The Crystal Cathedral

Interior of the Crystal Cathedral. Seating capacity is 2,890. The ninety-foot glass doors are o *behind the altar. Dr. Schuller appears on the Jumbotron donated by the Sony Corporation.*

ind the altar is the organ donated by Mrs. Hazel Wright of Chicago. The organ is composed '29 ranks and more than 13,000 pipes. Beneath the organ is the Crystal Cathedral Choir.

The last picture of Carol Schuller taken before the motorcycle accident in Iowa. Carol sold the horse she is on to help her Dad with Million Dollar Sunday.

Carol and Gretchen in Hawaii.

Medal winner Carol.

Carol Schuller Milner gets a double kiss from her husband Tim and her father, Dr. Schuller, on her wedding day.

Dr. Norman Vincent Peale   Dr. Peale had a tremendous influence on Robert Schuller.
Peale's best-selling book - The Power Of Positive Thinking - encouraged Schuller durin
his struggle in California. Dr. Schuller and Dr. Peale have remained close friends an
colleagues for over forty years.

Above: Norman Vincent Peale in the Crystal Cathedral with Dr. Schuller.

Left: Dr. Schuller and Norman Vincent Peale groundbreaking the Tower of Hope.

Below: Arvella and Dr. Schuller with Dr. Peale and his wife, Ruth.

The statue of Job symbolizing struggle and perseverance. The statue was sculpted by Dallas Anderson from a block of pure white Vermont marble. It was unveiled on Thanksgiving Day, 1983 and stands outside the Crystal Cathedral.

Photograph of Christ by Robert Schuller.

"Oh, hello, Mike," Schuller said groggily. "How are you?"

Nason took a deep breath and swallowed. He didn't know how to brace Schuller for what he had to tell him. So he just told him straight out.

"Bob, get a hold of yourself. I've got bad news. It's Carol. She's been in a motorcycle accident. They may have to amputate her leg."

Schuller was too stunned to speak. *It's a nightmare*, he thought. *I'm having another nightmare. I'll wake up any minute.*

"She's in the emergency room at Sioux City," Nason went on. "Have you got a pencil? Here's the number at the hospital." He read Schuller the seven digits off his pad. Schuller would know the area code in Iowa, so Nason didn't bother with that. Nason also knew that Schuller would know what it meant if they had already taken her to Sioux City.

"Thanks, Mike," Schuller said weakly. He had to sit down on the bed when he heard 'amputate her leg'. He wiped a handful of sweat off his forehead and said, "We'll take the first flight we can get. I don't know when that will be. Northwest is booked solid and I don't know the schedule for Korean Airlines."

Schuller took a deep breath. He felt a little dizzy. "Would you see what you can do about a flight from Los Angeles to Sioux City?"

"Sure, Bob. I'll get right on it."

"Thanks," Schuller said. There was a note of relief in his voice. "And Mike, I'm glad you were the one who called. It makes it easier to take."

Schuller hung up the phone and dropped his face into his hands. He knew what it meant to be taken to Sioux City. And he knew Arvella would know what it meant, too.

*   *   *

"Her femur is broken in four places," the Doctor said.

Uncle Henry listened quietly to the physician. They stood in the bright hallway, down from the operating

289

room. It was deathly still.

"Her left leg took most of the impact," the Doctor said in a low, serious tone. "Her entire left side, from the knee down is mangled and twisted. Even with all the transfusions, she hasn't responded well enough for us to operate yet. We'll have to wait until she's more stable."

Uncle Henry knew Carol had very little pulse or blood pressure when she arrived at the hospital. She had lost over seventeen pints of blood. The blood transfusions she had been receiving were barely able to keep up with the bleeding. The broken bone had ripped out of her thigh. By the time the ambulance had gotten to her, the infection had already started to spread.

"Henry, I want you to understand something," the Doctor said. "Her leg is gone. We can't save her leg. Right now, we're trying to save her life. We can't give her any drugs for the pain, for fear it will send her into shock. If she goes into shock, she might die instantly. She's just going to have to hang in there until her vital signs stabilize."

"She's only thirteen years old," pleaded Schuller's brother Henry. "She can't take that much pain."

"She'll have to. Or else she's dead."

The Doctor walked down the hall to the operating room. Henry Schuller was left standing in the hall by himself. He thought of his younger brother halfway across the world.

* * *

Arvella rapped on the hotel room door three times. It startled her when the door pulled open abruptly. She instinctively smiled when she saw Schuller standing in the doorway.

Schuller immediately wrapped his arms around her. Arvella could see Ike over Schuller's shoulder. Ike spoke hurriedly into the phone.

"Arvella," Schuller started, "Mike Nason just called from California." Schuller's voice dropped into a soft whisper as he said the next words. "There's been an accident. Carol's in the hospital in Iowa."

"What kind of accident?" Arvella asked. She could see in his eyes that it wasn't good.

"A motorcycle accident," Schuller said. "They may have to amputate her leg."

Arvella held onto him for a minute. She knew he needed to hold her as much as she needed to hold him. After a moment, they pulled apart.

"Ike is trying to get us on the nine o'clock flight tonight. It's the only flight until tomorrow morning." Schuller looked at her carefully. Arvella nodded to let him know she understood. "I've called Dr. Cho and asked him to excuse me from Sunday's speaking commitments."

Arvella nodded. Her eyes were starting to mist as she reached for the box of tissues on the nightstand. She walked over to the window and looked out.

She doesn't cry easily, Schuller thought. *She's not like me. She can hold it in and stay calm. I wish I was more like her.*

Inside, Arvella fell apart. She thought about her innocent young daughter lying on an operating room table halfway across the world. The family was scattered again. They were eight thousand miles away in Korea. Robert Anthony was in Jerusalem for the summer. Sheila and her fiance Jim Coleman were in California and Jeanne had gone back to college in Illinois.

Arvella looked at the bright yellow package that held the white lace dress she had bought for Carol.

*   *   *

"I'll take the evening flight out of Chicago tonight," Jeanne said.

291

"We're booked on the six-thirty out of LAX," Sheila said on the other end. "No, wait," she added, "Jim says it's the seven-thirty." Jim Coleman had waved the information to Sheila from the kitchen.

"So when will you get to Sioux City?" Jeanne asked.

"Not until about eleven," Sheila said. "Aunt Vi is picking us up at the airport. We'll just go straight to the hospital."

"Tell her we may get a rental," Jim told Sheila. "That way we'll have an extra car for your folks when they get there."

"Jim says we'll probably get a rental car, Jeanne."

"That's a good idea. Have you heard anything more from the hospital?"

"No. But I'm sure everything is okay. Uncle Henry or Aunt Vi would have called if it wasn't. I think they're still waiting for her to stabilize before they operate."

"I still can't believe this is happening," Jeanne said.

"I know," Sheila answered. "I can't either."

"I hope Mom's okay. You know how she's going to take it, Sheila."

"I know." Sheila responded sadly.

*   *   *

Schuller stared into the night as he felt the plane circle East. Slowly he turned to Arvella. She read the Bible that the women at the Ministry all talked about. They loved the special ivory cover she had put on it. Arvella never travelled anywhere without her Bible.

She sensed his quiet stare and slowly lifted her attention from the Bible. As they gazed into each others eyes, their silence admitted their pain. Schuller forced a gentle smile to his lips for her.

"Can I get you anything, Dr. Schuller?"

"No, no, thank you," Schuller said to the beautiful

stewardess. She was a tall girl with long, honey-blonde hair. *She can't be more than twenty-two,* he thought. She smiled and walked toward the front of the plane. Schuller couldn't help but notice her long, slender legs.

His eyes welled up with tears again.

His eyes had been red since they left Seoul. Dr. Cho had somehow gotten them on the evening flight. Ike had taken care of the luggage and Dr. Cho had even gotten them waved through security ahead of everyone else. The whole way home, Schuller's chest felt as if someone were sitting on it.

He tried to smile as often as he could, to try and forget the pain. But every time he did, he saw a picture of Carol astride her horse in California. He had taken the pictures of her himself, just before they left. She wore a sweater top and white shorts.

Carol had grown so much from the ages of twelve to thirteen. Her legs had grown long and shapely. She probably wouldn't grow as tall as Sheila, but she would certainly catch a photographer's eye the way Jeanne had. He thought about the modeling pictures that Jeanne had shown him from her first year at Wheaton College in Illinois.

Schuller looked over at Arvella and suddenly his head felt like it would explode. She was weeping. Schuller's head pounded harder and harder and he knew that he couldn't hold it in much longer. He touched Arvella's arm, ripped off his seat belt and sprang up.

He held his head high as he ran to the lavatory. The whine of the plane engines pounded in his ears.

Schuller opened the door to the tiny lavatory, squeezed in, and shut it behind him.

He let the grief overcome him and buried his head in his hands.

The plane streamed on through the night to California.

- 13 -

The Dragon Cage

The methodical pattern of the heart monitor slowly summoned her eyes to open. Carol's world seemed suspended in time as she scanned the room. Her eyes landed on a dimly lit bandage that concealed the newly formed stump. Pain killing drugs masked her emotions as she tried to imagine life without her leg.

"Carol?"

The voice pulled Carol's eyes to the bedside.

"Jeanne," she strained with a horse whisper.

Jeanne smiled and put her hand on the bed.

"How are you feeling?"

"Okay," Carol replied. "How long have you been here?"

"Not long," Jeanne replied. "Mom and Dad will be

here soon."

Jeanne stared at the barrage of wires and tubes emanating from her little sister and said, "Gretchen was here earlier, but she passed out when she saw the transfusion tubes."

"Jeanne," Carol began to cry, "They took my leg off."

Tears rolled down Jeanne's cheeks. "I know sweetie, I'm sorry."

Jeanne looked down at her own long slender legs. She couldn't even begin to imagine the life of pain and suffering her little sister was about to begin. She slowly reached over and wiped the tears off Carol's cheeks. There were so many tubes sticking out of Carol's arms, Jeanne knew that just to wipe her own tears, would cause agonizing pain to shoot through her body.

"How's Mark?" Carol asked groggily. "Have you seen him?"

"He's going to be okay. His leg is broken, but the Doctors say he's going to be all right. He keeps asking about you."

"Can I see him?"

"He's sleeping now, "Jeanne said. "And you need to rest now too, sweetie. I'll wake you when Mom and Dad get here."

Jeanne gently stroked her sister's hair. Carol closed her eyes and drifted off into the darkness.

Their footfalls echoed down the hospital corridor. Their hands tightly clenched together as the door to Carol's room came into view. Their eyes met each other in breathless anticipation at what lay on the other side. Schuller's hand gently began to push open the door. A silent prayer left his mind. *Dear God, let me be strong for Carol!* A quiet voice met them as they entered the room.

"Mom, Daddy." She said as she forced a smile through her pain.

Schuller paused, taken back by all of the tubes

flowing from their little girl's helpless body. Fine lines of tension clearly outlined Arvella's face.

Tears filled Carol's eyes as her mother rushed to the bedside. Gently she reached down to kiss her daughter.

Carol writhed in pain from her mother's touch. Arvella jerked her hand back and gasped, "Oh Carol, I'm so sorry!"

Carol bit her lip in agony, but her eyes found her Mother's as if to say, *It's okay.* They both felt the same pain of helplessness.

Schuller's hand gently reached down and touched Carol's remaining foot. It seemed to be the only place that she wasn't in pain. His soft caress seemed to block her pain, if only for a moment. Schuller squeezed the lump from his throat and said tearfully, "How are you feeling, sweetheart?"

"I'm okay, Dad. The painkillers help a lot."

Carol paused. She looked deep into her father's eyes. "Daddy, it hurt so much."

Schuller knelt down next to her bed and softly caressed her hand against his face. "I love you, Carol."

"Mr. and Mrs. Schuller?"

Arvella turned back toward the door, to see Carol's Doctor.

"Yes," she said.

"Could I see the two of you for just a minute?"

"Yes, of course Doctor," Arvella replied.

Arvella turned back to Carol. Her eyes had closed again and she had fallen asleep.

They stood with the Doctor in the hallway. He dug his hands deep into the pockets of his white coat. A heavy black stethoscope hung around his neck. "There is a chance that we may have to take more of her leg," he said straight out.

"What do you mean, take *more* of her leg?" Schuller questioned.

"There's still infection in her leg," the Doctor's face grew more serious.

"We've got her on antibiotics and pain killers right now. That's why she keeps losing consciousness. If the drugs aren't effective, we'll have to amputate again, this time above the knee."

Arvella felt her husband's strong arm wrap around her.

"How soon are you planning to operate again?" she heard him ask.

"We will know more in a few days," the Doctor told them. "I'm truly sorry."

Bob searched in vain for the right words. They never came.

"Mom?"

Sheila stood next to her mother. "There's a nurse down the hall that needs to speak to you. Something about some forms you have to sign."

"Thanks, Sheila," Arvella said. "It's probably for the insurance. I'll take care of it."

"Hello, I'm Arvella Schuller, Carol's mother. My daughter said you need me to sign some forms."

"Oh yes, Mrs. Schuller," said the nurse behind the counter. "I know it's been a long trip for you, and you must be very tired."

"That's all right. I have our insurance cards right here in my purse." Arvella pulled her wallet out and laid it on the counter. She looked up at the young nurse who was staring back at her.

"No, I'm afraid you don't understand Mrs. Schuller. These aren't insurance forms."

"Well what kind of forms are they?"

300

The young nurse hesitated. She slowly slid the forms across the counter to Arvella. "We have to bury your daughter's leg." The young nurse's eyes pleaded to Arvella, "We need your signature to do it."

The last bit of breath escaped from Arvella. "You need to do what?" she asked in disbelief.

"I - I'm sorry, Mrs. Schuller. It's the law."

Arvella's tears fell on the paper as she signed it.

*　　　　*　　　　*

"No, Bob, get her out of there. Get her out to California. They've got the new techniques out there. You won't have to worry about Carol losing any more of her leg."

Schuller listened to the advice over the phone. Cory SerVaas, A medical Doctor and the editor of the Saturday Evening Post had called Schuller as soon as she heard the news about Carol.

Schuller and Arvella worried about the operations the Doctors wanted to do next week. Carol's knee would be amputated next, then the Doctors would take more tests and decide what to do next.

"Do you think we could save the knee if we moved Carol to California?" Schuller asked Cory.

"What have you got to lose, Bob?" she answered. "Replantation centers are special hospitals where microvascular surgery is performed. They can go in and repair the tiniest blood vessels using microscopes. The one closest to you is in Irvine, at the University of California."

"That would have Carol near home and the Ministry," Schuller said. "It would keep the family together."

"Carol goes into surgery tomorrow for more amputation. How do we make arrangements to move her to California?"

"Let me make some calls, Bob," Cory said. "I'll call

you back as soon as I know.

"Thanks, Cory."

"I'll call you right back."

*   *   *

The ambulance jet waited on the runway. The doors spilled open and the medical team from UCI Medical Center stepped off. They had flown out from Orange County that morning to prepare Carol for the flight.

Carol lay in a special splint that would allow her to be moved the two thousand miles to California. She was still being given continuous blood transfusions, but her spirits seemed better now.

Schuller rode beside Carol's bed in the ambulance. Arvella held her hand on the other side. The whole family waited at the airport. It was a dark, early morning in Iowa.

The family rode back to California in the ambulance airplane - Schuller, Arvella, Gretchen, and Carol. They arrived in California early in the morning, at four a.m., and immediately took Carol to Children's Hospital.

*   *   *

"Sixteen million?" Schuller asked them calmly. He looked around at the serious faces in the board room. "It's going to cost sixteen million to finish the Cathedral now?"

Schuller tried to keep his mind on the meeting. He tried to focus on the figures, but he kept thinking about Carol. They had flown her home to Children's Hospital in Orange last week, and he and Arvella had been keeping the nightly vigils with her. He knew the circles under his eyes had blackened the last two days.

"The bank has agreed to lend us the extra money, at two over prime," Nason said. "Isn't that right, Fred?"

Fred Southard looked up from his notes. He had just come on as the new chief financial officer for the ministry. "The problem is that the Prime Rate went to twenty-one percent this morning."

Schuller looked at Fred. He had hired the former President of the U-Haul Corporation to help him manage the financial complexities of the ministry.

"What do you recommend we do?" Schuller asked.

"I don't recommend we borrow money to build the Cathedral. The payments on the debt service could put us in a negative cash position."

"So what are you saying?" Nason asked.

Schuller answered before Fred could reply. "He's saying we have got to dedicate the Cathedral debt free."

"I don't see how that is possible." Vic Andrews chimed in. "We lost a month when the scaffolding collapsed trying to put up the steel framework. We barely got the balconies done and we're already a million dollars over the latest budget figures. I don't think we can expect Bob to keep raising the millions we might need to finish it."

Schuller's head was pounding. The headaches had started last week, and now he was waking up with them every morning.

"Gentlemen, you handle the details among yourselves." Schuller said. He looked down at his watch. "I have to go see my daughter." He got up and left the room.

*   *   *

Carol's screams echoed down the hallway. The nurses at the reception desk looked up at the clock, and then at each other.

"They're changing her bandage again," one nurse said to the other.

Carol writhed in pain as the doctor slowly unwound

the thick white bandage from her leg. He carefully folded the bandage as he took it off. The nurse behind him checked the levels of the fluid in the I.V. bottles that hung over Carol's head. She checked the levels every three hours on the hour.

Arvella stood by Carol and held her hand. She knew the bandage changing was wearing on her daughter. It had been over a month since they had brought her back from Iowa. The doctors were still talking about more surgery, possibly removing her entire knee.

There had already been one surgery since they had come back. Carol's temperature had risen to one hundred and five degrees. They had to pack her entire body in ice and turn up the air conditioning in the room to bring her temperature down. She drank glass after glass of ice water. Nothing worked.

The infection from the hog yard had spread throughout her body. Her limp arms had turned black and blue down to her fingernails from the constant changing of the I.V. By the time evening came, the nurses would have to stick the I.V. needles in a dozen times before they found a vein.

Schuller brought her something special every day to cheer her up. There were cards, flowers and telegrams from Frank Sinatra, John Wayne, President Carter, and Senator Edward Kennedy. Tommy LaSorda and Steve Garvey called her to tell her how brave she was. Nothing worked.

The ghost pains kept coming and coming. Goliath wouldn't quit. Even the sponge baths were excruciating. The throbbing wracked her body, over and over again. The slightest touch would set the pain off. Every day was just another trial of poking and probing.

Schuller felt every bit of his daughter's pain as he watched the Doctor fold up the last layer of bandage. Tears flowed freely down his face as he saw her confined to the bed. The hospital room had become a cage for her.

Carol bit her lip as the Doctor peeled the last strip of bloodied gauze from her stump.

*   *   *

"It isn't going to work, Mike, it's going to fail for sure," Schuller said into the phone.

Schuller sat at his desk in the library of his home. It was quiet.

"Don't give up, Bob," Nason said. "We're still alive on this project. We'll make it somehow."

"A great big unfinished building will make us the laughing stock of the whole country," Schuller said.

Nason looked out his office window at the growing skeleton of the Cathedral. The crews had slowed down. Rumors had started to grow that the money was almost gone and another shut-down might be just around the corner.

"The way I see it," Schuller said, "No matter what I do. I lose. I feel like I'm in a cage, Mike."

Nason knew how Schuller felt. He had persuaded thousands of people to give him millions of dollars to build one of the greatest churches in the country. The project was way behind schedule, incredibly over budget, and they were almost out of money again.

Schuller was just as afraid of going on as he was of quitting. Quitting would mean letting down the millions of people who believed in him and his message of hope and optimism. Going on could mean letting down himself and his family.

Schuller had been in Time Magazine because of the Cathedral. He had been on the cover of the Los Angeles Times every other week and in the Wall Street Journal because of the Cathedral. He had been on national talk shows and radio. The Cathedral had made Schuller and the ministry he loved famous.

Now it was about to make him a famous failure.

The skeleton had become Schuller's private Goliath.

Schuller hung up the phone and looked around the library. He scanned the rows and rows of books on the shelves. There were countless volumes on motivation, inspiration, and problem-solving. Schuller had read them all. He looked over the titles for any help he could find.

He looked at the stack of messages on his desk that had been brought from the office that morning. Schuller had stopped going into the office just after the shut-down rumors had started. The negative feelings were just too strong. He couldn't seem to get anything done at the office.

Everyone had said he was just hiding out at home. Even he was beginning to think, maybe they were right.

There has to be a solution, and with God's help I am going to find it. He smiled to himself, *tomorrow was always a new day.*

- 14 -

The Cathedral

It wasn't the first time Arvella had discovered a lump in her breast. All the previous ones had been benign. Surely this one would be too. She had found the new lump two weeks ago. *Why upset the whole family,* she thought. *This one won't be any different.*

Sitting at the bedroom window, she stared out into space. The beautiful gardens of their two acre home, cheerfully greeted her gaze. She wasn't sure she wanted the house when her husband first took her through it.

The once prize-winning Hewes Park, of the early 1900's, was now an overgrown jungle. The forty-foot tall California Pepper trees were littered with vines. And weeds overpowered every flower bed on the property. The home was small and needed a lot of attention, with dust, spider webs, and rats nesting in the attic.

"We're buying the trees, Arvella," Schuller told her. "You can't find one-hundred-foot tall pine trees in Orange County anymore, and it's behind a gate so we can have a place of privacy."

Deep down she knew he was right. "Think of the prize-winning garden it used to be. With a little elbow grease, we can do it." If she ever forgot that she married a positive thinking preacher, he would always find the most unlikely ways of reminding her. But a hundred thousand seemed like a lot of money for a place that needed so much work. "Let's buy it," he had said. "Ten years from now, you will be glad we did." She was.

In the background she heard Schuller on the phone with the Doctor. His tone was quiet. He didn't have to say it, she already knew the test results.

"Arvella, the Doctor just called," Schuller said to her. She stood silently, her eyes not leaving the garden.

"It's malignant, they want to perform surgery as soon as possible." A shiver went down her spine. *If anything happens,* she thought, *Who's going to take care of Gretchen and Carol?*

"The Doctor wants you to come in for some more tests next week."

"Next week?" Arvella asked. She tried to keep her mind on what he was saying, but she found her thoughts drifting. Breast cancer. It didn't seem to be real somehow. Things like this were never supposed to happen. She felt her husband's arms gently wrap around her. His cheek softly caressed her hair.

"Next week will be fine," she said. A peaceful silence filled her heart. She turned and buried her face in Schuller's chest and wept.

"It's going to be okay, Arvella," Schuller told her. "Our vacation is only three weeks away. We will take some time off like we used to and spend it together."

"I hope you're right, Bob," she sobbed. "This last year has been the hardest one of all."

Schuller held her closer. "There isn't anyone that I would have rather spent it with than you."

Their lips met. She held him tightly, never wanting to let go.

*   *   *

Schuller watched the tiny colored lights dance around the Christmas tree. He couldn't remember ever being this tired on Christmas Eve before. The seven services he had given that evening, hadn't been any longer than usual. Why was he so tired?

"Okay, Santa Claus," Arvella said cheerfully. "The presents are in the closet. You put them under the tree, I'll start stuffing the stockings."

Schuller let out a long, deep sigh. "Okay," he said and started for the bedroom.

"Be careful with Carol's new stereo," Arvella called down the hall. "It's heavy."

"Yep."

Arvella knew what was on Schuller's mind. She just didn't know what to do about it.

Schuller slid the red package that contained Carol's stereo under the tree. He thought that having her home for Christmas would have made things easier for him. The all night vigils at the hospital were over, but now there were all these new problems he had never expected. For one thing, he never realized the attention someone in a wheelchair needed.

They had rearranged the furniture in the house to accommodate Carol's new wheelchair. She had to be helped in and out of bed. She had to be taken to the hospital every day for her therapy, tests or observation, and the ghost pains would stab at her relentlessly every night.

Carol would wake up in the middle of the night, complaining of cramps in a leg that was no longer there. Schuller would hold her quietly and stroke her hair. *It's not fair,* he thought to himself. *It's just not fair. No thirteen year-old girl should have to bear this kind of pain the rest of her life. Dear God, what's happening to my family? You promised me you wouldn't give me any more than I could bear. I have to believe that's still true, but I need your help. Please, Lord.*

Schuller wouldn't even try to stop the tears from rolling down his cheeks in the darkness. *Please, Lord.*

Schuller carried another heavy box down the hallway. He watched Arvella carefully fill the stockings over the fireplace with tiny presents. He smiled at how attentive she was to the task, because he knew the thought of cancer never left her.

The last time they spoke with the Doctor, he felt the cancer was contained, but you never knew for sure. It was unpredictable. Schuller quietly prayed that the Doctor was right and that the operation in June had removed all the cancerous tissue from Arvella.

And then there was the Cathedral. Those problems never seemed to go away. If anything, they grew bigger every day. Schuller figured he would need at least another five million dollars to finish the structure, and he had no idea where it was going to come from.

A bank loan was no good. Interest rates were much too high. He had already told everyone that they would finish the Cathedral without a bank loan. He had promised that there would be no debt on the building.

The trouble was, he had no idea how he was going to keep his promise.

Ten thousand windows had been delivered. There was only enough money in the bank to pay for half of them and there wasn't any money to pay for the installation. It seemed hopeless.

Schuller looked up at the lights on the Christmas

tree. He felt Arvella's arms wrap around him.

"Bob, stop worrying so much," she whispered to him. "It's all going to work out as long as we stay together."

"I can't get it off my mind. There never seems to be an end to it. I solve one problem and another rears up. It just gets worse and worse," Schuller sighed.

Arvella tickled his cheek with her slender finger. "Ho - Ho - Ho," she said.

Schuller managed a smile. "Are you saying my name is Scrooge?" he asked.

Arvella slid a red and white Santa Claus hat onto his head. The fluffy, white ball hung over his shoulder.

"You're out of practice, Mr. Ho-Ho-Ho." she said, "It's Christmas. Let's see a little Christmas cheer!"

"I love you, too, Mrs. Santa," Schuller said.

"I know, Bob," she smiled. "Let's make this the best Christmas ever."

They hugged and kissed each other and for a moment Schuller forgot all about the Goliaths that they had faced together.

*   *   *

"Bob?"

Mike Nason's voice echoed across the concrete floor of the unfinished Cathedral. Schuller stood looking up at the skeleton. The scaffolding climbed the steel, web-like structure. The inside of the space-frame was longer than a football field and half-again as wide. The peak of the steel Cathedral was over ten stories high. You could have hidden a 747 jet airplane inside the skeleton. But there was no place for Schuller to hide.

"Bob," Nason repeated as he came closer. "Is everything all right?"

Schuller took off his white hard-hat and took a deep

313

breath. "I didn't do very well yesterday, did I?" he said to Nason.

"It's only one talk show, Bob," Nason told him. "The Donahue Show isn't the whole world. You know he likes to stimulate the audience with no-win questions. Frankly, I thought you did pretty well."

"Why are you spending twenty million dollars on a glass church instead of giving it to the poor?" Schuller said. "I can't believe they asked me that."

Nason watched Schuller standing on the concrete floor of the Cathedral. He knew Schuller couldn't get the interview out of his mind.

"Let it go, Bob. You're letting it eat you up."

"The poor can't help the poor," Schuller said. "Is that so hard to understand, Mike?"

Schuller went on without waiting for an answer. He looked up at the space-frame. "I know this is different. I know it's never been done before, but it's really so easy to understand. There are almost a million people in our county alone who don't even know how much church can help them. They don't even know what religion is. People like that won't even think about coming to church unless you build something that screams out for their attention."

Schuller's face saddened.

"But all people really need is love. All they need is hope. And God is love, Mike. If you find God, you find love. That's as hard as it gets. We all need love. There isn't a single person in the whole world who doesn't need love."

"Why didn't you say that on the Donahue Show, Bob?"

Schuller looked at the unfinished Cathedral again. "I did say it, Mike," he said." I just don't think anyone heard me."

*   *   *

"Daddy," Carol struggled to sit up on the couch as

her father came down the hallway.

"Hi, sweetheart, how are you feeling today?" Schuller said as he knelt to hug her. Her face lit up as his strong arms wrapped around her body.

"I'm so glad you're home, Dad," she said.

"Really?" he said, genuinely surprised.

"Really," she said cheerfully.

"Where's your mother?" Schuller asked.

"Gretchen and Mom went over to Sheila's. They're working on the wedding plans. I'm so excited. Sheila's wedding is only a few weeks away. I've never been in a wedding before."

"How are you doing?"

"Better, I guess. The ghost pains aren't as bad as they were." Carol looked into her father's eyes. She had big news for him, but she wasn't sure how to tell him.

"What is it, Carol?" Schuller asked. "What do you want to tell me?" He knew that look on his daughter's face.

"Daddy. I've decided that I'm going to walk down the aisle at Sheila's wedding. No wheel chair, no crutches. I'm going to walk all the way up to the altar on my own." Carol's blue eyes lit up with the excitement of walking that far by herself. She had only been out of the hospital for a few months but she had been practicing walking with her artificial leg every day for the past few weeks.

"That's terrific!" Schuller said to her. He could barely contain his joy at his daughter's courage. "I know you can do it, too." he added softly.

At that moment, Schuller would have given the world for two healthy legs for his fourteen-year-old girl.

*   *   *

The sun splashed church was filled as the organ began its triumphal melody. Sheila's favorite piece, The Wedding March from the Sound of Music, began. Her flowing white dress, the beauty of her smile, and an aisle filled with white candles and flowers, were enough to make even the Von Trapp family proud.

The crowd held its breath as Carol started down the aisle. Her crutches were not disappointing enough to dampen her spirits. Sheila's tears were flowing as much for Carol, as for herself. She smiled proudly as Carol made it to the front of the church without a hitch.

One by one Schuller watched as his daughters made their way to the front of the church. Jeanne, tall, almost regal, with flowing brunette hair. Her slender frame had won her a third place finish in the Miss Indiana Contest. Finally there was Gretchen, his youngest, whose playful smile could light up any room.

Schuller watched them with living eyes. *Don't cry Schuller. Remember, you're paying for all of this!* He smiled broadly, almost laughing, as he led Sheila down the aisle.

*　　　　*　　　　*

The sun had begun to dip into the blue Pacific Ocean. They strolled along the sandy beach, hand in hand. Arvella smelled the sweet aroma of the fresh red rose Schuller had given her. She stroked the soft petals of the rose, marvelling at how beautiful, something so delicate could be.

"Looks a little different than the Floyd River doesn't it?" Schuller asked her. His gaze led her eyes out to the blue Pacific.

"The Floyd River?" Arvella asked. "What made you think of the Floyd River?"

"I was thinking of the day I came home from the Seminary, to ask you to marry me," he said. "I had the same thought when I was waiting for you to come out of surgery two weeks ago."

"Thoughts about what?" Arvella asked.

The sun was half set now. It sent a shimmering glow

across the waves. They walked up a pathway lined with small budding trees and bright yellow spring flowers.

"I thought about how much you mean to me," Schuller started. "And about how afraid I was of losing you. I love you, Arvella, more than I did the day I married you."

"Even after the mastectomy?" she asked softly.

"That doesn't matter. It never did." Schuller's voice deepened. "I fell in love with the person that's inside of you. Your bright smile, the strength that you always bring to me, the way the laughter dances in your eyes when you're excited."

Arvella blushed like a schoolgirl.

"I haven't seen you blush like that in a long time," Schuller smiled.

"I haven't felt like this since you wrote me those love letters," she said.

"I haven't either." Schuller said as he realized that he had fallen in love with her all over again. He felt like a teenager, out on his first date. It felt good.

He looked out at the sun as it dipped into the sea and thought about how important their love was.

"Arvella," he admitted. "I know I get all wrapped up in the dreams I have and all the things that I want to do, but I want you to know that the most important thing in my life has always been you. You made the difference. I couldn't have made it without you."

Arvella started to cry. She leaned over and quietly kissed him on the cheek. Schuller took her delicate hand, one which he loved to hold, and they walked down the path together.

*   *   *

Stacks of windows lay on the ground. Schuller looked down at them from his office window. The brainstorming session he had just adjourned, depressed him.

317

We need another four and a half million dollars, he thought to himself. *Where are we going to get another four and a half million dollars?*

Schuller searched through every idea they had come up with during the last six months. He was even having trouble coming up with fresh material for his weekly sermons now. All he could think about, was getting those windows in so they could finish the Cathedral.

It had been three years since they had first broken ground. It was almost Christmas again, 1979. The Cathedral had become the biggest project he had ever undertaken. He had raised almost fifteen million dollars so far. He had overcome rising construction costs and the labor disputes with the contractors. He had gone on national television and asked millions of Hour Of Power supporters for help. He had met with some of the richest people in the country and asked them for help. He had done things he thought were impossible three years ago.

And still the windows sat on the ground.

He discovered true possibility thinking meant making your dreams big enough for God to fit into.

We're so close, Lord. We've got to make it now. I'm not quitting. No matter what, we're going to find a way to finish it.

The door to the office flew open and Arvella rushed in.

"She's coming," Arvella shouted, "She said she would come and do the benefit concert!"

Arvella put the letter down on Schuller's desk right in front of him so he had to read it. She knew he would want to read it for himself.

Schuller read through the letter, but Arvella started to talk again before he could finish it.

"I knew they would help you, Bob." she said quietly. "Even famous people will help if you ask them."

Schuller looked up from the letter. She was right. As much as he wanted to believe that everything was lost, as much as he had wanted to quit, they had offered to help, just as Arvella had believed they would.

Frank Sinatra, Milton Berle, Mickey Rooney, Ted Mann and his wife Rhonda Fleming, had all agreed to lend their names to the benefit. And now Beverly Sills had agreed to perform the concert.

Beverly Sills would perform one of the last solo concerts of her career in the Crystal Cathedral. They would sell the seats for the concert at fifteen-hundred dollars apiece and be able to pay the remaining bills for the completion of the Cathedral.

The Cathedral could hold two thousand, eight hundred and eighty-eight people. Beverly Sills could sell that number out, with her eyes closed. They would hold the concert on May 13, 1980. It would be the first event ever held in the Crystal Cathedral.

It would finally be over. Schuller could see that now. There would finally be an end to it. They could do it.

"Now all we have to do is sell the place out," Schuller said to Arvella. "And we can finish it. We can do what they all said couldn't be done."

"I know we can, Bob. I know we can."

*　　　　*　　　　*

The Crystal Cathedral is built on the foundation of a four pointed star, reflecting the shape of the Star of Bethlehem. The structure is 207 feet at its widest point, 415 feet long from point to point, and 128 feet high at its highest point.

The Cathedral is an all-steel structure covered with glass windows. There are 10,600 glass windows in all. The Cathedral can withstand an earthquake of 8.0 on the Richter scale and winds of up to 100 miles per hour.

The Cathedral contains one of the largest pipe organs in the world, with over sixteen thousand pipes. There are two doors, each over ninety feet tall, that open up so that people sitting outside in their cars can still attend church, just as the original drive-in congregation did in 1955.

However, more than anything else, it is the soaring, sweeping roof of the structure and the striking gold leaf cross, standing proudly on the altar, that transforms the vast space of 3.5 million cubic feet, into the Crystal Cathedral, a place clearly meant to help people find God and his love.

* * *

It was a night filled with a thousand stars. The Crystal Cathedral glowed in the night sky as the theater lights burned in every color of the rainbow. The patrons, adorned in black tie and evening gowns, gazed in awe as their eyes captured the sight of the Cathedral's interior for the first time. Tickets were selling for fifteen hundred dollars. It was the price of hearing one of Beverly Sills' final solo concerts. Robert Schuller, pastor, consummate showman, and now fund raiser, had found a way to raise the final four and a half million dollars needed to complete this spectacular house of worship.

The orchestra filled the Cathedral with sound, as Ms. Sills began her melodic repertoire. Much like singing in the Grand Canyon, the opera star's voice began to echo off of every steel beam, pane of glass, and terrazzo surfaced floor. There are those who claim that if you listen closely enough in the Cathedral on Sunday morning, you can still hear Beverly Sills' final note.

Schuller and Arvella watched the gracious opera star as she worked her way through the performance. Arvella smiled, then looking at her husband, said, "Bob, they seem to be as enamored with the building, as with Ms. Sills."

"Good," he quipped back. "Maybe they won't notice the sound system." Their light-hearted exchange did little to replace the horror in Schuller's mind. *Is anybody going to be able to understand me when I preach? The greatest acoustical minds in the world were wrong!* "Arvella, what are we going to do? They can't understand a thing!"

"Bob," Arvella said, "It's only May, the building doesn't open until September. There's time to fix it."

Deep down, he hoped she was right. *Enjoy the concert, Schuller, tomorrow is a new day!*

*　　　　*　　　　*

The Goodyear blimp circled overhead in a slow, methodical pattern. Thousands of people lined the sidewalks around the Crystal Cathedral, waiting for the doors of the massive structure to finally open.

The soaring landmark designed to lift the spirit of man and glorify God, was finally finished. Schuller beamed with excitement and pride, now that opening day had finally arrived. He and Arvella, Robert Anthony, Sheila, Jeanne, Carol, and Gretchen led the procession from the walk-in, drive-in church to the new Cathedral. Entering the structure was like walking into the presence of God. Twelve stories high and a football field long, uninterrupted by walls or beams. The six story pipe organ soared majestically above the sanctuary floor, its pipes reaching for the heavens. His robe of deep blue and purple, concealed Schuller's graceful walk as he ascended the steps to the pulpit. The Bible was placed on the podium above three crosses, which had been mysteriously embossed in the salmon colored marble.

The people entered the building, reverently, excited, all colors, all races, and many religions other than Christian. The building and the ministry were truly a testimony to Schuller's ecumenical style of evangelism. From his pulpit vantage point, Schuller surveyed the crowd, smiling broadly at the number of unfamiliar faces this day had brought out. *It was worth it Lord! I can stand here and say that this day was truly worth the pain!*

As the choir finished their last chorus of Alleluia's, Schuller raised his hands to the heavens, and announced, "This is truly the day that the Lord has made. Let us rejoice and be glad in it!"

- 15 -

Tough Times

Schuller stepped out of the cab at the curb. The noise of honking horns was so loud in Chicago that summer, that he barely heard the driver yell out the fare.

"How much?" Schuller yelled back.

"Twelve-fifty," the fat driver shouted. He signaled with the stubby fingers of his right hand in sign language. "Twelve-fifty."

Seems like a lot for such a short cab ride, thought Schuller as he counted out the bills.

"Are you sure that's right?" Schuller yelled through the window.

"It's tough all over, Buddy," the driver said sarcastically as he took the bills. "Haven't you heard? There's a recession on."

Schuller knew all about the recession of 1982. It was the worst economic time the Midwest had seen since the Great Depression, a generation ago. Farms were being foreclosed upon left and right. Prime interest rates were 20%. People were out of work all over the country. Company after company had declared bankruptcy.

Schuller walked through the lobby of the Hilton Hotel. He headed toward the Grand Ballroom where he expected to find the Agri-Business Convention. Schuller entered the Ballroom and found himself looking into the despondent faces of thirty-five hundred people. He avoided their eyes and moved to the back of the speaker's platform.

Two big, burly men stepped in front of him.

"Dr. Schuller? Thank you for coming," the older one said in a somber tone.

Thank you for coming. The words reminded Schuller of a thousand other days that he had arrived at the scene of a tragedy. Hospitals, mortuaries, cemeteries. It always sounded the same. *Thank you for coming.*

The younger man spoke. "There are thirty-five hundred people out there waiting to hear you speak. These people are going through tough times. The toughest times of their lives. They don't want to hear your funny stories. They don't want to see you grinning from ear to ear and praising the Lord, the way you do on T.V."

"They don't want a pat on the back, with a hollow promise that everything is going to be okay," the older man added.

The two men moved shoulder to shoulder as if to block the silver-haired pastor from stepping onto the platform stage.

"That's right, Dr. Schuller," the younger man said. "These people are losing their farms. Their businesses are going bankrupt every day. Terrible pressures are mounting on their marriages and friends. They need help. And more than anything else, they need hope." His eyes were fixed on Schuller's. "Give it to them."

With that, the man turned and nodded to the sound man, who pinned a microphone to Schuller's lapel. Schuller heard a voice introduce him through the thin curtain.

"Ladies and Gentlemen, it is my pleasure now to introduce our key-note speaker. His name is Dr. Robert Schuller and he is the pastor of the Crystal Cathedral Church in California. No pastor, priest, minister or rabbi speaks to more people in the world than Dr. Schuller. Please welcome one of the most successful men in the world - Dr. Robert Schuller!"

The sound of hopeful applause filled the room. Schuller stepped up to the podium. All thirty-five hundred people rose to their feet, looking for something or someone they could cling to.

Inside, Schuller shuddered. The three jokes he had considered for warming the audience up, wouldn't work now. These people didn't come to hear any funny stories. They were serious.

Schuller didn't say anything. He paced back and forth, from one side of the stage to the other. Every so often, he looked up and searched the eyes of the audience, then he just kept on pacing. Back and forth. Back and forth. Finally, he stopped.

"They tell me you're having tough times here. Is that right? Is that true?" he asked them.

The audience sat quietly. They were the men and women who represented an industry that was vital to the survival of this country. They represented the core of the breadbasket of America. The food in the markets and on the tables of our homes came from the sweat and labor of these people.

Schuller took a deep breath and spoke forcefully. "Let me tell you about tough times."

"Let me tell you about poverty. I grew up on my father's farm not far from here, in Alton, Iowa. My father was one of those tough, willful farmers, like many of you here today. My father lost his parents when he was a child. He dropped out of school in the sixth grade and went to work. Back then in Iowa, you could always get a job shucking corn. It was the only job he could find, so he took it."

"What you did was, you went into the corn fields at the dawn of the day and you started in. You ripped all the leaves off the ear of corn, cracked off the six-foot stalk and threw it into a wagon. You got fifteen cents for every wagon that you filled up. If you were good, you could fill up a wagon in twelve hours. My father earned less than five cents an hour."

"He saved his nickels and dimes until he had enough to buy a farm. I grew up on that farm. I was seven years old when the Great Depression hit in 1933. I know there are a great many of you out there today who remember those times. I know there are a great many of you out there who will never forget those times. I know I never will."

"We lived on the top of a little hill, in a tiny, two-story wooden house. I grew up there with my father and mother, three sisters and my brother. The only protection from the cold winter wind outside were the trees that stood around the house. You never touched those trees. They were the only protection from the harsh wind in the winter and the only shade from the hot sun in the summer. You never even thought about cutting down those trees."

"We heated the house with two stoves. One was in the kitchen, which we used for cooking, and the other was in the living room, which we used for heat. There were little slots cut in the ceiling to let some of the heat rise upstairs to the bedrooms where we slept. In my room, the cracks in the wall let in more freezing air than the heat that came through the floorboards."

Schuller looked out over the thirty-five hundred

people. Every eye was fixed on him.

"We didn't have enough money to buy coal for the stoves. We barely had enough money to buy corn seed. Do you know what we did? Do you know how we heated the house at night?"

The audience sat quietly and listened.

"We burned corn cobs. That's right, corn cobs. It was my job to collect them. Every day, right before sundown. I would climb over a three-foot high, splintered, wooden fence and step into the hog yard. We had over a hundred hogs. And every one of them was a squealer and a squirmer. I walked through the slop and the mud with my empty basket and I picked up every dirty, filthy corncob left over by the hogs."

"I picked up every one. Every one mattered. Every one had value. When I had filled up the basket, I would carefully carry it into the house and fill up the buckets by the stoves. We would eat dinner and then I would go upstairs to get ready for bed. I still remember praying every night before bed. I prayed that I wouldn't freeze to death during the night, that I had found enough corncobs to keep the house warm. Then I would climb up into bed and hide under the covers and hope I could sleep until the morning came. In the morning, the floor would be covered with the snow that had blown through the cracks in the walls."

"Those were tough times!" Schuller bellowed into the crowd.

"In the summer, there was drought. We covered our faces with wet cloths when we walked from the house to the outdoor toilet. When we walked to the well, where we hoped we would be able to pump water, we wore the masks. We never went outside without our masks."

"I used to love to go down to the river. The Floyd River was about a mile from our house. The river was one of my best friends as a child. I'd lie on its green banks, looking at the wide open pastures nearby. I'd lay back and watch the billowy white clouds move across the blue sky and change shape. Those were great times."

"During the summer of the drought, I watched the river dry up. Little pools of water became dark brown mud holes, where squirming bullhead catfish died. We were surrounded by death - the river was dead, the fish were dead, and worst of all, the crops were dead."

"Those were tough times," Schuller stated matter-of-factly. "Those were tough times."

"Years later I asked my father how we had survived. After all, we had no money. We had no cash reserves, we didn't have any rich relatives or neighbors. We were just like everybody else. We were all in the same boat."

"I went to the bank," my father told me. "And I promised them that if they would help me, somehow I would return their money. I pleaded with them to refinance, rearrange the mortgage, postpone the due date, anything. For some reason, the bank believed in me and they helped me."

"I remember that bank!" Schuller exclaimed. "I remember going in there as a kid, in my patched overalls with my father. They had a slogan on the wall in that bank that read: 'Great people are ordinary people with extra-ordinary amounts of determination.' That's how we survived, that's how we made it through those tough times, determination."

"We replanted and the rains came. The farm grew and prospered. I graduated from high school and went away on a bus to try and make my own dreams come true. I wanted to get a college degree and then go on to seminary school. So I got on a bus and went off to school in Holland, Michigan. I went to school there for seven years."

"When I was nineteen, I remember coming home for the summer. It was a clear June day when I stepped off the bus at the bottom of the hill that led up to our farm. I unpacked my suitcase and helped my dad cultivate the corn fields that afternoon. At the time, my dad and I could hear an awesome roar, reverberating like the hum of a mighty organ. The eerie sound was like a hundred freight trains, rumbling above the threatening and gathering clouds."

"Sounds like we're in for a hailstorm," my dad said. "We had finished our evening meal in haste. From the vantage point of our front lawn, we could see more than a mile down the valley. Suddenly, a black lump, about the size of the sun, bulged out of the black sky. In an instant, it telescoped to the ground in a long, black funnel."

"Dad yelled to me, 'Get your mother, son. Tell her to take whatever she can grab and come quickly. We've got to get out of here - right away! There's a tornado coming!' "

"A moment later, we were driving crazily down the road, trying to get away. We parked on the crest of a hill and watched the wicked twister spend it's killing power. As quickly and quietly as it had dropped, it lifted and disappeared. It was all over. The storm was gone."

"We could go home now. We reached the crossroads, only to find a long line of cars. Curious sightseers, sensing that something terrible had happened, were already gathering. They were looking at the complete destruction of a nearby farm."

"Wondering if our house had been spared, we drove down the lonely road, criss-crossed by wires from broken telephone poles, toward our secluded farm. We came to the base of the hill that hid the view of our house. Before, we had been able to see the peak of our barn. But not now. Everything was gone. Where only a half-hour before there had been nine buildings, freshly painted, now there were none. Where there had been life, there was the silence of death. It was all gone - - all dead."

"Dad got out of the car and walked with his cane, around the clean-swept, tornado-vacuumed farmyard. We later found out that our house had been dropped, in one smashed piece, a half-mile out into the pasture. There was nothing left of it."

Schuller looked into the crowd. "Do you know what we did?"

"We went into a nearby town and found an old house that was being offered for sale by the county. We bought the house for fifty dollars and took it apart piece by piece. I got up on the roof with my Dad and we took off every shingle, one by one. We saved every shingle and every nail. We saved every board and every brick, and took them back to the farm."

"And from these pieces we built a new little house on that same farm. Nine farms were destroyed in that tornado, and my father was the only one to rebuild. A few years later, the market came back and prices rose. The farm prospered. Within five years the mortgage was paid off. My father died a successful man!"

"So you're having tough times? Are they tougher than the ones my father went through?" Schuller looked deep into the eyes of a new generation of farmers. "Are you burning corn cobs for fuel? Is the mortgage due and the cash not there? Have you lost everything in a tornado? Are you thinking about putting the place up for sale and walking away? Then let me tell you something about tough times."

"I have a teen-aged daughter who has to go through life with one leg, I've suffered through cancer surgery with my wife. Let me tell you something about tough times."

Schuller stepped away from the microphone. The audience sat on the edge of their chairs, waiting for the next words to come from his mouth. Instead of answering, Schuller paced across the stage again. *If they only knew I don't have the slightest idea what I'm going to say next,* he thought.

Schuller paced across the stage once more and stepped back up to the microphone.

When he spoke, the words came out like a thunderclap.

"Tough times never last. Tough people do!"

The crowd broke up in applause. Thirty-five hundred farmers who had lost hope, found it again that day.

"Don't ever give up," Schuller told them. "Always keep looking for another way. Because you can be the one who makes it through this. You can do it just like we did. You can be the one who helps their Dad rebuild his farm. You can be the one who lives with that memory for the rest of your lives."

The applause almost drowned out the last words Schuller said to the crowd of thirty-five hundred hopeful people.

*   *   *

The palm trees swaying in the evening breeze were a welcome sight for the weary traveler. The harsh Chicago ballroom began to fade from his mind as the lighted cross of his church came into view. Leaning forward, toward the cab driver, Schuller said, "Excuse me, What's that building over there?"

"Which one are you talking about?"

"That cross over there," Schuller said cheerfully.

"Ohhh, That there is a famous Catholic hospital. I've never been there, but I hear it's real nice!"

Unbelievable! Not knowing quite how to react, Schuller said, "Well, next time you have a problem, you should go check it out!"

The cab driver glanced over his shoulder and said, "Are you a Doctor?"

Playfully Schuller said, "You might say I'm a Doctor of the Mind!"

"Brain surgeon, huh? Well, I'll remember that if I ever need brain surgery!"

Incredible, Schuller thought. *By now, I wouldn't think that there would be any one in the county who didn't know about the Crystal Cathedral! Here I am, not five miles from home and*

this man doesn't know anything about what we're doing here!
I guess our work isn't finished here yet.

- 16 -

Seven Secrets

There's a lot of pain in the world. There are a lot of people who depend on Robert Schuller and The Hour Of Power every week for hope to ease that pain.

Shannon braced her back against the door. She was a frail girl, small for her age and underweight. She braced her feet and pushed back harder against the door. It was all she could do to keep the thin wooden door from being smashed in.

"I'm going to kill you, Shannon!" yelled the voice on the other side of the door. "I hate you and I'm going to kill you for what you did to me!"

Shannon kept her weight against the door. She was only thirteen, trapped in her bedroom.

"I'm going to kill you, Shannon!"

Shannon was more scared than she had ever been in her life. It was dark and she was alone in the house. There was a new terror in the voice now. There was an edge that hadn't been there before. Shannon was sure the voice meant what it said.

There was no mistaking that tone in her mother's voice. Her mother was going to kill her if she could.

Suddenly, the battering against the door stopped. Shannon listened for her mother's husky breathing through the door, but she couldn't hear anything. She listened harder. She heard her mother's footsteps run down the hall.

Shannon checked the doorknob. It was still locked and holding fast. Just minutes before, her mother had jostled the knob violently, trying to get in. Shannon had been so scared that the lock would give way, and her mother would be able to force open the door.

Shannon's mother was much bigger and stronger than she was, and Shannon was sure she wouldn't be able to stand up against her mother. Especially not now, not against the violent, drunken rage that her mother was in. Shannon had poured out the last bottle of gin, down the kitchen drain.

Shannon looked over at the phone on her nightstand. She thought about the secret phone number she had in her pocket. Her Dad had given her the secret phone number.

"Here, sweetheart," he had said when he handed her the slip of paper. "Always keep this with you, wherever you are. If you ever get in trouble, call the number on this piece of paper. No matter where I am or what I'm doing, I'll come running to help you."

The phone number was Shannon's secret. No one knew about it but her and her Dad. She hadn't even told her mother about it. She had kept it a secret for over a year.

She always had that slip of paper with her wherever she went. Shannon had lost other things - addresses, schoolbooks, even jewelry - but not her slip of paper. She made sure that she always had that phone number with her.

Shannon reached into her jeans pocket and took out the paper. She had never used the secret phone number before, but now it was time. She would call her Dad and tell him what had happened. She would tell him how she had come home and found Mom passed out on the couch again. Her mother had been an alcoholic ever since Shannon could remember. All the kids at school had been forbidden to associate with Shannon because of her mother's drinking binges.

Shannon looked at the phone and began to edge away from the door. She would just dial seven numbers and her Dad would come and take her away. Just one phone call and it would be all over, she thought.

The sound of footsteps racing down the hall towards her, startled Shannon. It was her mother coming back. She had probably searched the kitchen for another bottle and found that Shannon had poured them all out.

Shannon braced herself against the door again. She waited for the pounding and yelling to start. There was nothing, only silence.

Then suddenly a knife blade pierced through the door, missing Shannon's head by just inches.

"I'm going to kill you, Shannon!" her mother screeched through the door. "I hate you and I'm going to kill you!"

Shannon screamed when the knife came through the door a second time. She ran and crawled under the bed. She closed her eyes and wished it would all go away. But all she could hear was the splintering of wood and her mother's screaming.

Suddenly she heard a thump and the screaming stopped. Through the crack in the bottom of the door, she could see her mother's limp body. She realized that her mother had passed out again.

The knife blade was still sticking through the door, where Shannon's head had been.

Shannon lay under her bed for what seemed like an eternity. Should she get up and crawl out the bedroom window and run away like her brother had done? Should she call her Dad? Who would take care of her mother? Someone had to help her mother.

Shannon crawled out from beneath the bed and slowly cracked open the door. She kept herself ready, in case she had to slam it shut again, in case her mother woke up.

Her mother lay in a crumpled heap on the floor. Her hair was a tangled, stringy mess. She was still wearing her housecoat from this morning. The hallway reeked with the odor of alcohol.

Shannon's stomach felt queasy. She couldn't bear to see her mother lying on the floor like that. Shannon quietly shut the door and locked it. She sat down on her bed and reached for the phone on the dresser. She dialed the number on the secret white piece of paper and waited for her father to answer.

"Hello?"

"Daddy?" Shannon's voice cracked. "Daddy, help me. Mommy's trying to hurt me."

"Where are you, sweetie?" he asked.

"I'm at home in my room. I'm scared, Daddy. Can you come home and get me right now?"

Shannon's father didn't answer.

"Daddy," she sobbed again. "Did you hear me? Daddy, I want you to come and get me right now."

"I can't do that, Shannon."

Shannon heard the sound of a woman laughing in the background.

"I'll be home later, sweetheart. You're safe at home." And he hung up.

Shannon held the phone in her lap and listened to the dial tone buzz. Her mind was paralyzed. Her heart pounded as the tears welled up in her eyes. She needed help, and her precious secret number was gone. She looked down at the phone and found herself dialing another number. A number she had seen on television. Shannon had used the television to keep herself company on Saturday nights when her mother would go out on a drinking binge. She would watch the late movies until she couldn't hold her eyes open any more. Slowly but surely, her eyes would melt into blissful slumber, only to be awakened the next day by a silver-haired preacher on television. He would talk about hope, and love, and having dreams for your life. Shannon didn't know what he meant. *How can anybody have a dream for their life,* she thought. *I'm just trying to survive.* But now she found herself dialing the number that she had heard the kind man talk about on television. Her fingers pounded out the numbers, 1-714-NEW-HOPE. She waited anxiously as the phone rang on the other end of the line.

"Hello?" the stranger said. "New Hope counseling, can I help you?"

"My name is Shannon, and I need help."

Help arrived a few minutes later. Shannon was safe. She had found someone willing to help her.

*   *   *

The lights of Las Vegas glittered against the dark desert sky. The town bustled with cars on the boulevard. Throngs of people crowded into the lobbies of the Casinos.

Schuller didn't like being in Las Vegas. It wasn't the people, it was the atmosphere. Las Vegas had the atmosphere of being a place where people came to see other people, and then talk about who they had seen.

Schuller didn't want to be seen in Las Vegas.

People were watching the Jim Bakker scandals on television every night. Schuller had even been interviewed by Ted Koppel on Nightline, about what he thought of the state of televised ministries. Schuller had tried to point out that The Hour Of Power was a televised church service, not the tool of a televangelist, but Schuller wasn't sure that people would make a clear distinction between himself and Jim Bakker.

Every reporter in the country was looking for a story. They were all looking for a new secret to tell. Right now, Las Vegas was the last place in the world that Schuller wanted to be.

But he had promised a friend that he would speak at this convention. He always did his best to keep his promises.

Schuller sat in the back of the cab with Mike Nason.

"What a great town!" Nason declared. "Look at those lights. It's like Christmas time, don't you think, Bob?"

Schuller glared at Nason. "Look, we're here for a short talk at the convention," he said sternly. "We're staying one night and taking the first flight back to California in the morning." Schuller looked out the window at all the lights. *Lord willing, we'll be out of here before anyone even wakes up tomorrow.*

Nason knew Schuller was uncomfortable being in Las Vegas, but he loved to tease him anyway.

"Sure, Bob, sure."

A red-coated doorman opened Schuller's door, as the cab came to a stop in front of their hotel.

"Reverend Schuller," the doorman said loudly. "Welcome to Las Vegas!"

Schuller winced. He hadn't been in town fifteen

minutes and already people were recognizing him. Schuller smiled, quickly shook the man's hand, said 'Thank You' and started into the hotel.

"My wife watches your show all the time," the doorman said.

"Really," Schuller said, "How about you?"

The doorman looked uneasy. Then he straightened up and said with a toothy smile, "Whenever I can, Reverend. Whenever I'm not working."

"Oh, do you have to work on Sunday?" Schuller asked.

"More often than I would like, Reverend. This town never shuts down." The doorman's eyes flashed. "But that's all right, because my wife gives me your sermons when I come home at night."

Schuller cracked a big smile. "Did you ever think about taking your wife to church sometime? Maybe all she wants to do is go to church with you."

The doorman started laughing. "Me, in church? That's a good one, Reverend Schuller!" He opened the door to the hotel for Schuller. "I'll tell my wife you said that. Have a nice stay while you're in Las Vegas."

Schuller stepped into the crowded hotel lobby. His eyes swept over the busy gaming tables and roulette wheels. Young girls in low cut outfits circled the slot machines, looking for a winner.

Nason slapped Schuller firmly on the back. "Not exactly the Crystal Cathedral, is it, Bob?"

Schuller raised both eyebrows and glared back at Nason. "We're going straight to bed after the speech and catch the first flight out in the morning."

Nason tried a more serious tone. "Why don't you have a seat here in the lobby, Bob? I'll go get us checked in, then we'll grab a quick bite to eat before your speech."

Schuller sat down and reached into his briefcase. He took out the black leather-bound notebook in which he had jotted down the notes for his speech. He found it hard to concentrate over the crashing sounds of coins dropping into slot machines and the whine of the winners' sirens. He concentrated harder, trying to remember the opening joke he wanted to use to warm up the crowd.

Then over the sound of crashing coins, over the ringing sirens boomed the words, "Paging Dr. Schuller, Dr. Robert Schuller. Would Dr. Schuller please come to a white paging telephone?"

You've got to be kidding! thought Schuller. *Now everyone in the world knows I'm here!* Schuller looked around the casino to see how many people were staring at him. He was sure the whole casino would be looking at him.

No one stopped gambling. No one stopped doing anything. All Schuller heard was the sound of laughter coming from behind him.

He turned around and found Mike Nason leaning against the wall laughing. Nason stopped laughing just long enough to say, "Paging Dr. Schuller, paging Dr. Schuller."

Schuller's face turned bright red.

"Loosen up a little bit, Bob," Nason said. "Nobody cares if you came to Las Vegas or not."

Schuller turned away embarrassed. Then he put his black notebook away, grabbed his suitcase and started to walk toward the front desk.

"Where are you going?" Nason called after him.

"Never mind," Schuller called back. "This will only take a minute."

Nason silently watched Schuller lean over the front desk and speak to the concierge. After a short talk, Schuller turned around and walked back to Nason.

"What's going on?" Nason asked when Schuller was close to him.

"You'll see," Schuller answered. "Come on. let's go."

Nason picked up his bags and followed Schuller toward the elevator. As the elevator doors closed, they heard the concierge's voice boom through the casino.

"Paging Jerry Falwell, Pastor Jerry Falwell. Paging Mr. Roberts, Mr. Oral Roberts. Paging Dr. Graham, Dr. Billy Graham."

Schuller turned to Nason and said with a big smile, "Now they'll think there's a religious convention in town!"

Nason laughed all the way up to their room.

*　　　　*　　　　*

The scent of popcorn and coffee, filled the master bedroom. The lights were dim as Schuller and Arvella settled down for a late evening of television. As fourteen year old Gretchen bounced into the room, the sound of a southern minister bellowed from the screen. Full of energy, she said, "Whatcha' watchin'?"

Bob raised his eyebrows slightly and said, "Jimmy Swaggart."

"Jimmy Swaggart the televangelist? What for?!"

Arvella quickly chimed in, "It seems that Reverend Swaggart doesn't care much for your father's ministry."

"What makes you say that?" Gretchen inquired.

Reluctantly, Arvella said, "We've heard rumors that Mr. Swaggart has been going around to the stations that air our program, and offering them more money so he can air his program instead."

Shocked, Gretchen said, "You're kidding, is he getting away with it!?"

"Not so far, we do have contracts with the stations."

"Then what's the problem?"

Frustrated, Schuller said, "The problem is, that it's driving up the cost of our airtime. Each year we have to renew with the stations, so now they are asking us to pay what's being offered to them by others!"

"That doesn't seem like a very Christian like attitude on their part, now does it?" Gretchen said sarcastically.

Arvella said quickly, "It's not illegal, Gretchen!"

"No, but it sure doesn't seem ethical. What's his problem anyway? I mean we don't have any problems with other ministries like that, do we?"

"According to our station buyers, there are others that do the same thing." Schuller said. "But we do have very positive relationships with most of them."

Arvella said, "Oral Roberts has been on our program, and Pat Robertson–and you've been on Paul Crouch many times, haven't you, Bob?"

Curious, Gretchen said, "How come some ministries seem to fight so much!"

Schuller said, "The church has been fighting for two thousand years, sweetheart. It usually stems from doctrinal differences. One group interprets something in the Bible one way, and another group sees it another way, and pretty soon you have the Protestants splitting from the Catholics, or the Baptists splitting between the north and south!"

"Yeah, but they all believe in Jesus and God don't they?" Gretchen continued to question.

"Sure they do."

"So what's the problem?" Gretchen repeated.

"Human pride. My way is right, and your way is wrong, even though we're trying to accomplish the same things..."

The voice on the television once again drew Bob's attention. "When you attend a rock and roll concert, you're having communion with the devil himself! And the next time you hear a minister spouting off about possibility thinking, and self-esteem, you just remember that he is not a man of God!"

"Daddy, can he say that?! Where does he get off! I can't believe what I am hearing!"

Disguising his pain, Bob said quietly, "He just said it, what can you do about it? That's his opinion."

"Come on, Dad, the Bible tells us not to judge other people, and this guy just put you on trial and appointed himself chief justice and executioner!"

Bob smiled at his daughter's adamant defense of him, as he said, "Justice is mine sayeth the Lord!"

Suddenly a broad smile appeared on his face as he said, "However, I can control what we listen to in this house!"

Dramatically, he lifted his remote control to turn the dial. Temporarily satisfied by his solution, he reached for the bowl of popcorn.

*   *   *

She rose early in the morning as the sun peeked over the horizon. Arvella loved the sunrise. The still quiet of the morning. It had started when the children were small. Rising early. A chance to be alone with Bob, but more so with herself. Normally it was a chance to be creative. That divine gift of inspiration that had helped to build a world wide television ministry. But this morning was different.

As she slowly sipped her coffee, thoughts of romance filled her mind. She couldn't help but stare at the roses on the kitchen counter. "To Gretchen, with Love, Jim." Her daughter had told her that he was just a friend. Somehow she knew differently. *Six foot two, dark and handsome, doesn't stay friends for long.* Her baby girl was in love, she just didn't know it yet. She knew the look well. The look that filled her husband's eyes on the steps of the general store in Iowa. He was such a dreamer!

Gretchen's suitor had that look, she thought to herself. The look that makes young girls fall in love. The look that made her fall in love.

Her eyes gently smiled as she watched her sleepy daughter enter the kitchen. Like most college students, she hated mornings.

"Good morning, sweetheart."

Gretchen's voice was dull and lifeless as she responded, "Morning, mother." Arvella remembered that look too!

"Now Gretchen, what's his last name?!"

Gretchen abruptly stopped pouring her morning coffee.

"Excuse me?"

"Jim's last name?!"

She continued to pour. "Penner, why?"

Arvella seemed to pay no attention as she hunched over her desk mumbling, "James Penner." She quickly raised her head and asked, "And his middle name?!"

"Mother, what's going on?"

"His middle name, please!"

"Bradley."

Pleased with Gretchen's response, she turned her attention back to her desk, mumbling as she wrote, "James Bradley Penner."

Gretchen's voice began to improve as the coffee took effect.

"Mother, what's this all about?"

"James Bradley Penner–You know Gretchen, I'm going to have to get used to that name, how long have you been dating?"

"About three weeks."

Arvella sighed deeply, her eyes lost in a romantic dream as she said, "Well, if you don't marry him, I think you're stupid!"

"Mother, who said anything about marriage?!"

Arvella seemed to pay no attention as she continued saying, "But you have to remember that he is not perfect!"

Finally, she's making some sense, Gretchen thought. "Yes that's true, he's not!"

Arvella continued, "Because love can be blind, you know."

"Yes, mother, I'm aware of that."

Suddenly she was back as she focused intently on her daughter's eyes and said, "Which is probably a good thing, because if it wasn't, I wouldn't have married your father!"

Arvella grinned as she turned to walk down the hall.

Gretchen stood in the kitchen looking stunned-remembering why she hated mornings.

*   *   *

"Arvella, look at this."

Schuller sat perched on the kitchen stool holding up a two page photograph of a man lying in bed. He was talking on the phone, watching a big screen T.V. and reading the front page of the Los Angeles Times, all at the same time. All around him on the bed were tall stacks of books and bound reports. Against one wall, three more television sets were on; all set to different programs. It was clear that even while in bed, the man was hard at work.

"That's Armand Hammer," Arvella said. She recognized Hammer immediately from all the recent news articles about Occidental Petroleum. Arvella turned her attention back to the stove. She wasn't about to get side-tracked and spoil the dinner she had worked on that afternoon.

"Look at this, Arvella," Schuller repeated. He pounded at the corner of the photograph with his finger.

Arvella walked over to where Schuller sat. She knew he wouldn't leave her alone until she gave him her full attention, if only for a moment. "What, Bob?"

"Look, Schuller pointed, "Right there next to him on the bed. On top of that stack of reports."

Arvella looked closer at the photograph. She saw the face of Beau Bridges, the son of Lloyd Bridges, on the cover of Guideposts magazine.

"That's Guideposts!" she exclaimed.

"Incredible," Schuller said, "Armand Hammer reads Guidepost magazine. One of the world's greatest industrial giants reads a magazine published by Norman Vincent Peale." Schuller looked up from the photo. "Arvella, Armand Hammer's been a personal friend of every Soviet Premier since Lenin."

"I can see your wheels are spinning already, Bob."

Schuller got up and started to pace the kitchen floor. He walked to the back door and looked out at the Koi pond. He always found his mind worked better when he watched the Japanese fish swim around their garden home.

Schuller walked over to the kitchen wall phone and started to dial.

"Bob, can't you at least wait until she finishes dinner?" Arvella said. She knew he was calling his secretary, Marge Kelley.

"She won't mind," Schuller answered, "I'm sure she's used to it by now."

"I don't think anybody ever gets used to it, Bob."

Schuller knew she was right. He had heard it too many times at the office but the phone was already ringing.

"Hello, Marge?" he said after she answered, "I'm not interrupting your dinner, am I?" He mouthed 'I'm not' across the kitchen to Arvella and then went on.

"Good, you know I'd never call you during dinner. Marge, do we have Armand Hammer's phone number and address in The Book? Could you check it for me please?. . . Yes, now."

Schuller hung on the line while Marge checked on the number.

"We do? Good," he said after a minute. Schuller paused and looked out into the gardens. Arvella started to put the corn and carrots on his plate. The look on her face told Schuller to make it short. The food was already

350

getting cold.

"Marge," Schuller said, "I want to send a short letter to Armand Hammer."

Schuller knew he better have the 'Sincerely Yours' done before Arvella put the meat on the table.

Schuller dictated while Arvella put the meat on the dinner plates. Food on the table at the Schuller house was the same as saying 'time's up' at a Rams football game.

"Marge, I'll have to call you back later," Schuller said as Arvella sat down at the table, "I want to get Arvella's thoughts on this, too."

Schuller sat down at the table and reached over for Arvella's hand to say grace. He hadn't the slightest idea that a man lying in bed watching television was about to change his life forever.

Book III

GOLIATH

Dr. Schuller hard at work on another book. He has written over thirty books in his career, including four New York Times Bestsellers. Dr. Schuller's books have been translated into twenty-two foreign languages.

"Millions can benefit from Dr. Schuller's wisdom."
- Armand Hammer

Dr. Schuller signing copies of his latest best-selling book.

Another satisfied fan.

The haunting picture of John Wayne that hangs in Dr. Schuller's hallway.

A 'Thank You' note from The Duke to Dr. Schuller for helping Wayne fight cancer.

"You want somebody to treat you good, you better treat them good."
- Sammy Davis, Jr.

"Mr. Piano" - Roger Williams. Mr. Williams was one of the many celebrities who helped Dr. Schuller in his ministry.

Dr. Armand Hammer - Humanitarian and world-respected business giant.

Dr. Schuller with Armand Hammer aboard OXY ONE on their way to Russia.

Dr. Schuller and Arvella in Armand Hammer's Moscow apartment. The painting on the wall is 'Children At Piano' by Bogdonova Belsky. Schuller believed the painting represented democracy.

Dr. Billy Graham in the Crystal Cathedral.

Dr. Schuller's

Dr. Schuller, Sheila and Jim Coleman, Arvella

Jeanne Schuller Dunn and Dr. Schuller

Daughters

Arvella, Tim Milner, Carol Schuller Milner and Dr. Schuller

Dr. Schuller walks his youngest daughter Gretchen down the aisle. She was the last daughter to be married.

Love comes in all

sizes and colors.

Record catch at Cabo San Lucas, Mexico. Dr. Schuller with his son, Robert A.

Robert A. and Donna Schuller with President Bush

Dr. Schuller, Gretchen, Arvella, and Carol in Indonesia.

Dr. Schuller extends a warm 'Thank You' to American soldiers for serving their country. Schuller's 'Hour Of Power' is broadcast to American bases and ships at sea all over the world each week.

Left: Keeping informed of current world events.

One of the world's largest flags raised at the Crystal Cathedral every Memorial Day. The flag is approximately fifty-five feet wide by eighty feet high.

Aloha. Schuller and the girls in Hawaii. Gretchen is on the far left, Arvella is near middle with Carol to her left. Dr. Schuller is the one in the fishing hat paying the bills.

Dr. Schuller and Arvella in Moscow wearing fur hats.

James Penner and Dr. Schuller with hard hats.

Schuller clowns with Russian General.

The Schuller Family

Far left: **The Colemans**
Jim and Nicky,
Jason, Sheila, Christopher,
and Scott (left to right)

The Dunns
Paul holding Stephanie
Jeanne and Jennifer (seated)

The Penners
Jim and Gretche.
(The Bride and G

(Since this photograph was taken in the fall of 1988, Tim and Carol have had another son, Eth

Dr. and Mrs. Schuller

The Robert Schullers

Robert A. is standing holding Christina, Donna,
his wife, is seated. To her left are Bobby and Angie.
Dr. Schuller is holding their youngest, 'AJ', Anthony John.

The Milners

Tim, Carol and Rebekah

im and Gretchen had a daughter Julia. Both Jeanne and Carol are expecting as this book goes to press.)

*Left: The Orange Drive-In
1955*

Below: The Crystal Cathedral Campus in Garden Grove, California - 1992

Right: The Garden Grove Community Church - 1968

Above: Dr. Schuller on one of his cross-country book signing tours.
Below: Schuller the photographer.

Above: Dr. Schuller speaks at several conferences and seminars each year throughout the country.

Crystal Cathedral Ministries

Statement
of
Purpose and Mission

This ministry is a center for spiritual growth,
where positive attitudes are developed,
where good people become better,
where hurts are healed,
where lessons are learned,
where friendships are developed,
where marriages are strengthened,
where families are bonded,
where the restless find peace,
where love is alive,
where God is understood,
where Jesus Christ is Lord.

Dr. Robert and Arvella Schuller

You need faith, hope and love.

And the greatest of these is love.

Book III

GOLIATH

- 17 -

Coming of Giants

If there was one thing you could depend on in Robert Schuller's life, it would be that the right people always came along at the right time to help him. Armand Hammer was one of those people.

Schuller and Arvella sat quietly in the passengers cabin of the private plane. The interior of Armand Hammer's 'OXY One' was appointed with plush captain's chairs, a burled walnut planning table and several televisions and telephones. Heavy pleated drapes hung over the windows. There was a separate bedroom compartment for Dr. Hammer in the rear of the aircraft. The plane had been outfitted to act as the intercontinental headquarters for the eighty-nine year-old chairman of the sixteenth largest industrial corporation in the United States, Occidental Petroleum.

The plane had been fitted with extra fuel tanks which gave it an extended range of over four thousand miles, enough to fly from Los Angeles to Moscow. That was stopping only once for refueling. During the last five years, Hammer spent time in the air constantly. Traveling to China, Canada, New York City, London, Berlin, Yugoslavia, Rome, Columbia, Mexico City, Washington D.C., Moscow, Madrid, Peru, and Bermuda.

"Now *this* is impressive!" Schuller whispered to Arvella. He swiveled around in his captain's chair and looked around the cabin. "What do you suppose they have on the lunch menu on a plane like this?"

"I'm sure it's a little better than what you're used to when you're flying around signing books, Bob," Arvella smiled.

"That's for sure!" Schuller said as he peeked out the window. He saw the baggage handler load two large suitcases into the hold of the plane.

"Did you remember your winter hat, Arvella?" Schuller asked, "Dr. Hammer's secretary told me it wouldn't be much above zero in Moscow when we land."

"I even remembered your long underwear, Honey! The bright red ones you got for Christmas."

Schuller smiled. "Good. At least I'll be warm, if not fashionable."

Schuller watched Armand Hammer walk across the runway and begin to climb the short flight of steps up to the plane. He still couldn't believe that his simple letter had led to all this. He had written Hammer about how inspiring it was "To see one of our country's greatest business leaders gaining strength from a positive, religious publication such as Guideposts magazine."

Hammer had called between services on Sunday morning. He said how much he admired what Schuller had done for religious broadcasting and that he also watched 'The Hour Of Power' every week. Hammer told Schuller that he had heard about Rupert Murdoch recently hooking the show up to his European satellite and now Schuller's 'Hour Of Power' was being broadcast in twenty-two European countries. Murdoch then floored Schuller by offering him the airtime for Europe free! All Schuller had to do was send him the weekly tapes of 'The Hour Of Power.'

"Would you be interested in broadcasting in the Soviet Union?" Hammer had asked Schuller bluntly.

"You bet I would!" Schuller had replied. The thought of bringing an inspirational message to the Russian people lifted Schuller right out of his chair.

"The only two times I've been to Russia," Schuller told Hammer, "was once while smuggling Bibles and the other was to talk to the underground leaders. That second time, the KGB was watching me like a hawk."

"I'm sure they were," Hammer said with a chuckle. "You're well known in Russia, Dr. Schuller."

"Really?" Schuller said, "A pastor well known in Russia?"

Hammer chuckled a second time. "Things are changing in Russia, Bob. Mikhail Gorbachev's new *Perestroika*, which means restructuring, has already caused tremendous change. If you're willing, I'd like you to come with me on my next trip to Moscow and meet with Valentin Lazutkin, the head of Russian television. He can help you get your 'Hour Of Power' to the Russian people."

Schuller leaped right out of his chair. He could hardly believe what he was hearing! Here was one of the richest capitalists in the world offering not only to take him to Russia, but to introduce him to the head of Russian television programming! Schuller knew that Armand Hammer was much more than just a capitalist to the Russian people.

Hammer's great grandparents had been born in Russia. They had come to America in the late 1800's, before the rise of communism.

Hammer was born in the lower east side of New York. He had made his first million before he was twenty-one. While he was attending medical school at Columbia University in New York, his father turned over the family pharmaceutical business to him. Hammer discovered quickly how to run the company by day and study by night. A master at organization and motivation, Hammer graduated from medical school and sold the business for a million dollar profit the same year.

Shortly after graduation, Hammer heard the news of a great famine in Russia that was the result of the October Revolution in 1917. Flush with cash, Hammer made his first trip back to Russia. The sight of people starving in the streets, caused him to offer a deal to the Russian government. Hammer would purchase a million dollars worth of grain in America and ship it to Moscow. In return, Russia would grant Hammer the exclusive right to mine for asbestos in their country. The idea of an American buying grain to help starving Russians caught the attention of Nikolai Lenin himself. Hammer soon found himself attending Communist Party functions and shaking hands with the new elite of Russia.

Hammer subsequently made millions from his mining rights, and had forever endeared himself to the Russian people. Hammer never practiced medicine, but he spent his entire life working to fund other philanthropic causes, particularly the fight against cancer.

Now Hammer hoped to deliver another kind of food to the Russians, one that communism had forbidden the open existence of for the last seventy years - freedom of religion.

"I would be thrilled to go to Russia with you, Dr. Hammer!" Schuller said enthusiastically. "I can't think of anything I'd like to do more!"

"Wonderful," Hammer had told him. "I know you have to get back to your congregation. I'll see you tomorrow."

Schuller was glad that Arvella had come along on the trip. He had no idea what he was going to say or do when he met the Russians, but he knew that having her there would help.

Hammer entered the living quarters slowly. He still felt the discomfort of his new pacemaker.

"He shouldn't even be taking this trip," Schuller whispered to Arvella.

Arvella nodded her head in agreement. It was hard for her to imagine what was going through Hammer's mind. His wife lay silently in a coma, while he quietly traveled to Moscow, hoping to make a difference in the lives of hurting people.

Hammer carefully sat down across from Schuller and Arvella. A gentle smile appeared on his lips. His powerful eyes twinkled as he thought about their upcoming mission.

Hammer had made many contributions to the Russian people in his lifetime, but this gift was special. Personal. His gift was Robert Schuller.

The plane lifted into the clouds. Schuller noticed the worry in Hammer's tired eyes, a pain that only a husband can feel for his wife.

"We could have postponed this trip, Dr Hammer."

Armand took a deep breath.

"No," Hammer responded. "She was stable when I left her this morning, still in a coma." He paused briefly. "Besides, she would have wanted us to go. This is too important."

Hammer paused and looked out the window of the plane.

"She would have wanted it this way. She loved the

Russian people as much as I do."

Schuller nodded to his new friend. He understood that kind of love very well. A love for people.

"Besides," Hammer continued, "she liked to give presents, and we've got the greatest present anyone can give." "It's called Hope."

The long flight through the night ended, as 'OXY One' touched down in Moscow on Tuesday morning. The Boeing 727 taxied up to the gate. The giant door housed in the tail of the airplane opened up, and the three travelers walked down the steps to the tarmac. The bitter cold air slapped against their faces as they walked to the airport terminal. A small party, from Occidental's Moscow office, met them at the terminal entrance and walked with them to the customs counter.

The simple, airport terminal had not changed much since Schuller had last been there, eighteen years before. Schuller looked for the place where he had been detained by the KGB.

"There it is, Arvella," Schuller said, "right over there!"

"What's that, Bob?" Arvella asked.

"That's where I was detained for bringing Bibles into Russia." Schuller started to laugh. "Ike made it through scott free! They caught me and confiscated all the Bibles I had in my suitcase! I must have had a sign on my forehead that said 'I'm a Pastor from America.' "

Hammer smiled at Schuller. "You just have one of those faces, Bob!" he said. "You can't hide anything!"

"Yeah, Bob," Arvella added. "Not a thing!" She smiled at the look of innocence on Schuller's face.

"Well, I'm not that bad," Schuller said. He kept himself from laughing, but a wide grin spread across his face. Arvella grabbed his hand and together they followed Hammer through the customs gate. Unlike eighteen years ago, the customs people waved them through.

The group made their way to the cars waiting at the airport entrance. Russian faces gazed in awe at Hammer because they recognized him as one of their national heroes.

They stepped into the cars and drove through the icy streets of Moscow.

"Where are the Christmas lights?" Schuller said to Arvella, "Three weeks 'til Christmas, and no lights?"

"You're right," Arvella added. "There's no color at all. Anywhere!"

"I remember coming here," Hammer said, "just after the revolution in 1921. It was a cold, hard, place back then. The people had given up hope." Hammer paused-remembering. "Moscow was in utter desolation. The stores were empty. The people were all dressed in rags with hardly any pants or shoes and they had wrapped dirty cloths around their legs and feet to keep warm. The children all ran barefoot. No one seemed to smile. Everyone looked dirty and dejected."

"Later, I was sent out to the Urals to report on conditions there. What I saw changed my life forever. There were cholera, typhus, and every other epidemic that you can possibly imagine. My first experience with what Russian famine was, left me cold and empty."

"Children were begging in the streets because they hadn't eaten for days. They begged ceaselessly for any scrap of bread, for life itself, but we couldn't help them all."

Schuller and Arvella were shocked. Nothing Schuller had ever experienced in his life prepared him for the atrocities that Hammer related to him.

"Wasn't there any food anywhere?" Arvella asked.

"The winter had wiped out the crops." Hammer told her. "I saw stockpiles of platinum, furs, and gems, but no one had saved any food."

"Why didn't they sell the gems and furs for food?" Schuller asked.

"It was the new government," Hammer said. "The

Communists were in power. They said it would take too long to sell the goods and buy food." Hammer turned his head and looked out the window. The stony faces of gray, snow covered buildings stared back at him.

"The stretcher-bearers carried the dead into the railway stations," Hammer said, "where they stacked up the bodies in tiers."

Arvella grasped Schuller's arm. She knew his brother Henry had been a litter-bearer in World War II, and had seen terrible atrocities. They were so horrific, that he wasn't ever able to talk about them.

"They stripped the corpses naked because their clothes were too precious to waste." Hammer said. "There were grim tales of cannibalism, of mothers driven mad killing one child to keep their other children from starving. Worst of all, there were butchers selling human flesh for profit." Schuller thought of the Goliaths that Hammer and the Russian people had faced in their lives.

Hammer turned back and placed his hand on Arvella's wrist. "I'm sorry if I upset you," he said, "but I wanted you to know why helping these people means so much to me. Communism is dying. I believe that soon the walls between America and Russia will also begin to crumble. The Russians will need our help. I don't ever want to come to Russia and see the same things I saw back then."

Schuller grasped Hammer's hand. He felt the deep compassion in the man. He wished that he had the words to help this man.

Schuller looked past Hammer and saw the shiny golden arches of McDonalds, out the window. "There's one sign of change right over there." he said.

Hammer looked at the McDonald's. "It's sad to think that one of the greatest countries in the world lacks the ability to feed itself."

"Things have gotten a little better since the last time I was here," Schuller commented.

The newly built McDonald's was in full view now.

Hammer's face lit up as they passed by.

"Fast food in Moscow," he said, "Why didn't I think of that?"

"You did, Armand, seventy years ago with a shipment of wheat!" Schuller exclaimed. "You started something!"

Hammer looked at the golden arches and smiled back at Schuller. "Think they have a drive-through yet?"

The car crunched through the snow to the curb in front of Occidental headquarters. The building stood only a few blocks from Red Square. A well-dressed young man rushed out into the snow. He wore a heavy wool coat and fur hat.

"Good Morning, Dr. Hammer," he said in Russian.

"Good Morning, Yuri," Hammer responded cheerfully. "I've brought some very important friends with me from the United States."

Schuller and Arvella smiled at the young Russian. They recognized the Russian greeting words Hammer had spoken and understood that they were being introduced.

Schuller extended his hand warmly to the young Russian.

"Good Morning," Schuller said in broken Russian.

"Pleased to meet you, sir," Yuri said in perfect English.

Yuri smiled at Schuller's surprise and added, "And this must be your lovely wife, Arvella."

Arvella looked at Hammer in amazement. "I'm very impressed with the efficiency of your organization," she said diplomatically.

"Thank you, Arvella," he said. "I think you'll find the Russian people to be more open and friendly than you may have expected."

"We've prepared your office, Dr. Hammer," Yuri said. "Shall I see to the luggage while you show your guests inside?"

Hammer nodded his approval. "Thank you, Yuri."

Schuller and Arvella waited as Armand Hammer picked up the phone. His office was decorated with richly finished furniture and bright flowers. It was a simple office with a long table on one side, a bookcase along one wall and Hammer's desk with three chairs for guests. Schuller knew that Hammer was calling to see how his wife was doing in America, so he and Arvella stood near the windows.

"You know he's one of the few people outside the Kremlin to have a direct line to the United States," he said to Arvella. "He's also one of the only people allowed to fly a private plane in Soviet air space." Schuller's voice fell to a whisper. "I still can't believe we're here!"

Schuller heard Hammer questioning his personal Doctor back in Los Angeles.

"How are her vital signs?" Hammer asked. He listened to the response and said, "Is she in any pain?" His voice became quiet. "Has she spoken?"

Arvella squeezed Schuller's hand tightly. She knew the pain that comes from a loved one being in a hospital halfway around the world.

Hammer took a deep breath and hung up the phone. He walked over to Schuller and Arvella and spoke matter-of-factly.

"First of all," he told them, "There will be a reception at my apartment tonight. Georgy Arbotov will be there. He's a high ranking Soviet official and he's very close to Gorbachev. He could be instrumental in keeping you on television once you're on the air." Hammer's voice took on the tone of a seasoned executive. "I've set up a meeting for you with Valentin Lazoutkin. Lazoutkin, you will remember, is the head of Gostel Radio, the Soviet owned Television Communications Station. He has the power to put you on Russian television, Bob. That's no small feat," Hammer said to Arvella. "There's only one television station in Russia. There are no commercials;

there are no other channels to turn to. The Communist Party controls all programming on Channel One. This one channel reaches two hundred million people." Hammer's face lit up with excitement. He looked right at Schuller. "You could definitely make an impact with those numbers."

Schuller smiled in appreciation. *An American preacher on television in Moscow. Incredible!*

"I'm not quite sure how to thank you, Armand," Schuller said. "You've done so much for us."

"Thank me? Thank you for coming, Bob. These people need you. Russia needs hope, and you know how to give it to them. I can't do it sitting behind a desk talking on the phone. But you can. You know how to talk to people through television. You know how to touch their hearts."

Arvella looked at Schuller. He had been genuinely humbled by Hammer's words. She couldn't remember when she was more proud of her husband than at that moment.

They passed by the marble facing and walked through the entryway to Hammer's apartment complex. The building was multi-storied and was the new Russian design that had become so popular in the last ten years.

Hammer's apartment was tasteful. The masterpieces which hung on every wall in the apartment, disclosed its owner. Above the couch in the living room hung *Children At The Piano* by Bogdanova Belsky. Nicolas Kassatkin's *At Her Bedside* filled the entire facing wall. *Le Tete a Tete* by Vladimir Makovski graced the dining room. Hammer enjoyed one of the largest private art collections in the world, but his Russian masterpieces always remained close to his heart. He said they reflected the romantic soul of the Russian people.

Schuller found himself staring at the painting by Bogdanova - *Children At The Piano*. It was a large painting, at least five feet by four feet. It depicted three poor Russian children. One young boy stood next to the piano watching his sister. In the background, a second boy dressed in rags, looked aimlessly into the mirror at his own reflection. The girl sitting at the piano depressed a single white key with her index finger. Schuller stared deeply into the painting.

"When the revolution was over," Hammer told Schuller, "the government came in and took the personal property from the wealthy and distributed it among the poor. In this case, a poor family received this piano and the mirror. They had never seen either a mirror or a piano before."

Bob looked in fascination at the painting. He looked hard at the masterful strokes. "It's like Perestroika," he said to Hammer.

Hammer smiled at his friend's intuitiveness. "Yes, it is," he said.

Schuller looked into the eyes of the children. "The people of Russia have all gotten something," he explained, "but they don't know how to use it. The little girl has gotten a piano, but she doesn't know how to play it. Perestroika has given the Russian people freedom, but they don't know what to do with it."

"The little boy looking in the mirror has discovered, for the first time, that he's an individual. 'I am somebody,' he's saying to himself." Schuller looked to Arvella and said, "The mirror is called democracy, and the piano is called freedom."

Hammer smiled again. He knew he had brought the right people to Russia.

*   *   *

The Gostel Radio Complex doors opened wide. Armand Hammer led his delegation through the tall glass doors with a tight military precision. Schuller and Arvella

walked next to Hammer. Schuller wore a black suit with a
red tie and a white shirt. He had given his shoes an extra
buff that morning so that the edges would keep a crisp
sparkle.

Arvella wore a navy blue dress with simple white
earrings and no necklace. She was the only woman in the
delegation and she knew she would be the only woman
allowed in the meeting. Arvella presented herself as the
gracious lady that she was.

They were met at the doors by four Russian
television staff members who were wearing the standard
uniform of the Soviet bureaucrat, double breasted suits
and plain ties. The greetings were polite and courteous,
all in Russian. Schuller and Arvella listened closely to the
translator, trying hard to understand every word.
Hammer smiled warmly and led the delegation into the
building.

They strode down a long, tiled hallway to the
elevators. Hammer stopped midway to catch his breath.
He was still getting used to his new pacemaker. His
assistant was constantly at his side, as he had been the
entire trip. He took Hammer's arm and helped him into
the elevator.

By the time they had reached Lazoutkin's office,
Hammer was beginning to get his breath back.
Lazoutkin's fourth floor office looked out over downtown
Moscow. The streets were filled mostly with the heavily
clad women wearing scarves. They trudged toward the
marketplace carrying bags of goods to sell. Arvella
noticed that the women moved among Russian men, each
was wearing a suit and carrying a briefcase.

Valentin Lazoutkin was the well-dressed image of
the Russian ruling class. He was one of the top men in
the communication ranks of the Soviet Central
government. Lazoutkin could not speak English, which
meant he had been provided with an interpreter for the
meeting with the Americans.

Hammer, Schuller, and Arvella entered Lazoutkin's office as a family. Hammer strode right up to Lazoutkin and shook his hand earnestly. Hammer greeted him in Russian, the sign of utmost respect in the Soviet world.

Lazoutkin's eyes shone brightly as he looked at Armand Hammer. He was well aware of and very impressed with Hammer's relationship to the Russian Party Leaders. Lazoutkin also knew of the unwritten rule in the Kremlin which said that a request from Armand Hammer was not to be turned down.

Hammer knew the same rule. He chose his requests very carefully.

Lazoutkin motioned for Schuller and Arvella to sit down across from him at the large, board room table. Hammer sat down next to Schuller and slid an official looking, white document across the table to Lazoutkin. Hammer spoke in English and let the interpreter translate his words so that Schuller and Arvella could understand.

"Here is a letter I sent to your President Gorbachev," Hammer said to Lazoutkin, "informing him of this meeting. In the letter I requested the President's full cooperation."

Lazoutkin took a long drag on his cigarette and slowly exhaled the thin wisps of smoke. He grinned slightly, his eyes never leaving Hammer's.

Hammer went on, saying, "I have come here with Dr. Schuller, the most widely respected television pastor in the United States and I'm asking for your cooperation in letting him air his program on your network."

"I respect you, Dr. Hammer, very much," Lazoutkin said, "and I am honored you came to see me." Lazoutkin turned to Schuller and said, "And I am honored to meet your guest, Dr. Schuller. I'm sure we can come to some kind of arrangement, Dr. Hammer."

Each word was chosen and spoken carefully by

each man. Each word was important and had to be precise and clear. The word of God had never been spoken on Russian television before. This meeting would determine if Schuller would be the one who talked to the Russian people about God.

Hammer smiled at Lazoutkin. "I have every confidence that you will be able to work out the details with Dr. Schuller."

"Bob," Hammer said to Schuller, "I will see you back at my office. My driver will come back for you and Arvella."

Hammer excused himself and left Schuller and Arvella alone with Lazoutkin and the interpreter.

"Dr. Schuller," Lazoutkin asked in Russian, "How do I know there is a God? I have never experienced Him."

Schuller waited for the translator to complete the question and then thought for a moment.

"Oh, but you have experienced God, Mr. Lazoutkin," Schuller said. "You just didn't know you did."

"What do you mean?" Lazoutkin asked. "I'm not sure I'm following you."

"Do you have children?" Schuller asked Lazoutkin calmly.

Lazoutkin looked at Schuller for a long time.

"Do you remember being a child?" Schuller asked.

Lazoutkin smiled. He looked at Schuller and then to Arvella.

"Can you look into a child's eye and tell me you haven't experienced God." Schuller said.

A tear appeared in Lazoutkin's eye. Then he nodded his head that he understood.

Lazoutkin stood up and walked around the table. Schuller stood up as Lazoutkin approached, not knowing what to expect. Lazoutkin walked straight at Schuller with his arms held open. The two men hugged each other.

At that moment, Arvella knew that her husband was going on Russian television.

*   *   *

"Gretchen, come take a look at this," Schuller said enthusiastically. "Bob Hope is having an autograph party for his new book over at the Ala Moana Mall in Downtown Honolulu." The three Schullers, Bob, Arvella, and Gretchen were enjoying a much needed vacation in Hawaii. It had been a long year.

Schuller sat on the balcony of the hotel room over-looking the blue Hawaiian Pacific. The warm, tropical breeze rustled the edges of his paper as he read through the local advertisements.

"No he's not, Dad, stop teasing." "Let's go down to the beach!" Gretchen shot back.

"Yes, he is," Schuller smiled broadly. "Look, it's right here." Gretchen plopped down next to her father in a wicker lounge chair. "See, it's right here." Schuller continued. "He's signing his new book, '*Confessions of a Hooker,* My Life Long Love Affair with Golf.' "

Schuller raised a cheerful eyebrow and looked at his youngest daughter. He knew that she loved Bob Hope. She had seen every, "On The Road" picture Hope and Bing Crosby had ever made together, at least half a dozen times. As far as Gretchen was concerned, they could have re-run Bob Hope movies every Saturday afternoon of her life and she would never get enough.

"Do you want to go down to the mall with me and pick up an autographed copy?" Schuller asked.

Gretchen's eyes lit up like a decorated tree on Christmas eve.

"You're kidding, right?!"

"No, I'm serious, You've always wanted to meet him; here's your chance!" Schuller answered.

"You're going to stand in line, at a crowded mall on Saturday afternoon, with me so I can get Bob Hope's autograph?" Gretchen inquired.

"Sure, sounds like fun." Schuller laughed.

Gretchen grabbed her fathers hand excitedly and proceeded to pull him out of his chair.

"Come on then, let's get going!"

Schuller quickly rose to his feet and called into the hotel room. "Come on Arvella, we're going down to the mall."

"What for, Bob?"

"Bob Hope is signing autographs, and Gretchen wants to meet him."

"Never look a gift horse in the mouth, Mom," Gretchen said. "You don't have to give me an excuse to go to the mall!"

"Absolutely, Gretchen." Arvella said excitedly. "Let's go shopping!"

The small bookstore in the corner of the mall was crowded with people, as the Schuller family approached the entrance. The line to get Bob Hope's autograph, wrapped around one hallway and down the next. There must have been one hundred people in the long line when they arrived, and it seemed to grow larger by the minute.

"Well ladies, it looks like this is going to take a little while." Schuller said.

"Bob, why don't you and Gretchen get into line," Arvella said. "I'll go in the store and pick up a copy of the book."

"Good idea, Honey," Schuller responded. "We'll see you in a few minutes."

Schuller and Gretchen had been standing in line for about five minutes when the sounds of people whispering could be heard on both sides.

"Isn't that Robert Schuller? Yes, I'm sure it is."

Gretchen smiled proudly at the attention her father was attracting. *Sometimes it's fun to have a famous father!* she thought.

From behind, Schuller could feel a soft tap on his shoulder.

"Excuse me," Asked a young Hawaiian woman. "Aren't you Robert Schuller?"

Schuller smiled warmly and replied. "Yes, I am."

"I watch your program every week. You're terrific! You have really helped me you know!"

"That's great," Schuller said cheerfully. "I'm glad our program helps you."

"I really would be honored if I could have your autograph." The woman asked respectfully.

"Of course," Schuller said. "Do you have something for me to sign? I don't have any paper on me."

The woman thought for a minute. She quickly looked through her purse but came up empty. Her thoughtful look turned to a broad smile as she quickly handed Schuller a copy of Bob Hope's new book.

"Here, why don't you sign this!"

Schuller started to laugh. "Hope is going to love this!"

"Go ahead, Dad," Gretchen said excitedly. Schuller personalized his autograph by adding the words, *God loves you and so do I.*

"Here you go, Ma'am," Schuller added. "It was a pleasure to meet you."

The line of people waiting for Schuller to sign books had started to grow, slowly but surely. Ten to twelve people both ahead and behind Gretchen and Schuller, were passing their 'Bob Hope' books to Robert Schuller for his signature. Schuller autographed each book that was handed to him.

They finally reached a tiny table in front of the bookstore.

"Robert Schuller," Bob Hope's smiling face greeted him as he reached the table. "I thought this was my autographing party!"

Both men laughed heartily. Hope was clearly pleased to see his old friend.

"How are you, Bob, it's great to see you again!" Schuller responded.

"You too," Hope said. "What brings you all the way to Hawaii?"

Schuller chuckled and said,"I suppose you wouldn't believe me if I said we came all the way here just to get your autograph, would you?"

"You're on vacation, huh?!"

"We just got in yesterday," Schuller responded. "But we saw the ad for your book signing and my daughter Gretchen has been a fan of yours for years, and...well...she wanted to meet you."

"Good enough, Bob," Hope said warmly. Hope turned to Gretchen and said, "Gretchen, it's my pleasure to meet you, and I must say that you are much prettier than your father."

Schuller laughed as Hope shot a glance in his direction. He took Gretchen's copy of his book and sat down to sign the inside cover.

"There you go, Gretchen."

"Thank you Mr. Hope. Thank you very much."

"My pleasure, young lady."

Hope turned back to Schuller. "Thanks for dropping by, Bob. It was great to see you again."

"Take care of yourself." Schuller responded.

As they walked off down the mall, they heard Hope say, "And next time, sign your own books, Schuller!"

- 18 -

The Shepherd's Song

Vacations didn't mean just rest for Robert Schuller. He used his vacations to write books.

Schuller sat at his desk in the library writing. He had been back from Hawaii for two days now, but it felt like two weeks.

"I don't know, Arvella," Schuller said, "It isn't coming to me. I can't see how we're going to finish this manuscript by the deadline."

"Take a break for a minute, Bob," she said. "Go get yourself a cup of coffee. I've still got two more chapters to edit."

"Great idea," Schuller said. He got up from behind his desk and started down the hallway. He walked past the lighted wall display where Arvella kept her doll collection and saw the haunting photograph of John Wayne.

Schuller stopped dead in his tracks. He looked at the profile of John Wayne who was looking off into the darkness.

Schuller stood there and stared at the photograph. He looked at Wayne and then at the darkness, and then back at Wayne. Schuller's eyes opened wide as he rushed back into the library.

"Bob, what are you doing?" asked Arvella.

She watched Schuller sit back down at his desk. The excitement on his face was evident.

"I've got it, Arvella. I've got it!"

"What have you got, Bob?"

Schuller wrote rapidly across the pad of paper in front of him. "I never saw it before," he said. "All the time that photograph has been hanging in the hall, I never could see what he was looking at."

"What who was looking at?" Arvella asked. She had put down the manuscript she was editing. She walked over to his side and looked over his shoulder to see what he was writing.

"John Wayne," Schuller said. "John Wayne."

*   *   *

What do you say to a man dying of cancer?

Schuller pulled into the parking lot of Hoag Hospital in Newport Beach. He was lost in thought. *What should I say to him?*

The question haunted his mind as he slowly made his way up the elevator. *I've only seen him a couple of times at some of those Hollywood social events, but we haven't been very close. We're friends all right, but I've never had to face what he's facing now.*

Schuller couldn't get the image of *The Shootist* out of his mind. It was the only movie he remembered John Wayne dying in.

The elevator doors opened. He could see the door to Wayne's room. It was guarded by a young man in uniform.

"Can I help you?" the Guard said when Schuller got close to the door.

Schuller took a deep breath and said to the guard, "Hello, I'm Robert Schuller. He called last night and asked me to come."

The Guard slipped through the door and left Schuller alone in the hall..

Dear God, please give me the right words to say.

"Let'em in!" called a deep, gravelly voice from inside the room.

The Guard opened the door and Schuller walked into the room. He still didn't know what he was going to say.

"Reverend Schuller, come on in and have a seat. I'm glad you could come." Wayne drawled.

"Hello, Mr. Wayne."

"Oh, that's too formal, Bob. Call me, John."

"I was surprised by your phone call, John."

"Well, to be honest with you," Wayne said, "I've watched you for years. So you might say that you're my Pastor."

With great effort he rolled onto his side to look Schuller in the eye. Schuller smiled gently as he looked into Wayne's warm face.

"And you have been my screen hero," Schuller replied. "How are you?"

Wayne nervously rubbed his hands. "Well, they're going to operate this morning. Cancer, you know. And they aren't too optimistic about it."

Schuller listened intently. He realized that Wayne needed someone to talk to.

"You know," Wayne said, "A while ago, you had a

sermon where you invited people to become believers in Jesus. Do you remember that?"

"Yes, I do it often." Schuller smiled.

"Not too long ago, my daughter Marissa and I were watching you on television. You said that a person's faith made all the difference. You invited us to pray with you. I looked at Marissa and told her I thought it was time for us to get down on our knees. "

Schuller thought he saw a tear in the famous actor's eye.

"She held my hand and we prayed," Wayne said.

Schuller reached out and held Wayne's hand.

"Oh, Lord," Schuller prayed, "You have given this man the gift of faith. Be with him now in his fight. He has given so much to so many millions and now he needs your special touch."

Wayne smiled. "Thanks, Bob. Keep putting in a good word for me. I need all the help I can get."

"That's beautiful, Bob," Arvella said as she finished reading the passage. "You gave him hope."

"I know now what the darkness is in Wayne's photograph," Schuller said. "It's death."

Arvella touched her husband's shoulder.

*   *   *

"About a year after I lost my eye," Sammy Davis, Jr. told Schuller, "I got up one morning and thought, 'There's got to be something more to life than partying and being a success. There's got to be - - I've got to have a bottom rung.'"

Schuller sat across from Davis in the lavish Las Vegas suite. Davis had just finished his last performance of the evening, downstairs in the ballroom. Schuller had long wanted to interview the famous entertainer and he had finally gotten his chance.

"So, I started in," Davis said, "reading everything I

could on religion, every religion I could. And some of my friends were into some of the more exotic ones, you know."

"Where did you find your faith?" Schuller asked Davis.

"My Grandmother gave me all of the basics," Davis replied. "What we used to call in the neighborhood, 'mother wit.' She gave me the instincts, the basic tenets of things, like, 'You want somebody to treat you good, then you had better treat them good.' 'And if you ever get big time,' she used to tell me, 'Don't you come in this house with a swelled head.' "

Davis smiled into the camera that was recording the interview.

"She was very respectful to the Lord, Dr. Schuller," Davis went on. "Sunday was an important day and she always refused to do any work. 'This is the Lord's Day' she would say, 'I ain't doin' no work on Sunday.' "

"She cooked all of our meals on Saturday. She would stay up late sometimes until the wee hours of the morning. 'On Sunday, it's only going to be a warm-up,' she would say, 'and that's it. We ain't cooking on no Sunday, 'cause it's the Lord's Day.' And if you took the Lord's name in vain," Davis went on, "you were in big trouble."

Schuller thought of his mother Jennie who had died some years before. He remembered that it had been her who had taught him the importance of faith, just as Arvella had taught their children.

Thank you, Mom. Schuller thought to himself.

"Have you ever faced criticism?" Schuller asked Davis.

"Oh, yes, many times," Davis said. "But, you know, it's something that I obviously had to face." "A lot of it, I've deserved."

"Like what?" Schuller asked.

"In the early days, when I was really going places and doing a lot of different things, I was eager for success." "I discovered however, that I had come along at a time when there were a lot of barriers to overcome, as a performer."

"You mean racial barriers?" Schuller asked.

"Racial barriers, as well," Davis nodded. "But sometimes you get on that road to success and you're driven by good intentions, but you take it just one step too far, because you're so anxious to get there." "That devil of success is right there on your shoulder and now you've developed a taste for it. That devil just keeps saying, 'You can get more, you need more, you want more.'"

Schuller saw that Davis, too, had faced his own Goliath.

"And so you want more," Davis said excitedly. "'Cause that's the nature of our business. That's the name of the game. The bigger you are, the better you are."

"I used to wonder why I wasn't making more money." Davis said out loud. "I tortured myself every day over the reasons why I didn't have it all!"

Schuller listened intently.

"That was when I started to blame all of my personal and theatrical failures on the fact that I was black," Davis said. "I believed that my color was the reason I faced failure. Unfortunately, that was part of the reason, but not completely."

"Now, when I walk out on that stage, I don't have those same devils on my back. I just go out there with a sincere desire to help people."

"That's ministry, Sammy."

"Yes," Davis smiled back at Schuller, "I guess it is. I love it when I see you creating that, Dr. Schuller. Many years ago, if I watched a television show, I would count how many black people were in the audience as the camera panned the crowd. I don't do that when I watch you. All I see is people."

"Of course," Davis added, "there are people of every color there. It must be the Cathedral - -"

"Sinatra once said he was going to sing in the Cathedral," Schuller said. "He promised to sing anything I requested."

"I did it my way," Schuller sang.

Davis laughed.

"That relates to Christ you know," Schuller said. "He did it his way, too. And you do it your way."

"Yeah," Davis said quietly, "That's beautiful."

Davis glanced over at Schuller.

"Bottom line," he said, "is that we have to give people a lift. And we have to do it with integrity."

"That's right," Schuller said.

"Speaking of integrity," Davis inquired, "Why is it that I listen to some men of the cloth, and I don't understand what they are saying. But you seem to be blessed with the ability to say things clearly and to say things so simply that everyone understands."

"I think some people spend a lot of time calculating what they are going to say." "They memorize all the technical details and and deliver a speech that no one can understand."

"I've never been able to do that," Schuller admitted. "I have an idea, and then expound on that idea as I speak! I think the key ingredient in any ministry has to be integrity."

Davis understood what Schuller was talking about. He voiced his next question.

"Weren't you scared when you built the Cathedral?" Davis inquired. "After all, nothing like that had ever been done before."

"I was scared," Schuller admitted, "but it was a question of integrity. The point is, that I had taken money from people. It seemed like everybody I knew bought a window in the Cathedral. Each window was a five hundred dollar donation. Sinatra bought a window in honor of his mother. Her name is mounted on a window, along with ten thousand, five hundred and ninety-nine others. I took their money," Schuller said, "and I had to deliver the product."

"But, didn't it take a lot of courage?" Davis asked.

"I've never thought about courage," Schuller said. "I don't know what courage is, because I've never faced physical danger. Courage isn't the absence of fear, I believe it's facing horror in the eye."

"That's right, Dr. Schuller, "Courage is facing horror in the eye."

*   *   *

The Free University Hospital in Amsterdam grew quiet in the evening hours. The memory of finding Schuller collapsed on the hotel floor that morning, was still fresh in their minds.

Mike Nason sat patiently as Paul Dunn nervously paced the floor.

Those first, frightening words of Dr. Wolburs, still rang in Paul's ears. "We have to operate immediately, Mr. Dunn, or your father- in-law will not live."

Across the room, Mike Nason tried to write a press release, but the words wouldn't come. He knew that as soon as any word regarding Schuller's brain surgery reached the press, the hospital phones would be ringing off the hook.

Schuller's trip to Rome and Moscow had been widely publicized. Millions would want to know about Schuller's condition. *What am I going to tell them?* Nason thought. *Even Arvella doesn't know.*

*   *   *

Arvella sat in the corner of the waiting room and listened to Dr. Wolbers.

"He may not recognize you, Mrs. Schuller. Brain surgery affects many people differently. Some people become violent, others are withdrawn and become only a shell of the person they once were."

"What are the chances of a full recovery?" Arvella asked matter-of-factly.

"I think the chances are fairly good," he said. "But we can never tell for sure."

Arvella took a deep breath. "When will we know for sure?"

"It may take months."

"When can I see him?" Arvella said.

"You can go into the room right now," Wolbers said. "He'll still be groggy from the anesthesia, but he will know you are there."

Arvella closed the door behind her very gently. She looked at Schuller lying on the bed. A large white bandage swathed his head. The color was completely gone from his face. The doctor had told her to expect a drastic change in his appearance, but nothing could have prepared her for this.

Arvella walked to her husband's side. She touched his hand. Schuller opened his eyes and looked up at her. They were darkened from the pain, but Arvella still saw a tiny sparkle. He pursed his lips as if to kiss her. Arvella smiled. She leaned down and kissed him. With a faint smile, Schuller closed his eyes and drifted off to sleep.

No one seemed to know what had really happened. They said that he had been complaining of a headache the night before. Earlier that same day he had bumped his head on the door frame of a car that he was getting into. It hadn't seemed serious at the time.

Before dinner, Schuller complained of a headache and cancelled his plans for the evening. He said that he wanted to get plenty of rest before he met with the press the next morning. When he failed to appear for his early morning appointment, Paul and Mike had gone up to his room. They had found him unconscious, out on the balcony. As far as anyone knew, he had spent the entire night there. Schuller himself didn't remember. I guess we'll never really know all of what actually happened.

Now, twenty-four hours after the accident, a simple bump on the head meant the difference between life and death. The Doctors had found a burst blood vessel inside Schuller's skull. All through the night the blood had flowed freely into his brain, creating an intolerable pressure. The surgeon had informed them that it certainly would have killed him if it had continued to bleed even as much as thirty minutes longer.

Arvella looked down at her sleeping husband.

Dear Lord, thank you for saving his life, she prayed.

She sat down next to the hospital room window, her Bible was in her lap. For Arvella, the Bible was always a source of strength and comfort. She knew that she could never travel beyond God's care. Now, as so many times before, she turned to the word of God for help.

Sometimes, she just opened the Bible and read what she found. She had brought with her, a small, purse-sized Bible. She opened it and began to read the Shepherd's song that she had always loved.

> *The Lord is my shepherd; I shall not want.*
> *He makes me to lie down in green pastures;*
>   *He leads me beside the still waters.*
> *He restores my soul; He leads me in the paths of*
>   *righteousness for His name's sake.*
> *Yea, though I walk through the valley of the shadow*
>   *of death, I will fear no evil; for You are with me;*
> *Your rod and Your staff, they comfort me.*
>
> *You prepare a table before me in the presence*
>   *of my enemies; You anoint my head with oil;*
>   *my cup runs over.*

GOLIATH

*Surely goodness and mercy shall follow me all
the days of my life; and I will dwell in the
house of the Lord forever.*

Arvella closed the Bible and looked out the window. A sparrow sat perched on the sill. There was a single twig in its mouth.

She looked into the eye of the sparrow.
Thank You, Lord.

-19 -

The Light In The Darkness

The red neon line methodically traveled up and down the face of the heart monitor. Dutch nurses scrubbed and prepared the surgical instruments while the team of Doctors conferred.

Schuller lay awake on the operating table. His skull was still sore from the first surgery. The Doctors had delayed the second brain surgery for a day due to Schuller's elevated temperature and high blood pressure.

"We'll wait one more day," Arvella had decided. Dr. Wolbers had agreed.

"Waiting is better than the risk of giving him a blood transfusion. But we'll have to operate soon, Mrs. Schuller. His brain is still bleeding. The first surgery was not a complete success."

"Will this new surgery permanently repair the broken blood vessel in his brain?" Arvella asked.

"I hope so," Wolbers told her. "We have every indication that it will."

Arvella thought about being with Schuller in his hospital room. It had been three days since she had arrived in Amsterdam.

Schuller's eyes had sparkled and a hint of a smile had curled the edge of his lips. The nurse had finally arrived with lunch. His memory, though spotty from the accident and surgery, distinctly recognized the scent of hot apple pie. A sumptuous tray of Dutch delicacies, disguised as hospital food, lay before him. Several days of liquid dieting had left his taste buds yearning for solid food.

Schuller reached forward for the pie. His motions were stiff and shaky as he slowly lifted his fork. His fork plunged through the pie crust, releasing a sweet, torrent of steam. Slowly he brought the fork to his mouth, anticipating that first bite.

The fork poked him in the chin instead of going in his mouth. Confused by his lack of motor skills, Schuller looked over to Arvella. His eyes were filled with a mixture of fear and determination.

Arvella turned to Dr. Wolbers. "Is he okay? What's wrong with him?" Arvella's concern clearly registering in her voice.

"There still may be blood on his brain," Wolbers answered. "The left part of the brain controls the motor skills. Hands, legs, speech. The subdural hematoma, the bleeding on your husband's brain, has paralyzed those functions in your husband's body."

Nervously, she raised her hand to her mouth to disguise her anxiety.

"He can still recover, Mrs. Schuller," Wolbers said softly. "We'll know more in a few days, but we may have to operate again."

By the time those few days had passed, Schuller's condition had worsened.

Arvella knew she would have to authorize another operation when last night he had told her, "Good night, Dear. I love you," three times.

He had said those same words to her every night since the day they were married, but never three times in the same night.

The first night she was there, Schuller had said, "Good night, Dear. I love you," and Arvella thought to herself, *Oh, this is wonderful, he's going to be all right!*

An hour later, he had said it again, then rolled over and went back to sleep.

When he had awakened a third time, Arvella had asked him if he had a good night kiss for her. Schuller kissed her, but it was very weak.

Arvella knew they would have to operate soon.

*   *   *

The light streamed through the hospital window into Schuller's room. Arvella waited alone by the window. The operation might not be over for several more hours.

She looked at all the bright flowers that had been delivered that morning. The cards and telegrams from all over the world. The President of the United States had sent a personal telegram. Members of the Crystal Cathedral had been wonderful in their outpouring of love and concern for Schuller.

Supporters of 'The Hour Of Power' both in America and in thirty-five foreign countries around the globe, had rallied in prayer and love for their pastor. It was more than Arvella could bear.

She went over to the empty bed and knelt down. She put her head on the sheets and closed her eyes.

Lord, He was yours before he was mine and I just give him to you now. I give you the Ministry, because I can't handle it without him.

She had done all that she could do. She stood up and smoothed the bed.

Dr. Wolbers came into the room. "He's in intensive care now, Mrs. Schuller. I think we've done it."

Arvella felt the weight of Goliath lift from her shoulders.

"Can I take him home now, Doctor?"

Wolbers smiled. "Yes, I believe we can move him in a couple of days."

*   *   *

Schuller rose from his bed into the light. His frail body struggled to break the confines of the hospital bed. His eyes searched for the window in the corner, trying desperately to catch a brief glimpse of home.

The Cathedral was there, just outside his window, a mile down the road. It was the place where dreams had come true. He was home. *Thank you, Lord.* Schuller prayed silently.

He smiled gently as he watched the great church shimmer in the setting sun. He leaned back in his bed, closed his eyes, and shut out the world around him.

Arvella watched him carefully. The twelve hour plane ride home from Amsterdam had not been easy for Schuller. He had slept for most of it. A doctor from Amsterdam had made the flight with them to make sure there were no complications.

The doctors at University of California Irvine, Medical Center, had said he could go home in just a few days.

They would just have to celebrate his birthday in the hospital.

Sheila brought in a white birthday cake full of

candles. Robert Anthony followed close behind with his wife Donna. The middle daughter Jeanne, and her husband Paul Dunn followed, arm in arm. Carol and her husband Tim had already arrived. My wife, Gretchen, who is the youngest daughter, and I stood next to Arvella.

A sweet melody filled the air as everyone slowly filed in. A soft smile crept onto Schuller's lips as he listened to his family.

> *Happy Birthday to you,*
> *Happy Birthday to you,*
> *Happy Birthday, dear Dad,*
> *Happy Birthday to you.*

Sheila set the cake down in his lap and said, "Make a wish, Dad."

The three youngest daughters rang out in an echoing chorus, "Yeah, come on, Dad, make a wish and blow out the candles."

He picked up the cake crowned with burning red candles and held it away from his tapered jaw. Every movement was steady and sure. Schuller started to smile as he read the simple inscription. 'Happy 65th Birthday, Dad!'

As he blew out the candles, Arvella said, "Carol has a special present for you, Bob." His eyes became bright as he quietly said, "Did you get your new prosthesis? Let's see you walk!"

Excitedly, Carol hopped up and began to demonstrate the miracle of modern technology. With the grace of a runway model, Carol strode across the hospital room floor with her siblings cheering her on from behind. For the first time in almost fifteen years, he nearly forgot the artificial limb his daughter wore as her left leg. As she walked across the room, Schuller couldn't help but remember the pain of the wound that had torn through his daughter's leg, and this father's heart. His face filled

427

with emotion as he said, "Congratulations, sweetheart, I'm proud of you."

That infectious smile, inherited from her father, appeared on Carol's face as she knelt next to his bed. Her eyes glistened as she fought back the tears. "Daddy, you spent a lot of hours by my bedside. I think it's time for me to return the favor!" She held him tightly as he closed his eyes, embracing her warmth. He didn't say a word; he didn't have to.

The family hugged and kissed him. Arvella watched them leave. She walked over and gave her husband a kiss. It felt so wonderful to be home.

*   *   *

"Bob, get off that stool!" Arvella cried.

Schuller stood on the step-stool next to the fireplace. His speech was quiet, slower than usual as he said, "I just wanted a match for the fireplace."

Shaking her head, she said, "Bob, you don't have your balance back yet. If you fall and hit your head, it will kill you." Her words pounded him in the back as he walked to his desk. She knew he didn't believe it.

"Hi, Mom, how's it going?" Gretchen asked as she came in the room.

"I'm frustrated," Arvella said. "He wants to go into the garden and trim the roses. He climbs on stools. He wanders out for walks anytime he pleases."

Smiling broadly, Gretchen responded just loud enough for her father to hear, "He's being himself, huh?"

"I'm fine," Schuller said. "It wasn't that serious. They just vacuumed out all the negative thoughts!"

"And saved your life, I might add." Arvella observed.

"Maybe so, but I feel fine."

Laughing at their exchange, Gretchen said, "Sounds like he's ready to preach again!"

"Don't get him started on that!" Arvella said.

"The doctor told me four more weeks, no preaching until November 10." Schuller said with a smile.

Arvella turned to Gretchen. "He still has holes in his memory, and his energy level is low." She stopped short, and then continued. "Although you wouldn't know it by looking at him today!"

A sheepish grin curled the corners of Schuller's lips. With eyebrows raised, he said, "Why, thank you, Dear, I love you, too!"

- 20 -

GOLIATH

Christmas at the Schuller house is a very special time. It's a time of peace and understanding; a time for family.

Arvella and the rest of the mothers, worked away in the kitchen, while Schuller and all the fathers, watched the grandchildren and television in the library. Sheila, Carol, Jeanne and Gretchen helped their mother. Robert A. and Donna were on their way up from San Juan Capistrano. They were always the last ones to arrive, due to his 9:00 a.m. service.

"Gretchen," Arvella called. "Would you please go ask your father where the roasting pan is? He always hides it out in the garage somewhere." Arvella put the last

433

handful of stuffing in the turkey and reached over to set the timer on the built-in oven.

"Okay, Mom," Gretchen replied. She finished filling the crystal dish with cranberry sauce and wiped her hands off on her apron. Sheila was preparing the sweet potatoes and had to step aside so that Gretchen could get out of the kitchen.

Gretchen didn't realize how busy everyone in the kitchen was, until she found herself in the peace and harmony of the living room. The Schullers always decorated the library for Christmas, which is in the opposite end of the house from the kitchen. The only real sign of Christmas in the living room, were the cards and letters sitting on the piano and taped over the fireplace mantel. Schuller and Arvella treasured each card as an expression of love from their friends all over the world.

Gretchen heard the sound of the grandchildren playing down the hall in the library.

"Tell us a story, Grandpa," little Jason said as he pulled on Schuller's sweater.

Schuller reached down and picked the boy up. "What kind of story would you like to hear?"

"A good one," Jason told him. His bright blue eyes beamed up at the white-haired Schuller.

"A funny one," added Christopher. He wanted to make sure his brother didn't leave out any of Grandpa's jokes. Christopher liked Grandpa's jokes.

All the kids gathered around while the fathers stood next to each other in the background. I watched Schuller sit down in the big easy chair where Arvella had read me the Love Letters. Jason sat on one arm of the chair as Schuller placed baby Julia next to him.

The rest of the grandchildren – there are thirteen in all – sat around Schuller's feet on the floor. The room grew quiet. I knew Schuller was searching for a story that would appeal to all of us.

"Dad," Gretchen interrupted before Schuller could start. "Mom needs the roasting pan for the turkey. Where did you hide it this year?"

"The roasting pan?" Schuller asked innocently. Then he rubbed his jaw and creased his brow in deep concentration. He looked at each one of the grandchildren as if he were asking them for help. "Let's see," he said solemnly, "the roasting pan."

"Yes, Dad." Gretchen repeated. "The roasting pan."

Schuller looked at her innocently and asked, "Did you look under your mother's car? I think I used it to catch the oil drippings."

"Dad!" Gretchen exclaimed and shot a 'Help me' look over her shoulder to me. I gave her my best 'Don't look at me, he's your father!' expression and shrugged my shoulders.

"Maybe it's behind the trash cans," Schuller suggested, "Or how about in the storage closet. Did you look in the storage closet?"

Gretchen crossed her arms. I knew that she was thinking that it might be quicker just to walk over to our house and get her own roasting pan.

Schuller looked down at Rebecca. "Rebecca?" he said, "Have you seen Grandma's roasting pan?"

Rebecca opened her big blue eyes and smiled at her Grandpa. Rebecca had blue eyes and a smile just like her mother, Carol. Schuller had never been able to resist Rebecca's smile.

He beckoned her over with his finger and whispered in her ear. She ran over to Gretchen and relayed the information.

"Thank you, Rebecca," Gretchen said and opened the closet door in the hall. She reached up behind Schuller's collection of baseball caps and found Arvella's hidden roasting pan.

Schuller looked at the children gathered at his feet and said, "I suppose you're wondering why I like to hide things from your Grandma?"

Gretchen rolled her eyes and left the room with the roasting pan. *Here it comes,* she thought.

"Many years ago," Schuller began, "long before any of you kids were born, I wanted a new fishing pole for Christmas. I always loved fishing and wanted a pole that I could use to catch fish in the ocean. I wanted that pole so badly that I left notes on Grandma's pillow every morning for a month. Grandma got very annoyed with me after the first week of notes."

"On the night before Christmas, as soon as I arrived home from work, I went straight to the Christmas tree, and looked at all the presents. There, under the tree, was a bright red package that was about this round." Schuller made a circle with his thumb and forefinger. "And about this long." Schuller held his arms open wide.

"I was sure that present was my new fishing pole," Schuller told the children. "And I just couldn't wait until Christmas morning to open it up."

"What did you do, Grandpa?" asked Jason.

"I bet he peeked," offered his brother Christopher.

"No, Grandpa wouldn't peek," defended Scottie. Then he looked up at Schuller innocently. "Would you, Grandpa?"

Schuller smiled, picked Scottie up and put him on his knee.

"No, Scottie, I didn't. I didn't peek."

"See," Scottie scolded his big brother, "I told you."

"Well, what did you do, Grandpa?" asked Rebecca.

"He opened up his fishing pole," Scottie told her. He was sure he had the right answer again.

"Well, not exactly," Schuller lamented. He looked down at the circle of puzzled faces at his feet. "I went into the kitchen. Grandma was getting dinner ready. She knew I had looked under the tree, so she pretended she didn't see me. I told her that there was a new package under the tree, a long package that had my name on it."

"What did Grandma say?" Rebecca asked.

"She said I'd have to wait until Christmas morning to find out what was in that package," Schuller replied. "But I couldn't wait. I wanted to open my present right then!"

"You can't even wait until Christmas to give presents to your own kids!" Arvella said as she came into the room. "Remember last summer, when I bought that briefcase for Jim, the one they had on sale? You gave it to him in September."

"He needed it for work, Arvella," Schuller defended.

"Tell the rest of the story, Grandpa," Jason piped up.

"Well, to make a long story short, we agreed that each of us could open one package on Christmas Eve," Schuller said. "I ran back to the Christmas tree and grabbed the package. I was in such a hurry that I didn't even take time to read the card. I tore off the wrapping paper and found an empty cardboard tube inside."

"It was the kind of tube that wrapping paper comes on," Arvella added, smiling at the memory.

"What's this? I asked your Grandma," Schuller said to the kids. "Down inside the tube was a can of shaving cream! I couldn't believe my eyes!"

"You mean there wasn't a new fishing pole inside the tube?" Jason asked.

"I was astonished," Schuller said, " 'Where is it?' I asked Grandma, 'Where's my pole?' "

Schuller looked around and then answered his own question. "Grandma wasn't talking." "I said to her, you've hidden it in the garage! You're just playing a trick on me! 'No,' came Grandma's reply. 'I'm not.' "

"So, what happened?" Scottie asked.

"Well, Grandma was so mad at me because I had pestered her every day about getting me a fishing pole for

Christmas, that she didn't get me one at all!"

"But why?" asked little Rebecca, still not understanding why there was no fishing pole.

"Because Grandma believed that Christmas presents were supposed to be surprises," Schuller replied enthusiastically.

"So I gave your Grandmother a surprise. I began to chase her all around the house, squirting her with the can of shaving cream!"

Rebecca squealed with delight at the vision this conjured up.

"You mean you had a shaving cream fight with Grandma?" Scottie asked, unable to believe his ears.

"In the house?" Jason added. "Wow!"

"Can we have a shaving cream fight, too?" Rebecca asked. She looked at her Grandfather with pleading eyes.

"Well, maybe . . . "

"Dinner! Dinner! everyone," Arvella called down the hallway.

Saved by the bell, Schuller thought.

After we had eaten dinner, we went back into the library to open the gifts under the tree.

We came to the final present that Schuller personally gives to each one of the grandchildren. It had become a tradition in the family. Some years the presents were toys, some years they were just tiny stuffed animals.

This year, Schuller left the room for a minute and returned with a stack of envelopes in his hands. Each envelope contained a crisp, new, twenty dollar bill, one for each grandchild.

The room grew quiet as Schuller handed each grandchild an envelope. I watched as he went from child to child, trying to make the moment something extra special for each of them.

As he handed out the envelopes, Schuller cried.

Tears streamed down his face. He tried to hide it, but it was no use. We were all caught up in his emotion. We had almost lost him that year.

At first, the emotions seemed excessive. Then it hit me. Schuller was remembering the envelope that his mother had sent him when he didn't have enough money to buy milk for Sheila and Bobby. Arvella had told me that the first year they were in California, things were so bad, Schuller tried to sell stamps back to the Post Office to buy milk. He never forgot that. He never forgot what it was like to have nothing.

I watched Schuller cry as he finished handing out the envelopes.

Then I saw it. I don't know if the others did or not, but I was sure of what I saw. In that unguarded moment, I saw Schuller.

I saw what made him so different from everyone else. It was his faith. Schuller had a tremendous faith. He believed in something he couldn't see. Where others had to see it to believe it, Schuller believed it before he could see it. It was his faith that made him so different from everyone else.

But it wasn't faith that made Schuller great.

It was love. Love made Schuller great. Love made Schuller tick. It was what he was all about from the very beginning.

Goliath is the greatest obstacle to love. Goliath is the monster in the darkness. Goliath is what we all face when we try to make our dreams come true.

Goliath is failure.

We're all afraid of failing. And you know what? You know what Schuller taught me?

It's OK.

It's OK to be afraid. It's OK to be afraid of failing, because you have to come through the darkness to get into the light.

The light is love. The light of the world is love.

That's as hard as it gets.

Schuller knew that if you're going to face Goliath, and we all face Goliath, that love was your only hope. Love was the one thing in the world that Goliath, for all his size, could not overcome.

Schuller knew that you needed three things to overcome Goliath.

You need faith, hope and love.

And the greatest of these is love.